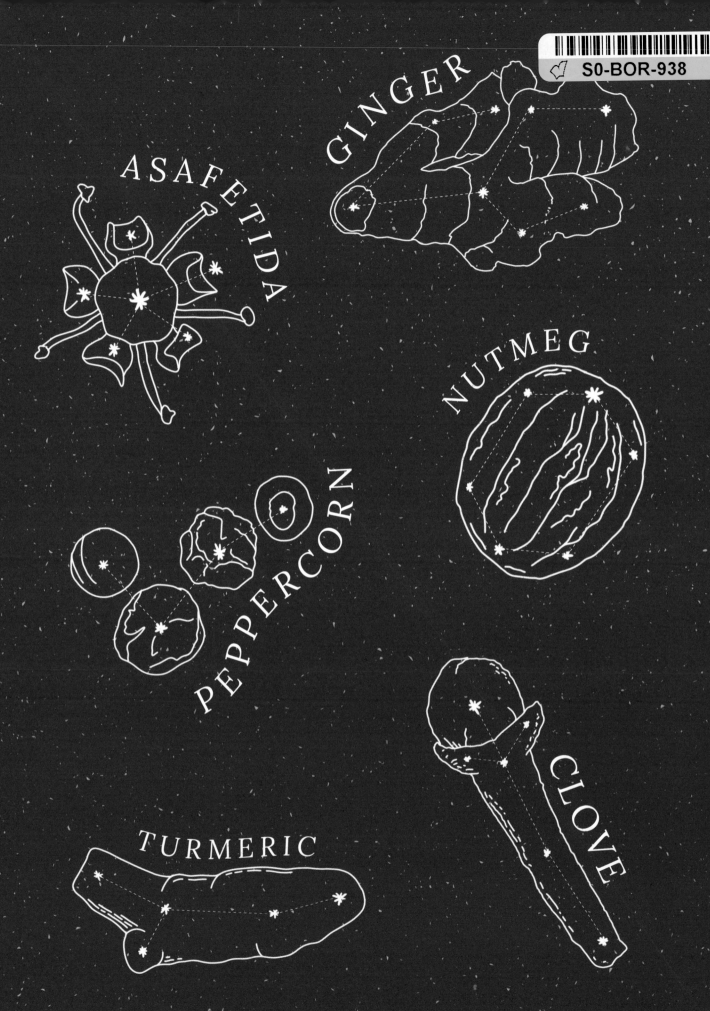

GINGER

ASAFETIDA

NUTMEG

PEPPERCORN

CLOVE

TURMERIC

OJAS

A COOKBOOK

OJAS

A COOKBOOK

Modern Recipes and Ancient Wisdom
for Everyday Ayurveda

NIRA KEHAR

DOVETAIL

DOVETAIL

Text copyright © 2018 by Nira Kehar
Photographs copyright © 2018 by Scott Gordon Bleicher
Design by Chris Santone

Published by Dovetail Press in Brooklyn, New York, a division of Assembly Brands LLC.

For details or ordering information, contact the publisher at the address below or email **info@dovetail.press**.

Dovetail Press
42 West Street #403
Brooklyn, NY 11222
www.dovetail.press

Library of Congress Cataloging-in-Publication data is on file with the publisher.

ISBN: 978-0-99873-997-7

First printing, March 2018

Printed in China

10 9 8 7 6 5 4 3 2 1

"More and more with less and less

until, eventually, you can do everything with nothing."

—R. Buckminster Fuller

CONTENTS

INTRODUCTION

I was 24 and just setting out on a less-than-exotic career path in computer engineering when I slipped. It was in the cafeteria at work, where grapeseed oil had spilled and sat in a puddle on the floor. Rarely has such a pedestrian food proved so vicious. I ended up landing in such a way that I hurt, of all body parts, my spine. I spent the ensuing year going through an agonizing recovery; it was the perfect setting for my first existential crisis. I had lots of time to think, and the thought of recovering just to go back to a life of computer engineering started to feel claustrophobic. I reflected on my choices and dared to dream bigger. A longing for creative expression was born.

But first, I had to get better. In my recovery, I decided against using any allopathic medication. I wanted to rely on my Yoga practice and Ayurvedic diet to heal through the pain, an alternative approach to wellness that had intrigued me since childhood. Growing up in Montreal as an Indian Canadian, I had fallen under the spell of Paramahansa Yogananda's *Autobiography of a Yogi*. When I was 10, I'd picked up the book during a visit to the library simply because it was the thickest book I could get my hands on. The pages were richly woven with stories about yogis exploring the world and themselves through meditation and Yoga. I was instantly enchanted. The promise of balance through self-exploration kick-started a lifelong practice of mindfulness. I tried to apply it to all aspects of life, including my diet. This was a world I wanted to be a part of.

It was grapeseed oil that brought me down; but it was food, too, that ultimately proved my salvation. During my recovery, I decided to enroll in a French culinary arts program in Canada. When the time came to set off on a three-month culinary internship, one of my teachers suggested New Delhi, a city where I could gain a unique experience of a culture for which I looked the part but had very little connection to. Although India is my parents' homeland, at that time I knew not a soul in the country.

What was supposed to be a three-month internship turned into a decade-long exploration. I quickly picked up on the country's pulse and began noticing a gap in the city's food scene. Despite India's rich food culture, when it came to dining out, most of the fancy restaurants were located in the ivory towers that were high-end hotels. The majority of Indians who came from more privileged backgrounds avoided sullying their hands and running their own kitchens. I sensed a need for a more distinctive and personal dining experience, and I was ready to get my hands dirty to achieve just that. There was a disconnect between the people who were working in the kitchens and those they were cooking for. I wanted to bridge the gap by opening a restaurant that was warm, creative, and run by the chef and owner.

I found a space in an old market where the government had granted living space to refugees pouring in from Pakistan during the Partition of India. To survive, many had opened small shops just outside their living quarters. Though the space was centrally located in a gorgeous part of Delhi, it was mainly the domain of tailor shops. To open a restaurant there, I was told, would be madness.

Ignoring the naysayers, my French brasserie, Chez Nini, soon opened its doors. I personally designed every smidgen of the restaurant: architectural drawings, furniture, menus, and crockery.

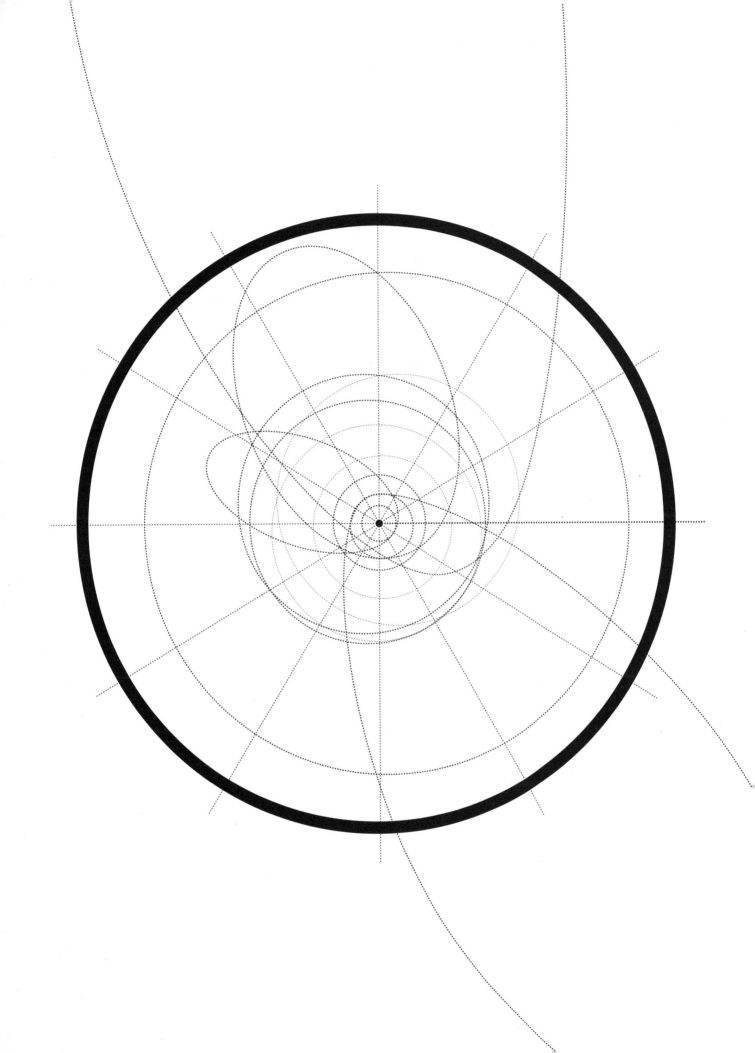

The menu developed in a very organic way as the restaurant came to life. Holding weekly food tastings familiarized me with the bounty of local ingredients I had at my disposal and with the tastes of my potential customers. As a result, I developed an array of dishes inspired by classic French cuisine and local offerings, including a spiced coq au vin and the best-selling duck burger. Eventually, we were recognized as the best new restaurant in Delhi by the *The Times of India* Food Awards, and received some great press in magazines such as *Vogue India* and *Elle India*. We'd introduced an imaginative and locally inspired cuisine to the city and received so much support from guests who came to dine with us from all parts of the country. I am incredibly proud of what Chez Nini achieved. It attracted people from all walks of life and backgrounds—from Bollywood hotshots to a couple who'd saved up for a special dinner and had never eaten non-Indian food before. As our tables filled, more and more restaurants with a similar contemporary approach opened in Delhi. A movement was born. Curiously, the old refugee market, which so many tried to dissuade me from, proved to be a great spot for a restaurant—and many more sprang up around us over the years.

After six years of running Chez Nini and collaborating with chefs and artists on a myriad of projects, it was time to move on. In my attempt to rediscover who I was as a person and a chef, I found myself revisiting my passion for Ayurveda. Its principles had been with me all along, silently guiding me through my growth as a chef and a home cook. I became determined in applying this broader, more wholesome perspective to the food I was making. I started on a path of holistically motivated fine gastronomy, and I wanted to become a part of the community that would bring Ayurveda to mainstream food culture. I was particularly inspired by the books and teachings of David Frawley, one of the most authoritative voices in the Ayurveda community, and Ayurvedic chef Richard LaMarita from the Natural Gourmet Institute in New York. Incorporating Ayurveda to the food I love prompted a drastic change in my wellness and vitality: eating for my body type translated into increased energy and an overall healthy glow that other people started to notice. The chronic health problems I'd developed while running a restaurant, like migraines, started to subside and were less frequent. I knew I had found my match, and wanted to become an advocate for the food that helped me feel in tune with myself.

During this time, I was introduced to the concept of *ojas* by Chef LaMarita at an Ayurvedic intensive course. Hearing him talk about it as a vital force within all of us that is extracted from the very essence of the food we eat, a concept that has not yet been quantified by modern science, was the most eye-opening experience on my journey. The dots started to connect. Suddenly, I understood my purpose with food and what I want to do for people when I feed them. It proved to be a true testament to the reality that you are what you eat.

This book is a journey of learning and uncovering a vast science that I want to bring closer to you through the lens of my own experience. Ayurveda is an ancient science that takes a lifetime to study and learn, and taking this first step, with food, will make you want to know more.

HOW TO USE THIS BOOK

The book consists of a brief introduction to the basic concepts of Ayurveda, with 12 chapters of seasonal recipes that represent the year according to the zodiac calendar, allowing for a more comprehensive view on seasonality. Although the zodiac year begins with Aries in March, the book starts with the Capricorn constellation at the start of the calendar year.

Each chapter contains recipes that will demystify the use of spices and herbs and show you how to achieve taste balances that are so critically important in Ayurveda—the tastes found in the foods we eat, which our bodies need to achieve physical harmony and avoid unhealthy cravings. You'll find recipes for snacks, main dishes, variations on a traditional Indian bowl called *khichdi*, desserts, and drinks incorporating ginger—a collection of dishes to inspire the use of seasonal ingredients as they become available throughout the year. Engaging with food in this way develops an intuition on how to balance all the tastes in our daily diet. I've developed spice blend recipes, one for each of the six tastes we need to satisfy daily, that will take the guesswork out of incorporating their flavor and healing benefits into your home-cooking routine. Food is best in its natural state because nature is perfect, and we can make delicious meals by gently accenting the inherent flavors and aromas of our ingredients. As you're cooking the recipes in this book, I hope this message hits home.

Before you start cooking, make sure to read about different types of constitutions (pages 16–17) and take the test on page 18 to figure out your own type, known as your *dosha*. Once you know your dosha, you can check the lists of ingredients on pages 22–27, for a guide on which foods to favor or avoid. Look out for doshic recipe tweaks in the Dosha Dos and Don'ts section of recipes, which will provide alternative ingredients and recipe adjustments you can use where possible. I'd suggest redoing the doshic test a few times as you start to understand the core principles of Ayurvedic practice to give yourself a more accurate sense of your dosha. If you cook for your loved ones, encourage them to take the test, too. Your well-being doesn't stop at you and your body—nourishing those around you through food is equally important.

You might notice that I don't follow Ayurvedic prescriptions to the letter, as I sometimes pair fruit and dairy in recipes. I also don't follow a strictly vegetarian or vegan diet. So if you love meat, don't worry—the recipes in this book simply advise moderation in meat consumption. Even eating just one more plant-based meal a week, or incorporating a ginger drink into your daily routine, is a great start to building better habits. I find that any rigid and overly restrictive lifestyle change we try to impose on ourselves only works for a short while. Sustainable change comes through small commitments we make. They are completely achievable and have a strong positive impact on our everyday vitality. As an introduction to the Ayurvedic lifestyle, this book intends to present an achievable and improved way of eating the foods we love. This book is designed for you to take what you want from it, and come away emboldened and inspired to make your own healthful creations in the kitchen.

AYURVEDA:
A Bird's-Eye View

What Is Ayurveda?

Ayurveda, the sister science of the now-widespread science of Yoga, is an ancient comprehensive system of life wisdom (translated directly from Sanskrit, *ayur* means "life" and *veda* means "wisdom or knowledge"). Like Yoga, it originated on the ancient Indian subcontinent more than 3,500 years ago. Rooted in the ancient sacred texts known as the Vedas, the holistic healing wisdom was revealed to great masters, seers, and yogis during deep states of meditation in response to their quest for alleviating the suffering of all living creatures. The revelations formed a matrix of knowledge about human physiology and health, as well as the medicinal properties of plants and minerals, to bring the body, mind, and spirit into a natural state of balance. Today, this comprehensive approach to health is quickly gaining popularity in Western countries by offering an innovative system of mind-body medicine for self-healing as an alternative to the illness-focused biochemical model of modern medicine.

A Common Misconception

Ayurveda is not a religious science, nor is it outdated folk medicine. It is simultaneously a science and a spiritual approach to self-healing. It is not necessary to study the Vedas or align yourself with the spiritual aspects of Ayurveda, but it is important to get a comprehensive understanding of its history and philosophy to use it successfully. The Ayurvedic lifestyle is enhanced by its spiritual wisdom, but it's nevertheless very effective when applied practically to maintain health and fitness, and prevent illness.

Ayurveda Today

Ayurveda is increasingly being practiced all over the world, with more and more Ayurvedic resources available to those who seek them. You can live an Ayurvedic lifestyle no matter where you are or what kind of resources you have access to. Use this book as a first step in your journey, and as soon as you figure out your constitution, you can start a process of self-discovery and improved wellness. Ayurveda emphasizes the importance of using seasonal and locally grown ingredients. Doing so helps us harness the benefits of nature's intelligence in providing exactly what our bodies need in a given climate and season. Nature provides perfect ingredients for us to balance our doshas with the doshas of the seasons.

A Unique Approach

The Ayurvedic way of life strives for a harmony of physiological, psychological, social, and environmental factors of the human microcosm and the universal macrocosm by using a personalized whole food diet, stress management techniques, and encouraging a sense of community with our fellow humans and with nature. By applying this nature-based knowledge to our daily lives, we support the inherent intelligent processes of our body. Unlike Western medicine, which primarily deals with symptoms, Ayurveda aims to treat the root cause of all ailments through a broader and more in-depth analysis of both our past and present state, and emphasizes that what is good for one person can be damaging to another. It is a perfect balance between the ancient and the modern, offering adaptable daily and seasonal health regimens. The knowledge and methods of Ayurveda develop and improve from our own internal resources and use the nature around us as our pharmacy. Unlike generic health systems, Ayurveda is based on customizable principles and practices according to each person's unique circumstances and needs.

Striking a Balance

When the balance in the body is interrupted, Ayurveda relies on the six tastes (sweet, astringent, sour, salty, pungent, and bitter) to restore it. These tastes, just like the doshas, originate from the five elements. How the natural ratio of the three doshas is affected by our diet depends largely on how much of each taste we include in our food. An Ayurvedic diet prescribes a nuanced intake of the six tastes, as determined by one's constitution, current state, and the season. In developing the recipes for this book, I've used Ayurvedic principles and seasonality to create dishes that focus on the use of herbs and spices. Evaluating your constitution (page 18) is the first step in toward embarking on an Ayurvedic lifestyle.

Universal and Timeless

Ayurveda is an integrative science, which is beneficial to every person. It is based on the idea that everyone is born with a completely unique blueprint for optimum health and opposes the one-size-fits-all approach to wellness and diet. This science remains as relevant as ever and it is enlivened every day as individuals around the world use its timeless wisdom in their day-to-day lives.

Customized Well-Being

Unlike Western medicine, which commonly deals with symptoms, Ayurveda aims to treat the root causes of all ailments by taking into account the whole, complete picture of a person. Understanding the individual is the key to finding a truly balanced diet. The foundational idea of Ayurveda is that every person is made of a unique composition of five basic elements found in the universe: ether, air, fire, water, and earth. These elements combine in the human body to form three life forces or energies, called doshas. They control how our bodies work. Therefore, good health and illness prevention is achieved when these forces are in balance. Food is considered to be just as powerful as medicine, making it imperative to eat foods uniquely suited to our physiology to achieve health and well-being. The good news is that your body is a regenerative entity, and you can reverse bad habits and improve your health at any point in your life. No need to feel defeated! Anything you do to improve your current situation can only lead to a better reality than the one you're facing today.

THE FIVE ELEMENTS:
Building Blocks of Everything

Ayurveda and the Elements

In Ayurvedic philosophy, all of creation is made up of five essential elements: ether, air, fire, water, and earth. More than just the physical elements we always associate them with, they represent ideas that are fundamental to nature and matter— they are the building blocks of all living things. Ayurveda recognizes the life-giving force that sustains the body as the same one that drives the universe. It is known as *prana* and is the source of life and existence for all things. Prana manifests in physical life through its division into the five elements. Each person is made up of a unique ratio of these elements, which establishes their basic constitution. This is the level on which Ayurvedic healing works. When the elements are strong and balanced within a person, they support healthy functioning on the concrete physiological level. The five elements are at work inside each of us, defining our body type, personality, and behaviors. Our particular elemental makeup dictates what balance looks like on an individual level.

A Common Misconception

Understanding the five elements is a cosmic approach to unraveling the truths of life and health. The elements don't represent any sort of pagan worship or ritualistic practice.

The Elements at Work

Each of the five elements has its own character, and together they combine to form life. Understanding the dominant elements inside a person, substance, or environment enables us to know what influences will be exerted upon the body and mind. All substances can be classified according to their predominant element. When we know which elements are primary for us, we can make dietary and medicinal choices that allow us to live balanced lives. In the body, ether corresponds to spaces like the mouth and the thorax. Air corresponds to all movement pertaining to muscles and organs. Fire corresponds to functions related to body temperature, digestion, and metabolism. Water corresponds to all fluids, such as blood and saliva. Finally, earth corresponds to solid structures and compact tissues, such as bones and skin.

A Tool for Balance

The five elements explain why substances of the natural world are harmonious with the human body. We easily utilize plants, herbs, minerals, and water because these substances are the same in composition and character as our own underlying makeup. Using the elements and their attributes in this way, we have a better understanding of the realm of cause and effect, anatomy and physiology, structure and function. Once you have a clearer picture of your own constitution and that of everything in your environment, you'll start to develop and strengthen your natural intuition to make choices that keep your body in tune. Each element corresponds to a season, a compass direction, a life stage, a color, a shape, a time of day, as well as to the aspects of the individual, such as emotions, activities, internal organs, and the senses. By focusing on each element and its corresponding season, we can see how the five elements can help keep our bodies harmonious.

Our Elemental Constitution

We are born with a specific elemental composition called our constitution, or *prakruti*. Many factors influence which constitution we're born with: heredity, our parents' health at our conception, our in-utero environment, astrology, and our past life karma. Our constitution is with us from birth and never changes. There are, however, different states and circumstances in life during which the ratio of the elements changes. This is known as your current state, or *vikruti*, and is examined in comparison with your prakruti to understand any deviation or imbalance you may be experiencing.

THE DOSHAS:
A FOUNDATIONAL TRINITY

In Ayurveda, five elements exist in our bodies as three doshas: Vata, Pitta, and Kapha. They are the forces that make up the layers of our being. The ideal state of health is when your body is in perfect balance of all five elements and therefore all three doshas. Since all three doshas are in everyone and everything but in different proportions (with one or two being dominant), all of our physical and nonphysical experiences affect our elemental balance. The doshas also combine to create different climates, foods, species, and even individuals within the same species. The three doshas construct and maintain our physical being, and they determine our unique characteristics and traits.

The ratio of each of the three doshas in our bodies constantly fluctuates according to the environment, our diet, the seasons, the climate, our age, and many other factors. One or more of the doshas can become aggravated (become excessive or depleted) signaling an increase or decrease of the elements they represent. Wellness and health is achieved when the three doshas move toward long-term balance, while long-term imbalance causes illness. A lack of understanding of our bodies' unique needs is akin to living in complete darkness. You can think of Ayurveda as an instruction manual on how to optimally "run" your body in order to successfully achieve your life's purpose. As you develop more knowledge on all the aspects of your dosha, a natural intuition will develop and assist you in balancing your health and preventing illness.

A person's doshic constitution is determined at the moment of conception, and is their own personal blueprint. The blueprint never changes, therefore, if the proportion of doshas in our current state is closely aligned to the dosha proportion we were born with, our health will be vibrant. A divergence between these states, however, will create imbalance. It is imperative to invest the time into figuring out how to relieve any excess or depleted doshic energy causing unwanted symptoms. Being aware of the dosha for the current time of year helps to determine what foods to eat to balance the dosha of the season, in combination with the needs of our individual doshic constitution.

Because an individual can have more than one dominant dosha, there are seven constitutional or doshic types: Vata, Pitta, Kapha, Vata-Pitta, Pitta-Kapha, Vata-Kapha, or Vata-Pitta-Kapha. The last two types are extremely rare, whereas the first five are the most common. Vata types are like gazelles—moving around all the time and rarely staying in one place too long; creative, inspired, and energetic. When out of balance, they tend to be indecisive, unpredictable, and overly sensitive. Pitta types are like tigers—natural leaders, brave, logical, organized, and ambitious, with type-A personalities. When out of balance, they can become overly critical, angry, and judgmental. Finally, Kapha types are like elephants—broad, strong, kind, patient, and slower to remember things (but once they do, they remember them for life). When out of balance, they become lethargic, complacent, and emotionally sensitive.

Vata, Pitta, and Kapha are present all over the body. But their activity can be especially observed in certain parts of the body. If you divide the whole body into three parts, the top is dominated by Kapha, the middle by Pitta, and the bottom by Vata. Furthermore, the three doshas exist in all aspects of life that go beyond just your physical body, including your emotions, psyche, and spiritual intelligence. Similarly, they are part of all aspects of nature and existence, including all physical and energetic forces we experience around us, including the seasons and the weather in our environment.

The proportion of each of the three doshas in the body constantly fluctuates based on numerous factors in the environment. As the doshas move in and out of balance, they can affect your health, energy level, and general mood. Finding out what your dosha type is requires nothing more than answering a few questions (page 18). To get a more in-depth analysis, you should contact an Ayurvedic practitioner to conduct a more thorough assessment. People often mistake their current imbalance for their constitution, so it's advisable to take the test at least twice. First, answer while thinking back to how you were as a child, which will reveal your prakruti, and then think about how things are for you currently, which will reveal your vikruti. The deviation between the two can help you understand your metabolic constitution and its physical rhythms, and can guide you to a greater understanding and evaluation of your nature in your present doshic state. You can use the appropriate principles and practices of Ayurveda to bring your mind and body back into balance.

Food has its own doshic constitution which determines its taste, as well as three other important characteristics: *rasa* or the immediate effect, *vipaka* or the short-term effect in temperature, and finally *vipak* or long-term post-digestive effect. The effects of food's tastes on the body are usually described as follows:

> *Sweet:* Heavy, Cold, and Oily
> *Sour:* Light, Hot, and Oily
> *Salty:* Heavy, Hot, and Moist
> *Pungent:* Light, Hot, and Dry
> *Bitter:* Light, Cold, and Dry
> *Astringent:* Heavy, Cold, and Dry

The rule of thumb when balancing tastes and qualities of food is that opposites attract. For instance, if you are dominant in one or two doshas, you should choose foods which increase the dosha you're lacking and avoid foods that increase the dosha you naturally have more of. A person with a dominant Pitta dosha (air and fire) should favor sweet (heavy, cold, and oily), bitter (light, cold, and dry), and astringent (heavy, cold, and dry) foods thereby increasing their Vata (ether and air) and

Kapha (water and earth) doshas and balancing their qualities (heavy, hot, and wet). By the same rule, Pitta types should avoid tastes which have the same elements and qualities as their dominant dosha, like pungent (air, fire, light; hot and dry), salty (water, fire; heavy, hot, and moist) and sour (earth, fire, light; hot and oily) ones. Once you've found your dosha type, you can refer to the ingredient section on pages 22–27 to figure out which ingredients agree and disagree with your dosha.

No constitution is better than another. A doshic constitution simply represents the natural tendencies and needs of different bodies. It is important to provide the body with what it specifically needs to operate at its best. So celebrate your individuality by being aware of your true nature. It will help you live the best version of your life, because that is the only one you are meant to fulfill to the best of your ability.

DOSHA TEST

The following checklist is a test that will help you determine your doshic constitution. I suggest you take the test twice with two different perspectives. First, think about the body type and tendencies you can remember having since childhood, then consider the current state of your body. This second perspective will give you a good idea of the deviations from your *prakruti*, which result from current dietary and lifestyle choices.

FRAME	☐ I am thin, lanky, and slender with prominent joints and thin muscles.
WEIGHT	☐ I have a tendency to lose weight easily.
EYES	☐ I have small and active eyes.
COMPLEXION	☐ My skin is dry, rough, and thin.
HAIR	☐ My hair is dry, frizzy, and brittle.
JOINTS	☐ My joints are thin, prominent, and have a tendency to crack.
SLEEP PATTERN	☐ I am a light sleeper with a tendency to awaken easily.
BODY TEMPERATURE	☐ My hands and feet are usually cold. I prefer warmer weather.
UNDER STRESS	☐ I become anxious and/or worried.
SPEECH	☐ Fast.
TEMPERAMENTAL FLAW	☐ I have a tendency to be impatient.
MENTAL ACTIVITY	☐ Quick, restless.
RESTING PULSE RATE	☐ 80–100.
PHYSICAL ENDURANCE	☐ I have poor endurance.
APPETITE	☐ I have an irregular appetite.
EATING SPEED	☐ I am a fast eater.
WEATHER PREFERENCE	☐ I have an aversion to cold.
DIGESTION	☐ I have a dry and hard elimination, and I am prone to constipation.
WALKING	☐ I walk at a fast pace.
TRAVEL	☐ I am a wanderer.
TOTALS	**VATA**

The dosha test will help you identify significant characteristics that fall into one of the dosha categories. As you go through the test, mark the answer that most accurately describes you in each category (if more than one answer applies to you, choose the one that is most accurate). Once you have completed the test, count the number of answers in each column. The column with the most answers is your dominant dosha. If your answers are pretty evenly split between two different doshas, it means both of them are equally influential, and your dosha type is a combination of the two. Once you determine your dosha type, you should consider the foods, spices, and herbs that are most suitable for you (see the ingredient section on pages 22–27), and follow the advice relevant to your dosha when looking at the individual recipes.

☐ I have a medium, symmetrical build with good muscle development.	☐ I have a large, round, or stocky build. My frame is broad, stout, or thick.
☐ It's easy for me to gain or lose weight if I put my mind to it.	☐ I gain weight easily and have difficulty losing it.
☐ I have a penetrating gaze.	☐ I have large pleasant eyes.
☐ My skin is warm, moist, reddish, and prone to irritation.	☐ My skin is oily, smooth, and thick.
☐ My hair is fine with a tendency toward early thinning or graying.	☐ My hair is oily, smooth, and thick.
☐ My joints are loose and flexible.	☐ My joints are large and padded.
☐ I am a moderately sound sleeper, usually needing less than eight hours to feel rested.	☐ I am a deep sleeper, and tend to awaken slowly in the morning.
☐ I am usually warm, regardless of season. I prefer cooler weather.	☐ I am adaptable to most temperatures, but I do not like cold, wet days.
☐ I become irritable and aggressive.	☐ I become withdrawn and/or introspective.
☐ Sharp, cutting.	☐ Harmonious, slow.
☐ I have a tendency to be jealous.	☐ I have a tendency to be clingy.
☐ Sharp intellect, aggressive.	☐ Calm, steady, stable.
☐ 70–80.	☐ 60–70.
☐ I have good endurance.	☐ I have excellent endurance.
☐ I have a sharp appetite and need food regularly.	☐ I can easily miss meals.
☐ I eat at medium speed.	☐ I am a slow eater.
☐ I have an aversion to heat.	☐ I have an aversion to damp and cool weather.
☐ I have a soft, normal, and frequent elimination.	☐ I have heavy, thick, and regular elimination.
☐ I walk at an average pace.	☐ I walk at a steady, slow pace.
☐ I am an adventurer with a purpose.	☐ I like to stay home.
PITTA	**KAPHA**

THE SIX TASTES:

Balance Is Health

Taste is assigned a much deeper significance in Ayurveda than we are accustomed to in the West, because it is considered critically important in determining the effect that various foods, spices, and therapeutic herbs have on our state of balance. It is with the dominating elements of each taste that diet is used to alleviate and sustain the doshas in harmony. Tastes are known in Ayurveda as rasas, and represent the essence of all food as sensed by the body. Ayurveda recognizes six tastes of food: sweet, sour, salty, bitter, astringent, and pungent. You can think of taste as a mechanism by which our bodies entice us to gravitate toward the foods they need in order to keep us in balance. Each taste contains all five elements, but two elements dominate, which is why each taste tends to exert a somewhat predictable influence on our physiology. All food contains all six tastes; however, it's the dominating taste elements that determine its essence. For example, if something is sweet, it means it contains all six tastes with sweetness being the dominant one. Knowledge of the different tastes brings awareness to our food cravings and how each individual should adjust the quantity of the tastes for his or her own body.

A Common Misconception

In today's world we are used to viewing cravings as weaknesses, but they are, in fact, our body's attempts to heal itself. All cravings come from unhealthy or deficient organs. By understanding taste and the nature of deficiency, we can understand the root of our cravings. When health and desire are one, our cravings become sacred.

The Power of the Tastes

Tastes combine in countless ways to create the incredible diversity of flavors we encounter throughout our lives. They can tell us a great deal not only about what we're ingesting, but also about the physical qualities and the energy we're taking in as a result. The moment food enters our mouths, our taste buds do much more than simply identify tastes. They unlock the nutritional value of foods and provide the initial spark for the entire digestive process. Tastes do not disappear with the food after it's been digested; they continue to influence our physical and emotional balance. Every meal should contain all six tastes, because that's how we can ensure that the signals that the brain is sending to our body for energy are adequately addressed, thus avoiding food cravings or overconsumption. In addition, in Ayurveda, the year is separated into 12 seasons, and each of them has a dominating dosha. The tastes play a big role in regulating the body's dosha with the dosha of the season through diet.

Signals for Your Body

The first experience of tastes happens on the tongue. In fact, the tongue is an integral part of the digestive system, just as much as the stomach or the intestines are. Different tastes create different perceptions in our taste buds, as well as different digestive reactions—a postdigestive effect known as *vipaka*, which takes place between 6 and 8 hours after ingestion of food. This is when the taste "emerges" in the stomach. For instance, lentils are considered to have a sweet taste, because even though they don't taste sweet while being consumed, they create a digestive reaction which increases water and earth elements. During digestion, the tastes are consolidated into three postdigestive tastes: sweet and salty consolidate to sweet, sour remains sour, while bitter, pungent, and astringent consolidate to pungent. The postdigestive taste has a significant effect on the long-term elemental constitution. Once brought into balance, a body's inherent intelligence takes over and naturally starts to gravitate to the foods and tastes it needs by enticing our senses.

Achieving Balance with Taste

Your body naturally desires tastes that balance its doshic makeup and shuns tastes of an aggravating nature. If we simply follow our natural inclinations, they would lead us to the foods we should be eating. As with most things in Ayurveda, the combination of tastes that are right for you depends on your constitution, your imbalances, your age, and your environment. In other words, while each of the tastes is necessary for all of us, the specifics are determined by the unique doshic makeup of each individual, and they may change over time. A balanced diet will include an appropriate quantity of each of the six tastes according to one's constitution or prakruti, current state or vikruti, and the season.

VATA INGREDIENTS

The following is a list of ingredients to favor and avoid in order to keep the vata dosha in balance.

Vata types should favor sweet, sour, and salty tastes.

FRUITS

Favor: Apples (cooked), apricots, bananas (ripe), berries, cantaloupe, cherries, coconut, dates (fresh, cooked, or soaked), figs (fresh, cooked, or soaked), grapefruit, grapes, kiwi, lemons, limes, mangoes, melons, oranges, papaya, peaches, pineapple, plums, prunes (cooked or soaked), raisins (cooked or soaked), tamarind

Reduce or Avoid: Apples (raw), bananas (green), cranberries, dates (dried), dried fruit (in general), figs (dried), pears, persimmons, pomegranates, prunes, raisins, watermelon

VEGETABLES

Favor: Asparagus, avocados, beets, carrots (cooked), chiles (in very small quantities), cilantro, cucumbers, garlic, green beans, green chiles, leeks, mustard greens, okra, olives (black), onions (cooked), parsnips, peas (cooked), pumpkin, rutabagas, spinach (cooked), squash (summer and winter), sweet potatoes, watercress, zucchini

Reduce or Avoid: Artichokes, beet greens, bell peppers, bitter melon, broccoli, Brussels sprouts, burdock root, cabbage, carrots (raw), cauliflower, celery, chiles (in excess), corn (fresh), dandelion greens, eggplant, Jerusalem artichokes, kale, kohlrabi, lettuce, mushrooms, olives (green), onions (raw), peas (raw), peppers (hot), potatoes (white), radishes, spinach (raw), sprouts, tomatoes, turnips

GRAINS

Favor: Amaranth, durum flour, oats (cooked), quinoa, rice (all types), sprouted wheat bread, wheat

Reduce or Avoid: Barley, buckwheat, couscous, millet, muesli, oat bran, oats (dry), pasta, rye, spelt, tapioca, wheat, wheat bran, yeasted bread

LEGUMES

Favor: Lentils (red), miso, mung beans, mung dal (split), pigeon peas, soy cheese, soy milk (served warm), soy meats, soy sauce, tofu (served hot), urad dal

Reduce or Avoid: Adzuki beans, black beans, black-eyed peas, chickpeas, kidney beans, lentils (brown), lima beans, navy beans, pinto beans, soybeans, soy flour, soy powder, split peas, tempeh, white beans

DAIRY

Favor: Butter, buttermilk, cheese, cottage cheese, cow's milk, ghee, goat's milk, ice cream (in moderation), sour cream (in moderation), yogurt (fresh)

Reduce or Avoid: Frozen yogurt, powdered milk

NUTS AND SEEDS

Favor: Almonds, Brazil nuts, cashews, hazelnuts, macadamia nuts, peanuts, pecans, pine nuts, pistachios, pumpkin seeds, sesame seeds, sunflower seeds, walnuts

Reduce or Avoid: Popcorn

MEAT, EGGS, AND SEAFOOD

Favor: Beef, bison, chicken (dark meat), duck, eggs, fish (freshwater and saltwater), seafood, turkey (dark meat)

Reduce or Avoid: Lamb, mutton, pork, rabbit, turkey (white meat), venison

OILS

Favor: Almond oil, avocado oil, castor oil, coconut oil, mustard oil, olive oil, peanut oil, safflower oil, sesame oil, sunflower oil

Reduce or Avoid: Canola oil, corn oil, flaxseed oil, soybean oil

SWEETENERS

Favor: Barley malt, date sugar, fructose, fruit juice concentrates, honey (raw), jaggery, maple syrup (in moderation), molasses, rice syrup, Sucanat, turbinado sugar

Reduce or Avoid: Artificial sweeteners, honey (heated or cooked), white sugar

SPICES AND HERBS

Favor: Ajwan, allspice, anise, asafetida, basil, bay leaf, black pepper, caraway, cardamom, cinnamon, cloves, coriander (seeds or powder), cumin (seeds or powder), dill, fennel seeds, garlic, ginger (fresh or powder), mace, marjoram, mint, mustard seeds, nutmeg, oregano, paprika, parsley, peppermint, pippali, poppy seeds, rosemary, saffron, salt, tarragon, thyme, turmeric, vanilla

Reduce or Avoid: Cayenne, chili powder, fenugreek, horseradish, neem leaves

PITTA INGREDIENTS

The following is a list of ingredients to favor and avoid in order to keep the pitta dosha in balance.

Pitta types should favor sweet, bitter, and astringent tastes.

FRUITS
Favor: Apples (sweet), apricots, berries (sweet), cherries (sweet), coconut, dates, figs, grapes (red, purple, and black), limes, mangoes (ripe), melons, oranges (sweet), papaya, pears, pineapple, plums (sweet), pomegranates, prunes, raisins, strawberries, watermelon

Reduce or Avoid: Apples (sour), apricots (sour), bananas, berries (sour), cherries (sour), cranberries, grapefruit, grapes (green), kiwi, lemons, mangoes (green), oranges (sour), peaches, persimmons, pineapple (sour), plums (sour), tamarind

VEGETABLES
Favor: Avocados, artichokes, asparagus, beets (cooked), bell peppers, bitter melon, broccoli, Brussels sprouts, cabbage, carrots (cooked), cauliflower, celery, cilantro, collard greens, cucumbers, dandelion greens, green beans, Jerusalem artichokes, kale, leeks (cooked), lettuce, mushrooms, okra, olives (black), onions, parsnips, peas, peppers (sweet), potatoes (white), pumpkin, radishes, rutabagas, sprouts (not spicy), squash (spaghetti, summer, and winter), spinach (raw), sweet potatoes, watercress, zucchini

Reduce or Avoid: Beet greens, beets (raw), burdock root, corn (fresh), daikon radishes, eggplant, garlic, green chiles, horseradish, kohlrabi, leeks (raw), mustard greens, olives (green), onions (raw), peppers (hot), radishes (raw), spinach (cooked), tomatoes, turnip greens, turnips

GRAINS
Favor: Amaranth, barley, couscous, durum flour, oat bran, quinoa, rice (basmati, white, and wild), spelt, wheat, wheat bran

Reduce or Avoid: Buckwheat, millet, polenta, rice (brown), rye

LEGUMES
Favor: Adzuki beans, black beans, black-eyed peas, chickpeas, kidney beans, lentils, lima beans, mung beans, navy beans, pinto beans, soybeans, split peas, tempeh, tofu, white beans

Reduce or Avoid: Fermented soybeans, soy sauce, urad dal

DAIRY
Favor: Butter (unsalted), cheese (soft, unsalted, not aged), cottage cheese, cow's milk, ghee, goat's milk, goat cheese (soft, unsalted), yogurt (homemade, diluted, without fruit)

Reduce or Avoid: Butter (salted), buttermilk, cheese (hard), frozen yogurt, sour cream, yogurt (store-bought)

NUTS AND SEEDS
Favor: Almonds (soaked and peeled), charoli nuts, flaxseeds, popcorn, pumpkin seeds, sunflower seeds

Reduce or Avoid: Almonds (with skin), Brazil nuts, cashews, chia seeds, hazelnuts, macadamia nuts, peanuts, pecans, pine nuts, pistachios, sesame seeds, walnuts

MEAT, EGGS, AND SEAFOOD
Favor: Bison, chicken (white meat), egg whites, fish (freshwater), rabbit, shrimp, turkey (white meat), venison

Reduce or Avoid: Beef, chicken (dark meat), duck, egg yolks, fish (saltwater), lamb, pork, salmon, seafood, turkey (dark meat)

OILS
Favor: Coconut oil, evening primrose oil, flaxseed oil, olive oil, sunflower oil, soybean oil, walnut oil

Reduce or Avoid: Almond oil, apricot oil, corn oil, safflower oil, sesame oil

SWEETENERS
Favor: Barley malt syrup, date sugar, fructose, maple syrup, rice syrup, Sucanat, turbinado sugar

Reduce or Avoid: Honey, jaggery, molasses, white sugar

SPICES AND HERBS
Favor: Basil (fresh), cardamom, coriander, cumin, dill, fennel seeds, ginger (fresh), mint, neem leaves, orange peel, parsley, peppermint, saffron, spearmint, tarragon, turmeric, vanilla, wintergreen

Reduce or Avoid: Ajwan, allspice, anise, asafetida, basil (dried), bay leaf, caraway, cayenne, cloves, fenugreek, ginger (powder), mace, marjoram, mustard seeds, nutmeg, oregano, paprika, parsley, pippali, poppy seeds, rosemary, sage, salt, thyme, trikatu

KAPHA INGREDIENTS

The following is a list of ingredients to favor and avoid in order to keep the kapha dosha in balance.

Kapha types should favor astringent, bitter, and pungent tastes.

FRUITS
Favor: Apples, applesauce, apricots, berries, cherries, cranberries, figs (dried), grapes (red, purple, black), lemons, limes, mangoes, peaches, pears, persimmons, pomegranates, prunes, raisins, raspberries, strawberries

Reduce or Avoid: Bananas, cantaloupe, coconut, dates, figs (fresh), grapes (green), grapefruit, kiwi, melons, oranges, papaya, pineapple, plums, rhubarb, tamarind, watermelon

VEGETABLES
Favor: Artichokes, asparagus, beets, bell peppers, bitter melon, broccoli, Brussels sprouts, cabbage, carrots, cauliflower, celery, chiles, cilantro, collard greens, corn, daikon radish, dandelion greens, eggplant, garlic, green beans, horseradish, Jerusalem artichokes, kale, kohlrabi, leafy greens, leeks, lettuce, mustard greens, okra, onions, peas, peppers (sweet and hot), potatoes (white), radishes, rutabagas, spaghetti squash, spinach, sprouts, squash, tomatoes (cooked), turnips, watercress, wheat grass

Reduce or Avoid: Avocados, cucumbers, olives, parsnips, pumpkin, summer squash, sweet potatoes, tomatoes (raw), zucchini

GRAINS
Favor: Amaranth, barley, buckwheat, couscous, durum flour, millet, oats (dry), polenta, quinoa, rice (basmati, wild), rye, spelt, sprouted wheat bread

Reduce or Avoid: Oats (cooked), rice (brown, white), wheat

LEGUMES
Favor: Adzuki beans, black beans, black-eyed peas, chickpeas, lentils, lima beans, mung beans, navy beans, pigeon peas, pinto beans, split peas, white beans

Reduce or Avoid: Kidney beans, soybeans (and all related products)

DAIRY
Favor: Buttermilk, cottage cheese, ghee, goat cheese, goat's milk, yogurt (freshly made)

Reduce or Avoid: Butter, cheese (processed), ice cream, milk, sour cream, yogurt (store-bought)

NUTS AND SEEDS

Favor: Almonds (soaked and peeled), charoli nuts, chia seeds, flaxseeds, pumpkin seeds, sunflower seeds

Reduce or Avoid: Brazil nuts, cashews, filberts, macadamia nuts, peanuts, pecans, pine nuts, pistachios, sesame seeds, walnuts

MEAT, EGGS, AND SEAFOOD

Favor: Chicken (white meat), eggs, fish (freshwater), rabbit, shrimp, turkey (white meat), venison

Reduce or Avoid: Beef, bison, chicken (dark meat), duck, fish (saltwater), lamb, pork, salmon, sardines, turkey (dark meat)

OILS

Favor: Almond oil, corn oil, flaxseed oil, ghee, sunflower oil

Reduce or Avoid: Apricot oil, avocado oil, coconut oil, evening primrose oil, olive oil, safflower oil, sesame oil, soybean oil, walnut oil

SWEETENERS

Favor: Fruit juice concentrate, honey (raw), natural fruit juices

Reduce or Avoid: Artificial sweeteners, barley malt, date sugar, fructose, honey (cooked, heated, or processed), jaggery, maple syrup, molasses, rice syrup, Sucanat, turbinado sugar, white sugar

SPICES AND HERBS

Favor: Ajwan, allspice, anise, asafetida, basil, bay leaf, black pepper, caraway, cardamom, cayenne, cinnamon, cloves, coriander, cumin, dill, fennel seeds, fenugreek, garlic, ginger, mace, marjoram, mint, mustard seeds, neem leaves, nutmeg, oregano, paprika, parsley, peppermint, pippali, poppy seeds, rosemary, saffron, spearmint, tarragon, thyme, trikatu, turmeric, vanilla, wintergreen

Reduce or Avoid: Salt

HERBS AND SPICES:

NATURE'S PHARMACY

Eating all the healthy, wholesome foods in the world is of little benefit if your body cannot absorb the nutrients and put them to use building healthy tissue. This is why spices and herbs are used as nature's pharmacy and are at the front and center of an Ayurvedic diet—they activate the digestive fire of the body known as *agni*, which is responsible for everything from breaking down what you eat, absorbing its nutrients, and assimilating it into the vital energy, known as *ojas*. Agni supports a strong metabolism, cleanses toxins from the body, and prevents digestive disorders.

There is a panoply of healing herbs and spices available for us in nature, and their taste composition serves to balance the three doshas. Turmeric, cumin, coriander, fennel seeds, mint, asafetida (or hing), black pepper, ginger, cardamom, cinnamon, nutmeg, and cayenne are among the most commonly used Ayurvedic spices, boasting an array of health benefits, such as anti-inflammatory, antibacterial, and anti-oxidant properties, aiding respiratory issues, helping regulate blood sugar levels, strengthening the immune system, lowering bad cholesterol, improving good cholesterol, treating skin disorders, and many more.

You should try to incorporate spices and herbs in each of your meals. They not only provide you with the six tastes, but are helpful in customizing a meal to your liking. This book will guide you through the use of spices at different times of year, in order to reap their benefits. Each recipe incorporates one of the six tastes as a dominant flavor profile, and you'll find recipes for the six main spice mixes on pages 30–35. Refer to the ingredient sections with recommendations for your particular dosha (pages 22–27) to get an idea of what herbs and spices are particularly good for you.

Buy spices in their whole form whenever possible, as they'll stay fresh about five to six months longer than preground versions. You will need to periodically replace them and keep them tightly sealed to ensure they don't lose their healing properties. As a general rule, dried herbs and ground spices will last 1 year and whole spices will last 2 years. Grinding them in small batches is the best way to use them. My go-to tool is a mortar and pestle, but you can also use an electric spice grinder or a coffee grinder designated solely for this purpose. Roasting dry spices is key to bringing out their flavors. Heating certain spices and herbs like turmeric, cumin, coriander, mustard seeds, fennel seeds, and dill is known as "blooming"—a technique that releases essential oils, which not only enhances flavor, but also enhances their healing properties. When blooming whole spices, you can either roast them on a dry, nonstick pan, or in ghee or oil. For powdered spices, blooming is best done in sautéed onions, garlic, ginger, leeks, or chiles. Be cautious not to overheat them, as their essential oils can be damaged and the benefits lost in the process.

People often think that adding spices to a dish will make it spicy, so they shy away from using them altogether. But spices can add a range of flavors and aromas from very intense to extremely mild; it's just a matter of getting the hang of using them. From more complex dishes to flavoring basic natural ingredients for simple homemade snacks, spices and herbs eliminate the need for various packaged foods. Ayurvedic physicians recommend against taking spices in supplement form, where the so-called active ingredient is isolated and put in a pill or a capsule. Take them as nature intended—in your food.

SPICE BLENDS

The following six recipes are for spice mixes that represent the six tastes in Ayurveda. You'll find them used throughout book. Consider these mixes templates for each flavor profile; they incorporate some of the most beneficial spices mindfully mixed together in combinations that work for a broad spectrum of dishes. Making and using them will establish a strong intuition about how to use individual spices, and you can eventually tweak the amounts of each spice according to your dish or personal preferences.

The representation of tastes in these spice blends shouldn't be confused for the way "taste" is used in everyday language. In Ayurveda, taste has everything to do with the essence of food and its effect on the body. For example, cinnamon is commonly associated with sweet flavors, but in Ayurveda it is also recognized as bitter, because of its postdigestive effect on the body.

SWEET SPICE MIX

MAKES 1 PORTION (ABOUT 1½ TEASPOONS)

1 teaspoon cinnamon powder
1 whole clove
⅛ teaspoon cardamom seeds (or seeds of one pod)
¼ teaspoon smoked paprika
A pinch of saffron (optional)

Combine all the spices in a mortar and pestle or a spice grinder. Grind the spices to the desired consistency.

SALTY SPICE MIX

MAKES 1 PORTION (ABOUT 4 TEASPOONS)

½ teaspoon celery seeds
1½ teaspoons garlic powder
1½ teaspoons onion powder
1 teaspoon kosher salt

Combine all the spices in a mortar and pestle or a spice grinder. Grind the spices to the desired consistency.

SOUR SPICE MIX

MAKES 1 PORTION (ABOUT 1 TABLESPOON)

1 teaspoon pink peppercorns
1 teaspoon sumac
1½ teaspoons sesame seeds, toasted
½ teaspoon fennel seeds
½ teaspoon black pepper
¼ teaspoon fine Himalayan salt

Combine all the spices in a mortar and pestle or a spice grinder. Grind the spices to the desired consistency.

PUNGENT SPICE MIX

MAKES 1 PORTION (ABOUT 2 TEASPOONS)

¾ teaspoon cayenne pepper
½ teaspoon ginger powder
½ teaspoon white peppercorns
½ teaspoon ajwain powder or anise seeds

Combine all the spices in a mortar and pestle or a spice grinder. Grind the spices to the desired consistency.

BITTER SPICE MIX

MAKES 1 PORTION (ABOUT 2 ½ TEASPOONS)
½ teaspoon turmeric powder
⅛ teaspoon ground nutmeg
1 teaspoon cocoa powder
1 teaspoon ginger powder

Combine all the spices in a mortar and pestle or a spice grinder. Grind the spices to the desired consistency.

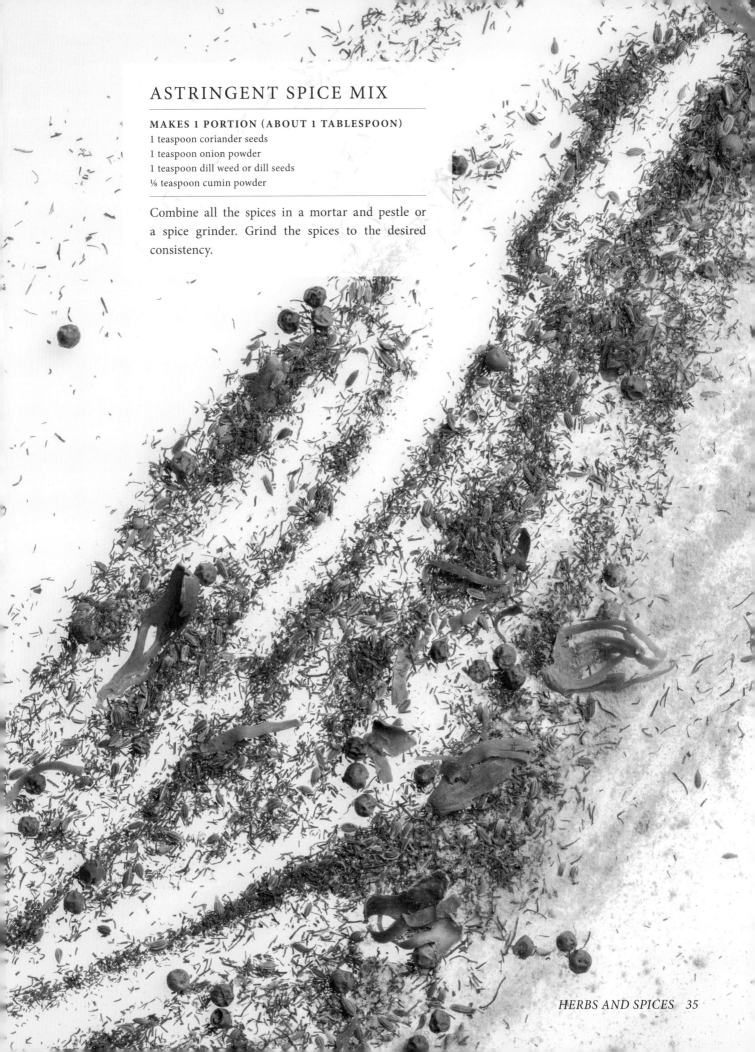

ASTRINGENT SPICE MIX

MAKES 1 PORTION (ABOUT 1 TABLESPOON)

1 teaspoon coriander seeds
1 teaspoon onion powder
1 teaspoon dill weed or dill seeds
⅛ teaspoon cumin powder

Combine all the spices in a mortar and pestle or a spice grinder. Grind the spices to the desired consistency.

OJAS:
The Life Force

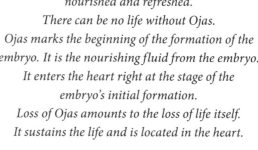

What Is Ojas?

The Sanskrit word *ojas* directly translates to "vital energy and bodily strength." Ojas is considered the most refined byproduct of digestion. It is the finest material substance in the body that contains life force (*prana*) and serves vital functions that maintain the body's energy reserves and proper immune status. It has been compared to a subtle glue or cement that binds the body, mind, and spirit into a contained functional whole. It is what is often described as "the glow" of a healthy person. The ancient classical text the *Charaka Samhita* describes ojas as follows:

It is the Ojas which keeps all the living beings nourished and refreshed.
There can be no life without Ojas.
Ojas marks the beginning of the formation of the embryo. It is the nourishing fluid from the embryo. It enters the heart right at the stage of the embryo's initial formation.
Loss of Ojas amounts to the loss of life itself. It sustains the life and is located in the heart.

You Are What You Eat

Like honey that's collected from fruits and flowers, ojas is "collected" in the body from our actions, qualities, habits, and diet. Since ojas is the final product of a perfect digestion, it makes sense that building it will require eating natural whole foods in accordance to our doshic constitution. The energy of the foods we consume is fully extracted by our bodies at different levels over a period of about 30 days. Understanding ojas makes you realize that we really are what we eat. Other than diet, there are many ojas-building activities that should become part of our daily routine, such as exercise, meditation, Yoga, self-massage, a good sleep schedule, and the use of herbs and spices. These routines are essential for longevity, resistance to illness, youthfulness, and vitality.

Ojas in the Making

Ojas is the first thing to be created in the body of all living beings and is used up when any of the five senses are engaged. It is the ultimate product of nutrition, digestion, and metabolism. While complete digestion of a meal takes about 24 hours, it takes 30 days for the body to digest food at the subtler levels of tissues and refine it enough to manufacture ojas. Through proper diet, rest, and attitude, ojas can be rebuilt in our system. During our teenage years, ojas is at its peak, and if one keeps up with a life of good eating habits and life routines, ojas will continue to thrive.

Ojas in the Body

Ojas is centered in the heart, but it exists throughout every part of the body and protects the health of every cell. It is both a mental and a physical factor, manifesting physically in the immune system. All functions of the body that act to preserve and protect it are manifestations of ojas. Signs of abundant ojas are clear, radiant eyes, lustrous hair, glowing skin, a strong immune system, a positive outlook on life, joy, mental clarity, and compassion. Signs of depleted ojas include dry skin, cold hands and/or feet, constipation, anxiety, pain, mental fogginess, negativity, loneliness, and fatigue. The strength of a person's ojas is visible in their body and physique. It manifests as bodily strength, the ability to resist illness, a well-functioning digestion, and fertility. Your ojas can be considerably diminished even though you are not experiencing overt illness. If you are feeling generally stressed out and fatigued on a regular basis, your ojas likely needs rebuilding.

THE ZODIAC CALENDAR:

A BROADER VIEW OF SEASONALITY

From our earthly perspective, it appears as if the sun, the moon, and the planets travel on a set path through the sky known as the ecliptic. The constellations (a recognized cluster of stars) that the sun passes through are known as the constellations of the zodiac. The zodiac signs reflect the position of the sun relative to a particular constellation during a specific period of the year. The cosmos and the human body are variants of the same energy principle. It is important to understand the energies that surround us in the universe, to establish a more seamless relationship between the macro and the micro aspects of life.

The positions of the constellations relative to the sun indicate seasons and have historically provided a forecast for the coming changes. This book is structured around the signs of the zodiac to provide an expanded view of our relationship to the universe—a month-to-month take on seasonality, as opposed to the conventional understanding of just four seasons. Two of the most important aspects of restoring balance in Ayurveda are tuning in to the natural rhythms of your body, then bringing your lifestyle into sync with nature and its cyclical patterns. This includes lining up your activity level, food choices, sleep schedule, and so on, with the time of day as well as the seasons. Living by nature's rhythm is the only logical solution to mankind's health problems. Zooming out from our subjective worldview will enable us to create a connection with where we originally came from, where we are today, and where we would like to go. Navigating the year based on the seasons of the zodiac and Earth's path around the sun enables us to eat in each season what nature has intended for us. Each chapter of this book contains recipes that help create a harmony of doshas and the seasons, by using fresh, local, in-season ingredients.

During each microseason there is an accumulation of extreme conditions characteristic for that time of year. When we eat locally and seasonally, we have an ideal monthly harvest to keep us strong, healthy, energized, and focused. Everyone in the world experiences general reactions and transitional changes through the seasons, which are ruled by the inherent intelligence of our body as well as Mother Nature. Pairing seasonal dietary guidelines with your individual needs anchors you to a fine-tuned routine throughout the year.

Keep in mind that the use of the constellations in this book is in no way related to your personal astrological birth sign.

THE SIX STAGES OF ILLNESS:

A PREVENTIVE APPROACH

Contrary to modern medicine, Ayurveda recognizes illness in six stages: accumulation, aggravation, dissemination, localization, manifestation, and chronicity or disruption. It is considered a preventive medicine that treats the root causes of an illness instead of just the observable symptoms.

Illness occurs when an increase in the amount of each dosha eventually spreads and settles in the weak tissues of our body over many years. When a dosha enters one of the bodily tissues—plasma, blood, muscle, fat, bone, nerve, and reproductive tissues—it begins to affect its physical structure and cause illness. Illness starts in the gastrointestinal tract, when toxins, known as *ama*, accumulate and aren't flushed out properly. In the first stage, illness is quite manageable through the body's natural abilities to heal itself—the body will attempt to correct the imbalance by intuitively guiding the individual away from the factors that are causing the problem. If the signals of the body are ignored, it will be unable to correct the imbalance and the symptoms will worsen. The symptoms will often become chronic, but an individual might brush them off or temporarily appease them with over-the-counter medication. If no effort is made to bring the body back into balance, toxins begin to spread from the digestive system and circulate in the body. After moving through the circulatory system, they find a weak tissue and they plant themselves in it. This is the beginning of actual illness, when serious physical symptoms start to occur. Western medicine considers this to be the beginning of an illness and makes a clinical diagnosis.

We are most vulnerable to illness when poor diet, stress, and other environmental factors interfere with the body's ability to heal and repair itself. Human health is optimized when the doshas are flowing out of the body freely and the tissues are properly nourished. When a person doesn't listen to their body's inherent biological intelligence, he or she will crave substances that hurt them and make negligent choices which disrespect the senses and disrupt a healthy rhythm of life.

Since illnesses develop in distinct stages, a good understanding of their progression will help recognize them early on. The first four stages are unique to Ayurveda because they are asymptomatic and allow us to detect and correct the problem before it manifests as a serious physical symptom. The good news is that illness usually takes years to fully develop, and there are many opportunities to intercept its path. If we bring the aggravated dosha back into balance before the fifth stage, we stand a good chance of reversing the progression of an illness and restoring our health.

Unfortunately, Western medicine often doesn't recognize the early stages of illness and only has tools to treat the final two symptomatic stages. Ayurveda can offer an insight into the early stages and enables the monitoring of the smallest imbalances that could lead to a serious illness. If we learn to recognize the warning signs, we stand a much better chance of reversing the progression of illness before it begins to damage our body's tissues.

A STEP FURTHER:
AYURVEDIC BITES OF KNOWLEDGE

FOOD COMBINING

When certain foods with different tastes, energy, and postdigestive effects are eaten together, they can hinder the digestive fire, which causes indigestion and the formation of toxins in the body. The most important rule about food combinations is to try and eat fruits on their own. Food is digested in the stomach in the order that it's eaten, and fruits will start to ferment and rot as they are waiting in this digestion line. They are one of the easiest and quickest things for your body to break down, so enjoy them for breakfast or as an afternoon snack. There are many Ayurvedic guidelines to appropriate food combinations available online, but pace yourself and test how you react to one change at a time. And remember, your diet is never going to be black or white, but the better choices you make daily, the more you are tipping the scales in favor of health.

DRINKING AND EATING

Ayurveda discourages drinking an excessive amount of liquid during meals, because it hampers good digestion. However, you can sip tepid water or warm tea in moderation throughout the meal, to moisten ingested food. For optimal hydration, make sure to get your recommended 6 to 8 glasses of water throughout the day.

NEVER HEAT HONEY!

Ayurveda has appreciated honey's healing qualities for thousands of years, emphasizing that it's vital to know how to eat it properly. Consuming honey that has been cooked, baked, or added to hot liquids contributes to bad health over time, because heated honey becomes similar to glue in your digestive tract. Enjoy honey at room temperature and preferably raw.

DIGESTION AND EMOTIONS

Emotions are our body's signal to action and attention. They are energy in motion and will become damaging if we don't let ourselves wholly experience them or if we overreact. Our emotional state has a strong impact on our physical health. Emotional health can be facilitated by improving digestion and steering clear of toxin buildup. We possess a "digestive fire" (*agni*) that processes emotions, not unlike the digestive fire that helps us process the foods we eat. This force is obstructed when faced with emotional upheaval and the aggravating stress of daily life, resulting in a direct effect on our digestive health, as well as our emotional state. By improving diet and lifestyle, one can ease emotional imbalances and vice versa.

A SIMPLE ROUTINE FOR STAYING YOUTHFUL

Having and maintaining a daily routine is crucial for creating sustainable change in the body and mind. Following a personalized daily routine is the most stabilizing and nurturing adjustment you can make in your life. The appropriate routine should be one that meets the needs of each individual's constitution and current state of health. The right daily routine can dramatically improve your life, so here are some simple practices you can start to incorporate into your day-to-day. It can be hard to make too many changes at once, so go at your own pace.

» Wake up an hour earlier than usual (aim for before sunrise).

» Brush your teeth and scrape your tongue. Toxins accumulate on the tongue while we sleep, and we don't want to introduce them back into our digestive system. Tongue scraping acts as stimulation and massage for internal organs.

» Splash your eyes with clean water. This practice strengthens the eyes, improves eyesight, clears the mind, and recharges mental energy.

» Drink a cup of warm water with lemon on an empty stomach—it will kick-start the liver and prepare it for a brand new day of work.

» Massage yourself with appropriate oils a minimum of three times per week. Self-massage ignites your vitality from within and stimulates all the systems of your body.

» Exercise daily. Do whatever makes you feel like a kid again—be it running, riding a bike, or walking your dog. Just get your body moving.

» Eat only when you're hungry, and make a maximum effort to eat local whole foods suited for your dosha and the season. Learn how to differentiate hunger from eating for the sake of eating.

» Sip ginger tea throughout the day, or enjoy any of the ginger drinks from this book (they are the last recipes in each chapter). Ginger is nature's treasure for your health.

» Take a 20-minute break after every 50 minutes of work. The brain is a muscle, and like every muscle, it tires from repeated exertion.

» Meditate every day in whatever way relaxes you, even if it means lying down and listening to your favorite tunes. A regular meditation practice calms and grounds the mind, and brings clarity and happiness.

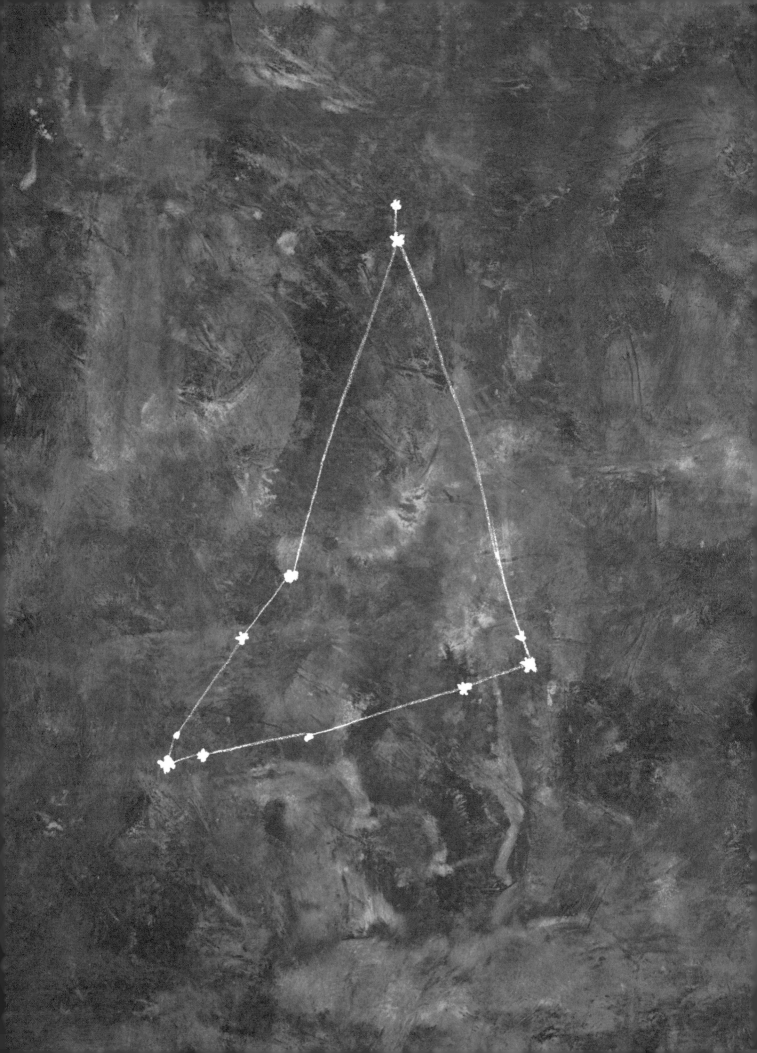

CHAPTER 1

CAPRICORN

Essential Ayurvedic Spice

CLOVE

» *Cloves are native to the Maluku Islands, now a part of Indonesia. Today, this evergreen grows naturally in India, Sri Lanka, Brazil, the West Indies, Zanzibar, Madagascar, and Tanzania. It is a spice that grows as a pink flower bud on a tropical evergreen tree. It is picked before it blooms, then dried into a brown bud that resembles a tiny nail.*

» *Beneficial for balancing the Vata dosha, cloves should be consumed in moderation for the Kapha dosha and can be aggravating to the Pitta dosha if there is already a tendency toward excessive heat in your body.*

» *Since cloves are very heating and energizing, it is important to use them more sparingly in the hotter seasons. Although they have a very hard exterior, their flesh features an oily compound that is essential to their nutritional and flavor profile. Among their long list of health benefits, cloves enhance circulation, digestion, and metabolism.*

» *Cloves provide one of the most powerful flavors of all the spices. They are simultaneously bitter and sweet, a mixture of flavors that can overwhelm the palate if overused. One of the tricks I have learned when using cloves is to pair them with some citrus juice or zest, which breaks up their strong, earthy aroma with a fresh and uplifting scent that brings back memories of holiday meals.*

» *Cloves can be used whole or ground to add a peppery flavor and should be used in moderation to avoid overseasoning or overpowering other flavors. It's best to grind whole cloves into powder right before using them to ensure flavor and freshness are at their peak.*

» *Cloves have a long shelf life; they last up to a year if they're kept in a cool, dark place.*

December 22–January 19

CAPRICORN

Capricorn is Latin for "the goat" and is commonly represented in the form of a simplified drawing of a half-goat, half-fish mythological creature known as the sea goat. It is the tenth sign of the zodiac. The first half of Capricorn falls into the general Vata season, then makes a transition to Kapha season in the second half. As the sun enters Capricorn, nature rests. Cold and gray skies create a sense of roughness in a hibernating world.

Balance your diet with lightly sweet and nourishing foods, like amaranth, avocado, apples, cashews, raisins, and yogurt, which will help combat the cold. Try to avoid storing any more fat in the body. Start to moderate sour foods when transitioning seasons, as they can cause water retention and an increased appetite. They remain helpful for countering the tendency toward dryness at this time, so don't cut them out altogether. Moderate your intake of salt, as it helps keep the body warm and prevents dryness, but it can cause an excess of moisture and heaviness as you move toward the seasonal change. Increased fats, excess water retention, an increased appetite, and heaviness will all hinder the natural detox cycle your body is entering as it transitions into the Kapha season in the second half of this period.

At the beginning of the winter season, your energy settles down and turns inward. Try to get adequate sleep, which is imperative during this period.

JERUSALEM ARTICHOKE FRITTERS *WITH CHILE-YOGURT SAUCE*

This crispy comfort snack is packed with healthy ingredients. It's a perfect way to start providing your body with some of the healthy insulation it needs in the cold season. Jerusalem artichokes (also known as sunchokes) are one of my favorite ingredients. They are low in calories and fat and can be used as a healthy alternative to potatoes. They are also one of the finest sources of dietary fiber essential to good digestive health. You should take advantage of their versatility and serve them as a mash, in a stew, a roast, or even as a side dish, just as you would potatoes or carrots. This red pepper sauce works well as a dressing or even a light spread, so I always make extra and keep it in the refrigerator for a couple of days.

Dosha Dos and Don'ts: *Vata types can substitute the Jerusalem artichokes with sweet potatoes; otherwise, they should indulge in this snack moderately to avoid too much of their bitter taste and other airy qualities, which can be aggravating for Vata and cause bloating.*

SERVES 4 TO 6

Chile-Yogurt Sauce:
2 large red bell peppers
One 1-inch piece fresh ginger
1 tablespoon fresh lime juice
2 teaspoons cinnamon powder
1 cup plain organic yogurt
Kosher salt

Jerusalem Artichoke Fritters:
1 pound Jerusalem artichokes, scrubbed, coarsely grated, and kept in ice water to avoid browning
1 cup amaranth seeds
2 tablespoons yellow cornmeal
¼ cup brown rice flour
3 medium shallots, finely chopped
1 Indian green chile, finely chopped
1 teaspoon kosher salt

½ teaspoon baking powder
1 portion Bitter Spice Mix (page 34), finely ground
4 large organic eggs, whisked
Sunflower oil, for frying

To Finish:
2 tablespoons chopped chives
2 tablespoons chopped mint

For the sauce: Preheat the oven to 450°F. Place the bell peppers on a parchment paper–lined baking sheet and roast for 25 minutes, or until the peppers are shriveled and the skins are charred. Remove from the oven, transfer to a mixing bowl and cover with a plate to allow the peppers to steam in their own heat. When the peppers are cool enough to handle, peel and seed them.

Place the peppers, ginger, lime juice, cinnamon, and yogurt in a blender and blend until smooth. Add salt to taste and refrigerate until ready to serve.

For the fritters: Lower the oven temperature to 250°F.

Drain the Jerusalem artichokes and squeeze them with your hands to remove excess water, then place them in a mixing bowl. Add the amaranth seeds, cornmeal, flour, shallots, chile, salt, baking powder, and spice mix, and stir, mixing well. Add the eggs, and mix to combine into a thick batter.

Pour ½ inch of oil into a large skillet and heat over medium-high heat until it starts to sizzle. Take about ¼ cup

of the fritter mixture in your hands and shape it into a round patty about ½ inch thick, then use the back of a spoon to flatten it down slightly once in the skillet. Fry the fritters 4 at a time until both sides are crispy and golden brown, 3 to 5 minutes. Place the fritters on a parchment paper–lined baking sheet and transfer to the oven to keep them warm while frying the rest.

To finish: Place the yogurt sauce in a small bowl, top with chives and mint. Serve alongside the hot fritters.

CAULIFLOWER MISO SOUP

This soup is comforting and gives your body the warmth it needs during the cold season. You can also enjoy it in warmer months, in which case you should omit the nuts to make a lighter version. Nature gives us clues as to what foods help what part of our body by mirroring the body parts they provide nutrients for. Because of its shape, cauliflower is said to be good for the brain.

Dosha Dos and Don'ts: *Pitta types can halve the amount of miso because the sour taste of such fermented foods can cause overheating in an already heat-prone Pitta. Vata types with a tendency to experience bloating should enjoy this soup in moderation (too much cauliflower can further aggravate this condition). However, the spices used with the cauliflower are very effective in making the soup suitable for Vata types.*

SERVES 4 TO 6

1 medium head cauliflower, chopped into small florets

2 medium shallots, quartered

3 tablespoons olive oil, plus more for roasting garlic

Kosher or sea salt

1 teaspoon coarsely ground white pepper, plus more to taste

6 garlic cloves

2 tablespoons fresh thyme leaves

1 tablespoon white miso

1½ teaspoons Dijon mustard

One ½-inch piece fresh ginger

¼ cup cashews, soaked in hot water overnight, or for at least 20 minutes, plus 2 tablespoons toasted in a dry pan and chopped

1 portion Sweet Spice Mix (page 30), coarsely ground

2 tablespoons sultana or golden raisins, soaked in hot water for 15 minutes

4 cups Vegetable Broth (page 242)

1½ teaspoons fresh lemon juice, plus more to taste

Preheat the oven to 400°F. Place the cauliflower and shallots in a mixing bowl and toss with 2 tablespoons of oil, 1 teaspoon salt, and some pepper. Spread the vegetables on a parchment paper–lined baking sheet.

Wrap the garlic cloves, along with a drizzle of oil and a pinch of salt, in a piece of parchment paper and place it on the baking sheet with the vegetables. (The garlic will caramelize when it's roasted, becoming soft and milder in flavor.) Roast for up to 40 minutes, checking on the garlic as well as the cauliflower and shallots regularly to avoid burning them.

When the cauliflower is browned around the edges, remove all the vegetables from the oven and let cool slightly. The garlic may need more time to cook, so make sure to check if it's tender. Set aside 1 cup of the smaller cauliflower florets for garnish.

In a blender, combine the remaining cauliflower, shallots, roasted garlic, 1 tablespoon of thyme leaves, miso, mustard, ginger, soaked cashews, spice mix, and raisins, and blend until smooth. Gradually add the broth until the mixture reaches a smooth consistency. Add the remaining 1 tablespoon of oil, the lemon juice, and a pinch of salt and pepper, and continue to blend. Taste and adjust the seasonings, adding more salt, pepper, and lemon juice as needed. If the soup is too thick, add some more broth or water, a few tablespoons at a time, and blend to the consistency of a heavy cream.

To finish: Serve topped with a drizzle of oil, the reserved cauliflower florets, toasted cashews, and the remaining 1 tablespoon of thyme leaves.

KHICHDI:
THE PERFECT TEMPLATE

An old favorite in Southeast Asia, khichdi is a mixture of grains and legumes stewed in water or broth and flavored with a mix of spices (its components and preparation haven't been altered for centuries). It is an ancient staple recipe in Ayurveda because it balances all three doshas, making it a tridoshic food. No matter what your taste or dietary preferences, you'll enjoy the comfort of this dish once you find the right combination of ingredients for you. Anyone with a busy life will appreciate khichdi for its simplicity—ingredients can be prepared ahead of time and the dish made with minimal supervision.

The dish is most popular in India, Nepal, and Pakistan, where common additions to it include cauliflower, potato, and green peas. In Southern India, khichdi is prepared with curry leaves, mustard seeds, cashews, and onions. In the Northeast, it is made with lots of ghee and pickled vegetables, and served with meat curries, fish, potato chips, and omelets. Versions of khichdi can be found in other parts of the world: in Egypt, a dish called koshary is made with rice, lentils, and macaroni; the Middle Eastern dish mujaddara traces its influences back to khichdi; in Britain, a breakfast version of the dish made with rice, boiled eggs, and haddock is called kedgeree.

Khichdi was once considered a delicacy reserved for Indian royalty, but it became best known in modern-day India as a food eaten when sick or to relieve stomach ailments. The combination of rice, lentils, and ghee provides carbohydrates, protein, dietary fiber, vitamins, calcium, magnesium, phosphorus, and potassium. You can also use it as a way to reset your digestion when you've overindulged in things that are less than great for you.

There are endless variations of khichdi, depending on the grains, beans, or lentils, stock or broth, herbs, spices, and vegetables used. It can be made with or without meat, the latter version easily adjusted to being vegan, as well as gluten-free, by choosing gluten-free grains like brown rice or quinoa. A basic khichdi is usually made from white rice and yellow, green, or split mung beans and topped with some ghee. You will find 12 khichdi recipes in this book, one in every chapter, which is plenty to get you to experiment until you come up with your own version. I've varied the grains, legumes, oils, spices, and toppings across these recipes to create an array of khichdis you can enjoy all year.

BASIC KHICHDI

Anyone who's grown up with Indian parents, no matter what part of India they come from, often share a memory of being given khichdi to eat when they were sick. The basic idea is to have a very well-cooked combination of a whole grain, a lentil or a bean, some form of cooking liquid (i.e., water, broth, stock, etc.), spices, herbs, and any sort of toppings. They can be cooked into a variety of consistencies (anything from a soup to a drier risotto), but the goal is to cook the grains and lentils until they are very tender and easy for the body to break down.

Dosha Dos and Don'ts: *You can create different versions using ingredients suited to your body type (refer to ingredient sections on pages 22–27). Vata types can easily get bloated, so they can replace the black beans with lentils and mix half the barley with any type of rice.*

SERVES 4 TO 6

¾ cup dry black beans
2 teaspoons asafetida powder
¾ cup barley
1 tablespoon ghee
2 medium white onions, diced

3 medium carrots, scrubbed, trimmed, and cut into 1-inch slices
1 portion Sour Spice Mix (page 32), finely ground
3½ cups Vegetable Broth (page 242) or water

1 teaspoon kosher salt, plus more to taste
2 tablespoons poppy seeds, toasted in a dry pan until they pop
½ cup chopped parsley

To prepare: In a medium heavy-bottomed saucepan, cover the beans with water, add 1 teaspoon of asafetida, and bring to a boil; boil for 2 minutes. Turn off the heat, cover the pot, and let the beans soak for 60 minutes (preferably overnight). Presoaking the beans makes them easier to digest; it also helps them cook more evenly and become tender all the way through.

It's also good to soak the barley, which makes it easier to digest. Cover the barley with water and soak for 1 hour.

After soaking the beans and barley, drain and wash thoroughly with cold water.

If you don't have time for any soaking, you can cook the dish directly from the dry ingredients, but it will take additional time to achieve the desired tenderness.

For the khichdi: In a medium heavy-bottomed saucepan, heat the ghee, then add the onions, carrots, and spice mix. Cook until the onions are translucent, then add the barley, beans, remaining 1 teaspoon of asafetida, and broth, and bring to a boil.

Reduce the mixture to a simmer and cook for about 1 hour, making sure there is always enough liquid in the pot. Simmering the beans gently helps them cook evenly until tender, retain their shape without losing their texture (getting mushy) too quickly, and keep their skins intact. After about 45 minutes, add the salt and stir (the best time to add the salt is about three-quarters of the way into the cooking process, when the beans are tender but still partly firm).

After cooking for 1 hour, taste the khichdi, and if the beans and barley are not very tender, continue cooking for up to 30 minutes longer. Depending on your preference, you can adjust the texture of the khichdi for a drier risotto-like consistency or a wetter soup-like one by either allowing the excess liquid to evaporate or adding more liquid.

To finish: Place 2 large spoonfuls of khichdi in each serving bowl. Sprinkle with the poppy seeds, parsley, and a sprinkle of salt.

SOCCA *WITH* TOMATILLO ROMESCO, STEWED BANANAS, *AND* GOAT CHEESE

A great alternative to pizza dough, socca has a deliciously smoky flavor and is much lighter. It is essentially a large gluten-free pancake made out of chickpea flour (also known as besan), which is less caloric than wheat flour. Cooking the socca in a heavy cast-iron skillet (with plenty of oil) and then finishing it in the oven creates the best texture. The combination of tomatillo and banana seemed odd to me, but I was pleasantly surprised by the interaction of the sweet and tangy flavors of the two ingredients when a Somalian friend introduced me to the pairing. It's been my favorite socca topping ever since.

SERVES 4 TO 6

Tomatillo Romesco:
½ cup raw almonds, soaked in water a minimum of 15 minutes (preferably overnight), then peeled
1 red bell pepper
1 yellow bell pepper
5 garlic cloves
¼ cup raw flaxseeds, lightly toasted in a dry pan, then cooled
¼ cup canned tomatillo puree
2 tablespoons chopped rosemary
1 tablespoon sherry vinegar

½ cup flaxseed oil or extra-virgin olive oil
1 teaspoon Himalayan salt, plus more to taste
1 tablespoon smoked paprika
1 portion Pungent Spice Mix (page 33), coarsely ground

Banana Stew:
½ teaspoon cinnamon powder
1 tablespoon ghee
2 tablespoons white miso
2 ripe bananas, cut into ½-inch slices

Socca:
1 cup chickpea flour, sifted
1 cup water
2 tablespoons ghee
1 teaspoon finely chopped rosemary
½ teaspoon fine sea salt
½ teaspoon finely ground black pepper
2 teaspoons olive oil

Toppings:
½ cup crumbled goat cheese
2 teaspoons chile flakes

For the tomatillo romesco: Lightly toast the almonds in a dry pan until they're golden brown, about 5 minutes. Toss regularly and watch them closely, as they can burn quickly when almost done. Remove from the heat and let them cool.

Roast the peppers over an open flame on a gas stove or grill until the skins are blackened and wrinkled. Place the peppers in a bowl, cover with plastic wrap, and let sit until cool enough to handle, about 20 minutes. Remove the charred skin, seeds, and cores.

In a food processor, pulse the peppers, almonds, and the remaining ingredients until smooth. Salt to taste and refrigerate until ready to assemble the socca for baking.

For the banana stew: In a frying pan over medium-high heat, heat the cinnamon, ghee, and miso and stir until well combined.

Add the banana slices and cook for 4 minutes on each side, or until they start to caramelize and turn golden brown. Adjust the cooking time and heat to avoid burning the bananas.

For the socca: In a medium bowl, combine the flour, water, ghee, rosemary, salt, and pepper. Whisk until smooth, cover, and let sit in the refrigerator for 30 minutes. The batter should be about the consistency of heavy cream.

Preheat the oven to 450°F.

Position an oven rack 6 inches below your oven's broiler. Place a 10-inch cast-iron skillet under the broiler and turn it on; let the skillet get hot. Take the skillet out of the oven (careful—it will be very hot) and coat with the oil by brushing or swirling the pan to coat it evenly. Pour the batter into the center of the pan, immediately tilting the pan to spread the batter evenly. Broil the socca for 6 to 8 minutes, until the surface starts to brown and crack lightly. If the socca is browning before it's evenly cooked and set, then lower the rack. The texture should be soft in the middle and crispy on the edges.

Remove the socca from the oven (leave the broiler on if you plan to finish it now), use a spatula to release it from the pan, then slide it onto a wire rack.

At this point, you can assemble and broil the socca and serve, or you can cool it, then wrap in a clean dishcloth, and refrigerate for later use.

To finish: Spread the tomatillo romesco over the warm socca, then top with the stewed bananas and crumbled goat cheese.

Put the socca back in the oven, and broil until the top is browned evenly, about 3 minutes. Remove from the oven and let cool for a couple of minutes. Cut the socca into wedges, sprinkle with chile flakes, and serve hot.

COCONUT-CRUSTED AVOCADO *WITH* CURRY LEAF *AND* PINE NUT PESTO

Curry leaves actually have very little to do with "curry," the Westernized dish most people think of when think think about Indian food. Curry leaves are some of the most flavor-imparting leaves and have a very distinct aroma. They have been used extensively in cooking Eastern cuisines, but I'm always looking for ways to incorporate them in more unexpected ways in "Western"-style dishes. The pesto in this recipe is the best one I know of, and it can be eaten in many ways. Make an extra batch, and you can keep it in the refrigerator for about a week. The coconut-crusted avocado makes for great leftovers that can be used in a sandwich with green chiles and any leftover pesto. Eating half an avocado a day helps satisfy hunger and prevents snacking later in the day.

Dosha Dos and Don'ts: *Kapha types should limit themselves to half an avocado, as it can cause lethargy and heaviness if not eaten in moderation. Pitta types can replace the sour cream with yogurt to reduce the sour taste that can cause an excess of digestive heat.*

SERVES 4 TO 6

Curry Leaf and Pine Nut Pesto:
1 cup tightly packed curry leaves (available at most Indian supermarkets)
1 cup watercress, with stems on
5 garlic cloves
1 cup raw pine nuts, toasted in a dry pan
1½ teaspoons honey, preferably raw
1 Indian green chile, cored, seeded, and chopped
3 teaspoons yuzu juice
One 1-inch piece fresh ginger
½ teaspoon asafetida powder

¼ teaspoon green peppercorns, freshly ground
1 portion Salty Spice Mix (page 31), coarsely ground
3 tablespoons almond oil or extra-virgin olive oil, plus more if needed
Kosher or sea salt (optional)

Coconut-Crusted Avocado:
3 tablespoons ground flaxseeds
1 tablespoon water, plus more if needed
2 ripe avocados
Lemon juice
1 teaspoon garlic powder

½ teaspoon onion powder
½ teaspoon smoked paprika
¼ teaspoon freshly ground black pepper
3 tablespoons arrowroot powder
¾ cup unsweetened coconut, shredded

To Finish:
½ cup sour cream
1 tablespoon coriander seeds, toasted in a dry pan
10 curry leaves, pan-fried in oil
1 lemon, cut into 6 wedges

For the pesto: Place all the ingredients except the oil in a food processor, and process for a couple of minutes.

Start adding the oil through the feeder and continue processing on medium speed until the mixture becomes a very smooth paste. Feel free to add additional oil if you prefer a smoother, runnier texture. Taste and add salt as needed. Cover and set aside.

For the avocado: Preheat the oven to 400°F and place a rack in the center position. Line a baking sheet with parchment paper and set aside.

In a shallow bowl, combine the flaxseeds with the water and mix well, then place in the refrigerator for about 15 minutes.

Using a chef's knife, cut each avocado in half, rolling the knife around the pit. Twist the halves to separate, then strike the pit with your knife and twist to pull the pit out. Peel each avocado half, making sure the flesh stays intact. Cut each half into 5 slices, drizzle with a bit of lemon juice (to avoid browning), and set aside.

Combine the garlic powder, onion powder, paprika, and pepper into a seasoning blend. Place half the blend and the arrowroot powder in a shallow bowl, combine and set aside.

Remove the flaxseed-and-water mixture from the refrigerator and add more water if needed to loosen it up. In a third shallow bowl, combine the shredded coconut and the remaining half of the seasoning blend.

Dip one avocado slice in the arrowroot mix, then in

the flaxseed mix, and finally the coconut mix, coating the avocado liberally.

Place the coated avocado on a parchment paper–lined baking sheet, then repeat the process for the remaining avocado slices.

Bake the avocado in the oven for up to 10 minutes, checking on it halfway through. The avocado is done when it's golden and crispy.

To finish: Place a dollop of sour cream in each serving dish, then add a tablespoon of pesto, top with a few avocado slices, and add another tablespoon of pesto if you like. Drizzle each portion with a squeeze of lemon.

Garnish with some coriander seeds, crispy curry leaves, and a squeeze of lemon.

TEA-INFUSED SPICED APPLESAUCE

Does an apple a day really keep the doctor away? In Ayurveda, the answer is yes, as long as the apple is cooked. Raw apples aren't easy to digest, especially with the skin on, while cooked apples go through your digestive system in a snap. This sauce is a more aromatic version of the beloved classic comfort dish. It can be made ahead of time, covered, and kept in the refrigerator for about four days. It tastes great at any serving temperature.

SERVES 4 TO 6

4 cups water

2 jasmine tea bags

1 black tea bag

3 sweet red apples, peeled, cored, and sliced

3 green apples, peeled, cored, and sliced

2 pears, peeled, cored, and sliced

4 tablespoons crushed jaggery

2 vanilla pods, split

1 tablespoon plus 1 teaspoon fresh lemon juice

2 teaspoons cinnamon powder, plus more for serving

1 tablespoon plus 1½ teaspoons organic honey, preferably raw

½ portion Astringent Spice Mix (page 35), finely ground

1 cup cottage cheese

In a heavy-bottomed saucepan, bring the water to a boil. Remove from the heat, and steep all 3 tea bags for 10 minutes with a lid covering the pot. Discard the bags.

Add the apples, pears, jaggery, and split vanilla pods to the pot with the tea. Bring to a boil, stirring occasionally. Reduce to a simmer and cook until the fruit is very tender, about 25 minutes. Pick out the fruit slices and place them in a bowl, then add 1 tablespoon of the lemon juice and the cinnamon and set aside. Let the fruit mixture cool for 30 minutes, then use a fork (or a potato masher) to mash the contents until you get a chunky consistency.

Meanwhile, continue cooking the liquid for another 30 minutes, until it reduces significantly and starts to caramelize. Remove from heat and pour the reduced liquid over the mashed fruit; stir to combine.

In a small bowl, stir the honey, spice mix, the remaining 1 teaspoon of the lemon juice, and cottage cheese together.

To finish: Serve the applesauce in small bowls and top with the cottage cheese mixture.

PRUNE *AND* AVOCADO SHAKE

Prunes have gotten a bad reputation by commonly being associated with digestive aid. Prunes are simply dried plums, and it's time to start enjoying them for their rich and smoky-sweet flavor, as often as we would other dried fruit. Soaked in tea, prunes blossom beautifully, and this recipe makes a luxurious shake. It definitely doesn't hurt that they also do wonders for your digestion—and aid in preventing diabetes and lowering cholesterol. If you can, soak them overnight (or at least for as long as you can).

Dosha Dos and Don'ts: *Soaked prunes and almond milk are good for all three doshas (they are a tridoshic ingredient). If you're a Pitta body type, use half the amount of honey, or skip it altogether and supplement the prune's natural sweet taste with maple syrup.*

SERVES 4 TO 6
2 cups water
2 tea bags of your choice
1 cup prunes, pitted
One 1-inch piece fresh ginger

2 cups cold almond milk
2 tablespoons organic honey, preferably raw
1 tablespoon plus 1½ teaspoons almond butter

1 avocado, peeled and pitted
Almond flakes, toasted (optional)
Cocoa powder (optional)

In a heavy-bottomed pot, bring the water to a boil. Remove from the heat and steep the tea bags in the water for 10 minutes, then add the prunes and cover with a lid. Let the mixture cool to room temperature, then remove the tea bags.

Drain the prunes, and reserve the soaking liquid.

Add the soaking liquid, prunes, ginger, milk, honey, almond butter, and avocado to a blender, and blend until you achieve a smooth consistency.

If you want a thinner consistency or a cooler temperature, add a couple of ice cubes to the mixture and continue to blend.

Pour the shakes into glasses and top with almond flakes or cocoa powder before serving.

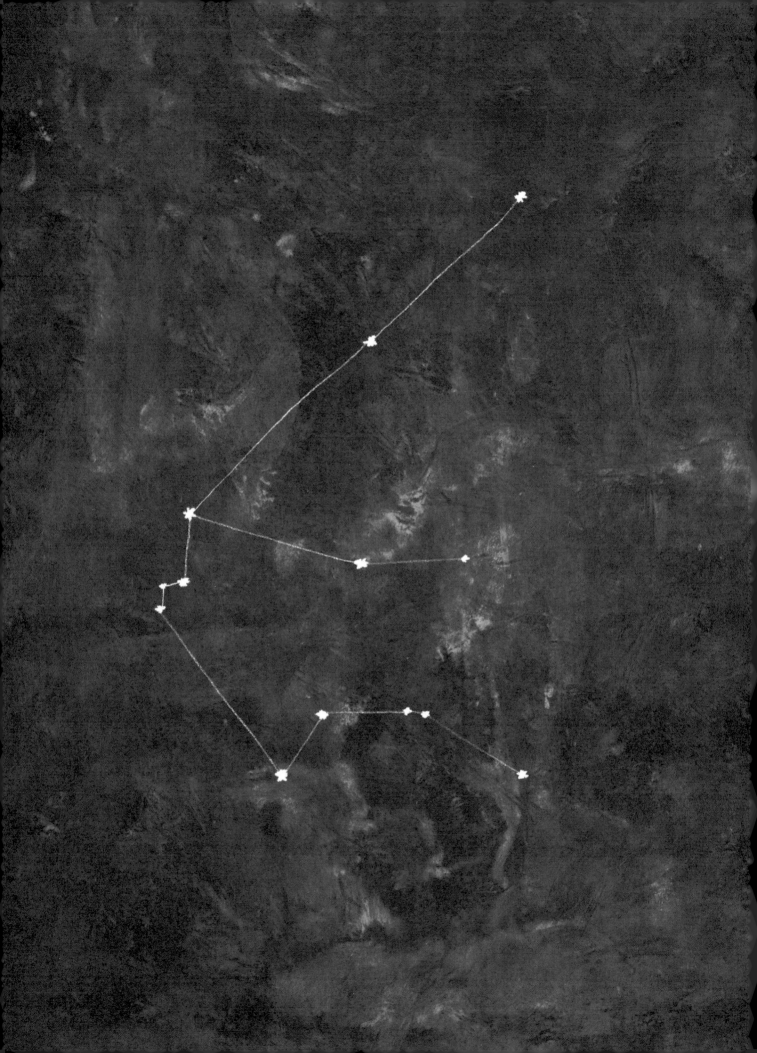

CHAPTER 2

AQUARIUS

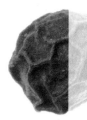

Essential Ayurvedic Spice

PEPPERCORN

» Peppercorn is native only to the tropical evergreen rain forest of Kerala, a province in southwest India. Today it is grown in Vietnam, India, Indonesia, Malaysia, and Brazil.

» Peppercorns grow on a flowering vine and are available in the market in varying colors. However, although there are different varieties of peppercorns, they are all the same pepper fruit picked at different stages of maturity and subjected to various methods of processing. The unripe fruit can be picked and treated to retain its green color, then sold as green peppercorn. Left to dry under the sunlight, the unripe green fruit shrivel and turn black, resulting in black peppercorn, the kind most common. Red peppercorns are fully ripened and they become white peppercorns after they're dried and processed.

» Black peppercorn is beneficial for balancing the Vata dosha, excellent for the Kapha dosha, and can aggravate the Pitta dosha if not used sparingly. To avoid overheating the body, moderate consumption of black peppercorn when it's hot out.

» Among its long list of health benefits, black peppercorn is most used to aid digestion by kindling the digestive fire (agni), improve circulation, stimulate the appetite, and flush out toxins.

» White peppercorn holds the most heat, while green peppercorn has a more subtle flavor. Black peppercorn adds a familiar sharpness and pungent aroma to any dish.

» An adaptable spice, black pepper can enhance a wide range of savory dishes. Its flavor is best when freshly ground and added to a dish just before serving. Pepper is not commonly used for dessert, but it is actually a great way to bring out the sweet taste and add a unique and unconventional flavor profile. I love to use a mix of freshly ground black, white, and/or pink peppercorns in tangy sweet drinks and desserts, especially ones that contain berries, lemon, lime, or chocolate. It's a great way to sharpen the sweetness and accentuate tartness.

» Available year-round, black pepper should be purchased as whole peppercorns. The alternative, pepper powder, can contain adulterated spices.

January 20–February 18

AQUARIUS

Aquarius is Latin for "the water bearer" commonly represented by a simplified drawing of water waves. It is an air sign ruled by Saturn and is the eleventh sign of the zodiac. Falling into the general Kapha season, it is the second sign of the winter triad. During the duration of Aquarius, we experience the coldest days of the year. There is a freshness in the air that both cleanses and stimulates. As the earth reaches its darkest point, it holds the promise of future life. Underneath the ground, the roots are starting to prepare for new beginnings.

February comes with a limited spectrum of available ingredients as the seasons turn from the bitter cold of winter to the rising temperatures and moisture of the spring. Seek out foods that will promote the natural detox process of your body, like garlic, leafy greens, broccoli, green tea, and citrus fruits, to help you shed some of the accumulated heaviness. You may experience waves of bitterness, which are natural emotional symptoms indicating that your body is preparing for spring by releasing stored winter fats. Steer clear of rich, fatty, and sweet foods, which deter the natural cleansing process of your body.

During the darkest part of winter, the light comes from within. Avoid cabin fever by trying new recipes with family and friends. With physical activity being limited, it's a time to discuss ideas, plans, and goals for the future.

RICOTTA CROSTINI *WITH* GARLIC CONFIT

This crostini is indulgent and grounding during this cold season, but it's also gluten-free and packed with nutrients. The list of different flours called for in the recipe for the rolls may seem a little extensive but it's worthwhile if you can manage it. However, if you want a simplified version, you can use just one good-quality gluten-free flour mix to replace all the others, as long as you make sure to use the same total amount. Garlic is one of those rare ingredients that can satisfy almost all our taste cravings (sweet, salty, bitter, astringent, and pungent), which is why it's considered a powerful superfood in Ayurveda. You can keep this garlic confit in an airtight container in the fridge for a few weeks, and use it in a whole array of dishes.

Dosha Dos and Don'ts: *Pitta types, whose elemental constitution is primarily fire, should indulge in garlic in moderation to avoid an excess of its warming effect.*

SERVES 4 TO 6

Rolls:
1½ cups brown rice flour
½ cup potato starch
¼ cup tapioca flour
¼ cup white rice flour
1 teaspoon xanthan gum
2 teaspoons instant yeast
¼ cup sugar
1 teaspoon salt
1 cup warm water
2 tablespoons melted ghee, plus 1½ teaspoons for brushing the rolls, plus more for greasing the pan

1 large organic egg, at room temperature
1 teaspoon cider vinegar

Garlic Confit:
3 heads garlic, cloves separated and peeled
1½ cups sunflower oil, plus more if needed
½ portion Sweet Spice Mix (page 30), coarsely ground

To Finish:
2 tablespoons ghee, for toasting the rolls
½ portion Sweet Spice Mix (page 30), finely ground
1 cup ricotta cheese
1 teaspoon cinnamon powder
½ Himalayan salt
2 tablespoons honey, preferably raw
1 tablespoon poppy seeds (optional)

For the rolls: In a medium mixing bowl, combine all the flours, xanthan gum, yeast, sugar, and salt, then add to your food processor or electric mixer. Start the machine at low speed, add the water, 2 tablespoons melted ghee, egg, and vinegar, and mix at medium speed about 3 minutes.

Grease a 9-inch round cake pan with ghee.

Using a ¼-cup measuring cup, scoop the dough into 12 balls and place them in the pan, far enough apart that they aren't touching. Dip your fingertips in warm water and smooth out the tops of the balls, then cover them with a dry towel and let them rise in a warm place for about 45 minutes to 1 hour.

Meanwhile, preheat the oven to 400°F. When the rolls have risen, bake them for 25 to 30 minutes, or until they become golden brown, then remove them from the oven and brush them with the 1½ teaspoons melted ghee.

For the garlic confit: Preheat the oven to 250°F.

Place the garlic, oil, and spice mix in a small ovenproof saucepan (add more oil if cloves aren't completely submerged). Cover and bake until garlic cloves are golden and tender, about 2 hours. Let the garlic cool, then transfer it and the oil to an airtight container and chill. Bring to room temperature before using.

To finish: Melt some ghee in a pan, add the spice mix, then slice each roll in half and toast in the pan, sliced-side down, so the rolls can soak up the ghee. Do this in batches until all the rolls are toasted.

Take about 1 cup of the garlic confit and drain the oil, then roughly chop the garlic. Spread a tablespoon of ricotta over each roll and top chopped garlic. Sprinkle with cinnamon, salt, and top with a thin stream of honey and poppy seeds (if using).

BROCCOLI AND CAULIFLOWER SALAD *WITH BUTTERMILK DRESSING*

The beauty of this salad is that it works whether it's served hot or cold. Broccoli and cauliflower are packed with nutrients, are high in fiber, and keep us satisfied for a long time. Pumpkin seeds give this salad a nutty, chewy crunch and are good for all three doshas. You can toast a larger amount of pumpkin seeds and keep them in an airtight container to have them on hand.

Dosha Dos and Don'ts: *Vata types experiencing digestive sensitivity should have this salad in moderation to avoid bloating, which can be caused by the light and airy qualities of these two vegetables. However, the use of pungent spices significantly remedies this aggravating effect. Kapha types who are feeling heavier can avoid the sesame seeds and add some flaxseeds instead. Pitta types can replace the buttermilk with more yogurt or with coconut milk and reduce the pungent spices in the dressing to half the amount.*

SERVES 4 TO 6

Salad:

2 shallots, finely chopped

5 scallions, white and light green parts only, finely chopped

3 garlic cloves, thinly sliced and lightly fried in olive oil

4 tablespoons white balsamic vinegar, plus 1 tablespoon for finishing

Kosher or sea salt

1¼ cups raw pumpkin seeds

⅓ cup extra-virgin olive oil, plus more for toasting pumpkin seeds

3 cups coarsely chopped broccoli florets

3 cups coarsely chopped cauliflower florets

⅓ cup sesame seeds, toasted

1 tablespoon nigella seeds, lightly toasted

3 dates, pitted and finely chopped

Buttermilk Dressing:

⅓ cup buttermilk

⅓ cup organic Greek yogurt

1 tablespoon coconut sugar

1 teaspoon Dijon mustard

2 tablespoons orange juice and zest

1 jalapeño or other green chile, finely chopped

1 portion Pungent Spice Mix (page 33), finely ground

1 teaspoon fine kosher salt

For the salad: In a small bowl, mix the shallots and scallions with the garlic, vinegar, and ¼ teaspoon of salt. Cover and refrigerate for at least at 30 minutes.

Meanwhile, preheat the oven to 375°F.

Spread the pumpkin seeds on a parchment paper–lined baking sheet and drizzle with some olive oil and a pinch of salt. Toast for 7 to 10 minutes, or until you hear them starting to pop. Remove them from the oven and set aside to cool. You can also toast the seeds in a dry pan, but they taste much better when toasted in the oven.

Place the broccoli and cauliflower florets in a large bowl and add the sesame seeds, nigella seeds, dates, the pumpkin seeds, the shallot-scallion mixture, and the oil.

Season with some salt and remaining 1 tablespoon of vinegar. Toss and refrigerate until serving.

For the buttermilk dressing: In a bowl, whisk the buttermilk, yogurt, sugar, mustard, orange juice and zest, jalapeño, spice mix, and salt together. Cover the bowl with plastic wrap and refrigerate for 1 hour before serving.

To finish: Take the salad out of the refrigerator and toss with most of the dressing. Top with more dressing if you like.

MILLET POLENTA *WITH CELERY,*
CHICKPEAS, AND PARMESAN

This hearty bowl is as satisfying as a creamy risotto, but it's dairy-free. Millet is one of the world's oldest grains. It can be grown in the harshest of conditions and is sustainable in many different environments. It's a great source of protein for vegetarians and pairs nicely with a broad range of flavors. Those with thyroid issues should avoid millet, but the rest of us should give it a shot and try incorporating it into everyday cooking.

Dosha Dos and Don'ts: *Pitta and Vata types feeling out of balance can replace half the amount of millet with amaranth seeds to moderate any possible aggravation. If Vata types are experiencing any type of digestive distress or bloating, they should eat this dish in moderation.*

SERVES 4 TO 6

Millet Polenta:
¾ cup millet
1 tablespoon ghee
3 scallions, thinly sliced
2 garlic cloves, thinly sliced
1 portion Pungent Spice Mix (page 33), coarsely ground
2 leeks, white and light green parts only, halved, rinsed, and thinly sliced
4 cups Vegetable Broth (page 242)

1 tablespoon tamarind pulp
1 teaspoon kosher salt

Topping:
1 tablespoon ghee
4 celery stalks, tough fibers peeled off, thinly chopped
1½ cups cooked chickpeas (page 247) or one 15-ounce can chickpeas, drained and rinsed
¼ teaspoon Himalayan or sea salt

2 tablespoons white sesame seeds, toasted
2 tablespoons black sesame seeds, toasted
½ cup shaved or grated Parmesan cheese

For the millet polenta: Pulse the millet in a blender or food processor to break down about half the grains. Transfer to a bowl, set aside, and rinse out the blender.

Heat the ghee in a large pot over medium heat, then add the scallions, garlic, spice mix, and leeks. Cook for 10 minutes, or until the vegetables are very soft, stirring often to avoid burning. Add half the broth and the tamarind pulp to the pot and bring to a simmer, then whisk in the processed millet. Bring to a boil, then reduce to a simmer and cook, stirring continuously, for about 45 minutes. Add the remaining broth in ¼-cup amounts while whisking as the mixture dries out and thickens until all the liquid is incorporated. Taste the mixture to make sure it is cooked and has a loose dough-like texture. It should not be watery at all. Add salt and stir.

If you want a perfectly smooth polenta, transfer the mixture to a food processor and blend until smooth. Add more broth, if needed, to achieve a smooth mixture. If you need to reheat the polenta, transfer it back into the pot (otherwise it's ready to serve).

For the toppings: In a pan, heat the ghee to medium heat, add the celery, and cook for about 10 minutes.

Add the chickpeas and cook for about 5 minutes, or until they're browned, and season with the salt.

To finish: Scoop 2 serving spoons of millet polenta into shallow bowls. Using the back of a serving spoon, create a small well on top of the polenta, top with the celery-chickpea mixture, and sprinkle with a mixture of sesame seeds and Parmesan.

BEET KHICHDI

So much of our food enjoyment starts with the eyes, and beets add a beautiful color to any dish. It's not always possible to plate your dishes with care and take the time to enjoy them visually, but it's worth the effort, even if you're just cooking for yourself. This simple khichdi is as delicious as it is visually appealing. So go ahead—serve it at your next dinner party.

Dosha Dos and Don'ts: *Pitta types can limit the tahini and sesame, or preferably replace them altogether with cashew (or almond) butter and nuts. Vata types can add even more of the sesame essence to this dish by replacing the sunflower oil with toasted sesame oil.*

SERVES 4 TO 6

¾ cup dry black-eyed peas

2 teaspoons asafetida powder

¾ cup red rice

1 tablespoon any vinegar or lemon juice, for soaking the rice (optional), plus 1 tablespoon for the beets

1 tablespoons olive oil

2 medium red onions, diced

1 portion Sour Spice Mix (page 32), coarsely ground

3 cups Vegetable Broth (page 242) or water

2 teaspoons kosher or sea salt, plus more to taste

4 medium beets, washed and scrubbed

1 tablespoon plus 1½ teaspoons balsamic vinegar

2 tablespoons tahini

Toppings:

½ cup crumbled goat cheese

½ cup toasted sesame seeds

½ cup roughly chopped dill

To prepare: In a medium heavy-bottomed saucepan, cover the black-eyed peas with water, add 1 teaspoon of asafetida, and bring to a boil; boil for 2 minutes. Turn off the heat, cover the pot, and let the black-eyed peas soak for 60 minutes (preferably overnight). Presoaking the black-eyed peas makes them easier to digest; it also helps them cook more evenly and become tender all the way through.

It's also good to soak the rice. In a medium bowl, cover the rice with 2 cups of water and add the vinegar (if using); soak for as long as possible, preferably overnight.

After soaking the black-eyed peas and rice, drain and wash thoroughly with cold water.

If you don't have time for any soaking, you can cook the dish directly from the dry ingredients, but it will take additional time to achieve the desired tenderness.

For the khichdi: In a medium heavy-bottomed stockpot, heat 2 tablespoons of the oil, then add the onions and spice mix. Cook until the onions are translucent, then add the black-eyed peas, rice, remaining 1 teaspoon of asafetida, and broth, and bring to a boil.

Reduce the mixture to a simmer and cook for about 1 hour, making sure there is always enough liquid in the pot. Simmering the black-eyed peas gently helps them cook evenly until tender, retain their shape without losing their texture (getting mushy) too quickly, and keep their skins intact. After about 45 minutes, add the salt and stir (the best time to add the salt is about three-quarters of the

way into the cooking process, when the black-eyed peas are tender but still partly firm).

Meanwhile, place the beets in a large pot, cover with water, and add 1 tablespoon of vinegar to prevent the beets from bleeding. Bring to a boil, then reduce to a simmer until tender, about 45 minutes to an hour. Peel the beets and cut them in half, then into ¼-inch half-moon slices. Set aside.

After an hour, taste the khichdi, and if the black-eyed peas and rice are not very tender continue cooking for up to 30 minutes longer. Depending on your preference, you can adjust the texture of the khichdi for a drier risotto-like consistency or a wetter soup-like one by either allowing the excess liquid to evaporate or adding more liquid.

Mix the tahini and the remaining 1½ teaspoons of balsamic vinegar into the hot khichdi, and add salt to taste, if needed.

To finish: Serve 2 large spoons of khichdi into each serving bowl. Using the back of a spoon, create a small well on top of each serving and top with the beets, goat cheese, toasted sesame seeds, and dill. Sprinkle with salt and serve.

ROASTED OKRA *AND* SOFT-BOILED EGG *IN* MUSHROOM-HORSERADISH BROTH

Okra is a tridoshic vegetable that takes some getting to know before you get it right. My favorite way to eat okra is roasted, almost to a crisp, which brings out a smoky flavor and makes it less sticky than the raw version. When buying okra, choose young, tender pods (overly mature ones can be fibrous and tough). This recipe is a lighter way to enjoy the flavor and texture of eggs—it calls for a 6-minute boiling time and then cooling the egg down to achieve that perfectly creamy yolk. You can also make this recipe with egg replacements like tofu to keep it even lighter.

Dosha Dos and Don'ts: Kapha types are especially sensitive to eggs, so when trying to balance your dosha, it may be best to forgo eggs completely and replace them with some semifirm tofu. Pitta types experiencing too much heat in their body should do the same.

SERVES 4 TO 6

Roasted Okra:
16 pieces of okra, sliced in half lengthwise
1 tablespoon olive or sunflower oil
1 teaspoon kosher salt
2 teaspoons freshly ground black pepper

Broth:
1 tablespoon ghee
1 medium carrot, diced
1 medium leek, white and light green parts only, halved, rinsed, and sliced crosswise into 1-inch pieces
1 medium white onion, diced
6 garlic cloves, thinly sliced
2¼ pounds white button mushrooms, stems trimmed, then cut into quarters
8 parsley sprigs
6 thyme sprigs
1 bay leaf
1 tablespoon horseradish paste
One 1-inch piece fresh turmeric, grated
One 1-inch piece fresh ginger, grated
1 portion Bitter Spice Mix (page 34), coarsely ground
12 cups water
¼ teaspoon kosher salt

Eggs:
8 to 12 large organic eggs (2 per serving)

For the roasted okra: Preheat the oven to 450°F. Layer the okra halves on a parchment paper–lined baking sheet. Drizzle them with the oil, sprinkle with the salt and pepper, and bake for 10 to 15 minutes.

For the broth: In a large pot over medium-high heat, bring the ghee to a simmer.

Add the carrot, leek, and onion to the pot, and cook, stirring occasionally, until the onion and leek have softened, about 8 minutes. Add the garlic and cook until fragrant, about 1 minute. Add the mushrooms, parsley, thyme, bay leaf, horseradish, turmeric, ginger, and spice mix to the pot. Stir and cook until the mushrooms start to release some moisture, about 4 minutes. Add the water and salt, and bring to a boil.

Reduce the heat to a simmer, and cook until the vegetables are soft and the broth has a strong mushroom flavor, about 1 hour.

Remove the broth from the heat and strain through a fine-mesh sieve into another pot, then discard the solids. Salt to taste.

For the eggs: Bring a medium pot of water to a boil. Set a timer to 6 minutes. Gently add the eggs to the boiling water and cook until the timer goes off. Remove the pot from the heat and place the cooked eggs in a bowl of ice water for 1 minute (to stop the yolk from cooking any more), then remove and peel the eggs.

To finish: Place the roasted okra in serving bowls and pour a cup of hot broth over each portion. Top with warm eggs and add more broth, if desired.

BARBERRY CRUMBLE *WITH* COCONUT FLAN

Grapes are considered a superior fruit in Ayurveda, and I'm always looking for ways to incorporate them into desserts. In this recipe, the grapes' crunch and burst of natural sweetness pairs well with the toasted crispiness of the crumble. If you can't find dried barberries, you can replace them with cranberries or raisins here without compromising the texture. This recipe can also be simplified by using store-bought wholesome granola if you don't have the time to make the rye crumble at home.

Dosha Dos and Don'ts: *Kapha types can moderate the amount of coconut flan and crumble to avoid feeling too heavy.*

SERVES 4 TO 6

Flan:
4 large organic eggs
3 tablespoons maple syrup, plus more
    for finishing
1 cup organic full-fat coconut milk
½ teaspoon vanilla extract
¼ teaspoon fine kosher salt

Crumble:
2 tablespoons ghee
2 tablespoons dried barberries (or
    raisins or cranberries)
1 cup brown sugar
¾ cup old-fashioned rolled oats
¾ cup rye flour
1 portion Sour Spice Mix (page 32),
    coarsely ground
1 stick (½ cup) cold butter

To Finish:
1½ cups red grapes, sliced in half
    lengthwise
Maple syrup

For the flan: Preheat the oven to 325°F.

Fill a kettle or a pot with water and bring to a boil to use for the water bath later.

Meanwhile, in a medium bowl, whisk together the eggs, maple syrup, coconut milk, vanilla, and salt. Pour the mixture into individual ramekins or small glass baking dishes.

Put ramekins in a 13-by-9-inch (or larger) rectangular baking pan and add the boiling water until it reaches halfway up the ramekins. Bake for 30 to 45 minutes, checking on the consistency of the flan halfway through. The custard is usually done when the outer edges are firm and the center a bit jellylike.

Take the ramekins out of the water and let them cool completely to room temperature. For best results, refrigerate them for at least 4 hours.

For the barberry crumble: Preheat the oven to 350°F.

In a pan, heat the ghee over medium heat, add the barberries, and cook for 2 minutes, to allow them to bloom and release their flavor. Transfer the barberries to a bowl, add the sugar, oats, flour, and spice mix and mix everything together. Add the cold butter and use two forks to mash it into the mixture until it resembles coarse crumbs.

Spread the crumble on a parchment paper–lined baking sheet. Pat the top gently until it's even. Bake in the oven until golden brown, about 40 minutes.

To finish: When ready to serve, remove the ramekins from the refrigerator and run the tip of a paring knife around the edges to release the flan. Place large spoonfuls of crumble in individual dessert dishes and flatten out to serve as a base for the flan. Place a plate over the top of the ramekins (one at a time) and, holding both firmly, flip the ramekins over to release the flan onto a plate. Slide a serving of flan on top of each crumble-dressed dish. Top with sliced grapes and drizzle with maple syrup before serving.

SPICED CHAI

Chai, a delicious spiced-tea concoction that traces its origins to India, has been around for centuries, and many people all over the world enjoy the drink (in many languages, chai is the word used for "tea"). The health benefits of chai mostly come from the blend of fragrant spices like cardamom and cinnamon.

Dosha Dos and Don'ts: *Sugar isn't ideal for Kapha types—they should try to keep it to a minimum and instead add more spices, as they fortify the metabolism during the cold season. Vata types can enjoy the chai as is, and even indulge in a bit more sugar. Pitta types can enjoy the sweetness but should reduce the amount of spices if they feel overheated.*

SERVES 4
2 cups water
One 1-inch piece fresh ginger, peeled
   and thinly sliced

4 green cardamom pods, crushed
1 cinnamon stick
1 star anise pod
3 black tea bags

2 cups almond milk (or soy milk), at
   room temperature (page 239)
4 teaspoons unrefined cane sugar, plus
   more for serving

Place the water, ginger, cardamom, cinnamon, and star anise in a saucepan over medium heat. Bring to a boil, then reduce to a simmer, and cook for a few minutes; turn the heat off. Add the tea and milk, and let the mixture steep for 2 to 3 minutes. Pour the tea through a fine-mesh sieve into cups, and discard the spices. Add a teaspoon of sugar to each cup, plus more to taste.

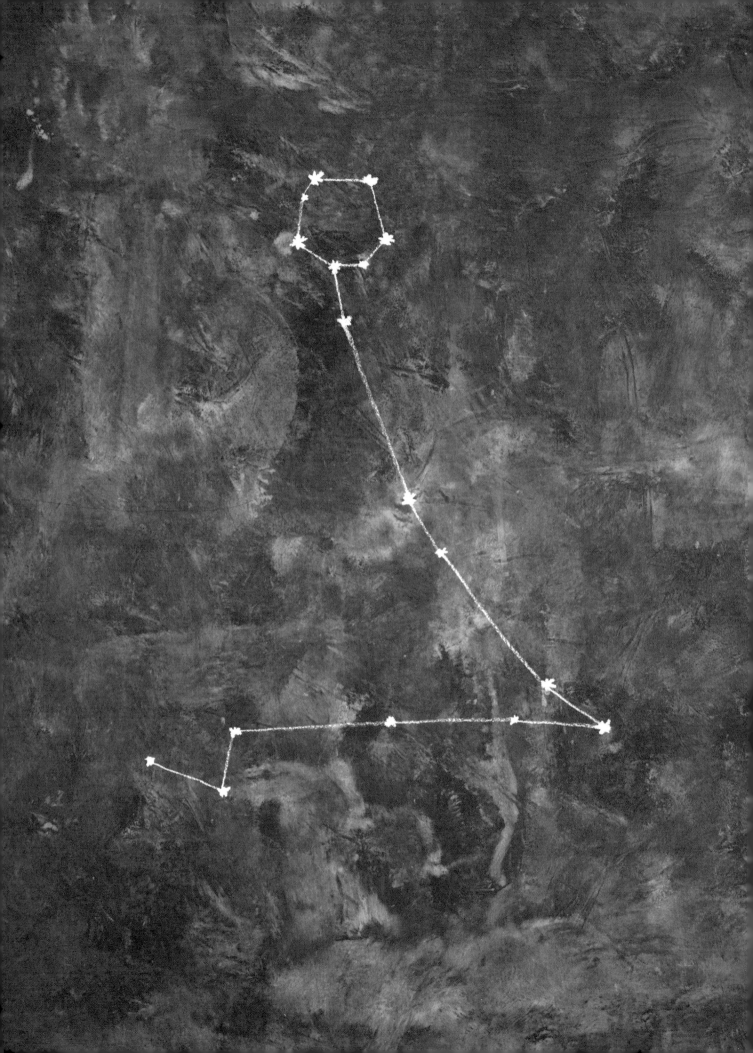

CHAPTER 3

PISCES

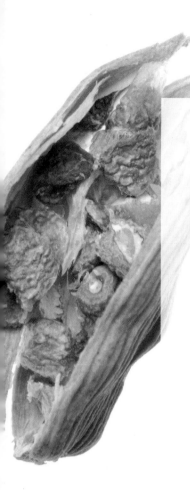

Essential Ayurvedic Spice

CARDAMOM

» *Guatemala grows and exports the majority of the world's cardamom. Sri Lanka, India, and Tanzania produce the spice on a smaller scale.*

» *Part of the ginger family, cardamom is the seed found in oval-shaped tropical fruit pods. You can find cardamom pods in two colors: green and black. Green is more commonly used than black.*

» *Cardamom is good for balancing all three types of doshas (known as tridoshic), but Pitta types should use it with some moderation.*

» *Cardamom can be used in both cold and hot seasons. In hotter weather, it is beneficial when used in combination with other warming spices and added to warm foods. In summer, it can be cooling when added to an iced tea, smoothie, or another cold drink.*

» *Among numerous health benefits, cardamom is most used for its anti-inflammatory benefits, detoxification properties, as a good source of dietary fiber, to manage food cravings, and to refresh the palate.*

» *Cardamom is a heating spice with an intense flavor, contributing both sweet and pungent tastes. A little cardamom goes a long way. It can be used in cooking both as a pod (split open to expose the seeds) or by directly crushing (or grinding) and adding the seeds to your recipe. The seeds have a sharp flavor and are used in combination with sweet recipes, while the whole pods are preferred in savory dishes, as they give more of a pungent taste. One of my favorite ways to use cardamom is to crush its seeds into a powder and add it to some crunchy peanut butter with some sea salt. Spread on a multigrain cracker—it's as good as a slice of cake.*

» *Available year-round, cardamom pods stay fresh for more than a year when they're stored in an airtight container. Buying cardamom whole is preferable because when seeds are removed from their pods, they start losing their flavor and healing qualities as soon as they are exposed to air. Ground seeds should be used immediately, before their flavor fades.*

February 19–March 20

PISCES

Pisces is Latin for "the fish" and is commonly represented by two fish tied together, swimming in opposite directions. The symbol expresses the duality of Pisces. It is a water sign ruled by Jupiter and is the twelfth sign of the zodiac. A Kapha duration, it is the last sign of the winter triad. Pisces marks a transitional period between the end of winter and an approaching spring. By the time the sun reaches the constellation of Pisces, the days are getting longer, the nights shorter, and the temperatures higher. Underground, the frozen earth begins to thaw, and water starts to flow. Deep within the ground, dormant life begins to stir and growth that won't show itself until spring is taking place. All of nature hovers in a state of limbo.

As the warm weather moves in, your body is ready to lighten up. Kapha subsides in the spring when your body is naturally letting go of winter weight. Your body releases much of the winter fat through your skin. Eat light food to support your body's shedding process, like raw vegetables, fresh greens, lentils, and fish, to build vitality and energy. Astringent, pungent, and bitter foods, including herbs and teas, will help in this transition by draining the excess moisture from your body and strengthening your blood flow.

According to the zodiac calendar, the year is coming to an end. This is an opportunity to enhance nature's inherent process for renewal by making the right dietary choices and building up your energy for the new year to come.

CRUDITÉS *WITH* CHAMOMILE HUMMUS

Infusing dishes with chamomile adds a delicious floral aroma and note of calmness during this Kapha season. Chamomile is one of the oldest and most widely used medicinal plants in the world, lauded for its versatility and applications in skincare, stress relief, and as a sleep aid. When I was in college, I often found myself drinking too much coffee, which started to affect my sleep. I changed to drinking tea after 2 p.m. and finally got introduced to the world of tea culture. After reaping the calming benefits of chamomile and falling in love with its aroma, I started using it to infuse flavors into different foods. You can do the same with all teas, often adding a unique flavor dimension.

Dosha Dos and Don'ts: *Vata types should lightly steam their crudité vegetables, making them easier to digest. They should also enjoy the hummus in conservative amounts as is or replace the chickpeas with mung beans. Pitta types trying to control an excess of their dosha can reduce the amount of tahini or replace it with almond butter or coconut oil.*

SERVES 4 TO 6

Hummus:

3 cups cooked chickpeas (page 247) or two 15-ounce cans chickpeas, drained and rinsed

1 tablespoon baking soda

⅓ cup tahini

¼ cup chamomile tea (made from 3 tea bags)

2 garlic cloves

1 portion Bitter Spice Mix (page 34), finely ground

¼ cup flaxseed oil or extra-virgin olive oil

⅓ cup plus 1 tablespoon fresh lemon juice

1 teaspoon kosher salt

Crudités:

¾ pound asparagus, tough ends trimmed, sliced in half crosswise

4 celery stalks, tough fibers peeled off, cut into 4 sticks each

1 kohlrabi, cut into 4-by-¼-inch sticks

1 head cauliflower, cut into medium florets with stems

Toppings:

Sweet paprika

2 tablespoons chopped parsley

2 tablespoons chopped cilantro

2 tablespoons flaxseeds

For the hummus: Place the chickpeas in a bowl and sprinkle with baking soda to remove the skins (if you don't mind the skins, you can skip this step).

In a medium bowl, combine the tahini and tea and stir vigorously with a fork to soften, about 2 to 3 minutes. Place the chickpeas in a food processor and grind to a coarse meal. Add the tahini-tea mixture, garlic, and spice mix, and pulse for about 45 seconds. Slowly add the flaxseed oil and lemon juice, alternating between them, and continue to process for about 5 minutes, until the hummus becomes smooth and creamy. Add the salt and process for another 30 seconds.

To finish: Transfer the hummus to a serving bowl and sprinkle with paprika. Garnish with parsley, coriander, and flaxseeds and serve alongside the crudités.

BREADED MUSHROOMS *WITH* CORN-BUTTERMILK CREAM

This recipe calls for button mushrooms, but other meaty mushrooms would work just as well—just make sure you serve them hot. As the poster child for the industrial food complex, corn cultivation has a dark side. Ayurveda recommends you eat organic corn only. If you cannot find fresh organic corn, look for frozen organic corn. The corn's sweetness and the buttermilk's light sour taste lift the fried mushrooms' earthy richness.

Dosha Dos and Don'ts: *Vata types could use half the amount of corn in the Corn Buttermilk Cream to avoid the dryness, which can lead to bloating and hinder digestive flow. Pitta types can reduce the egg yolks from six to three to balance their warming effect.*

SERVES 4 TO 6

Corn-Buttermilk Cream:
4 ears organic sweet corn or 2¼ cups frozen organic corn boiled for 3 minutes
2 cups buttermilk
2 cups heavy cream
½ vanilla bean, split, seeds scraped and reserved (or 1 teaspoon vanilla extract)

1 portion Salty Spice Mix (page 31), finely ground
1 tablespoon jaggery
6 yolks from extra-large organic ys, beaten
½ cup finely chopped mint
½ cup finely chopped dill

Breaded Mushrooms:
1 cup dry rolled oats

6 tablespoons chopped rosemary
½ cup almond flour
2 cups buttermilk
Zest of 1 lemon
½ teaspoon fine kosher salt
Freshly ground black pepper
24 button mushrooms, stems trimmed, cut into ¼-inch slices
⅓ cup sunflower oil, for frying

For the corn buttermilk cream: Remove the husks and corn silk from the corn and cut each cob into three pieces. Using a sharp knife, cut the kernels from the cobs; reserve the cobs. Put the kernels in a blender or food processor with the buttermilk and heavy cream and pulse into a coarse puree.

Pour the mixture into a heavy-bottomed pan, and add the cob pieces, vanilla bean pod and seeds, spice mix, and jaggery. Bring to a boil, then remove from the heat and cover.

Let the mixture steep for 1 hour, then discard the corncobs and vanilla pod.

Strain the mixture through a fine-mesh sieve, pressing down firmly to remove as much liquid as possible. Discard the solids. Pour the liquid back into the pan and place over medium heat.

Place the egg yolks in a bowl and temper them by adding a little of the hot cream to the bowl. Add the yolk mixture to the pan. Cook the cream, stirring constantly with a wooden spoon, until it's thick enough to coat the back of the spoon. Stir in the chopped mint and dill and set aside to cool.

For the fried mushrooms: Place the oats and rosemary in a food processor and pulse until finely ground.

Set up three shallow bowls for breading the mushrooms. Fill the first bowl with almond flour, the second with buttermilk, and the third with the oats and rosemary mixture; add the lemon zest, salt, and some pepper to the third bowl and mix. Dip each mushroom slice into the almond flour, then the buttermilk, and then the oats. Place the mushroom on a plate and continue breading the remaining mushrooms.

Meanwhile, heat the oil in a medium skillet to medium high. Fry the breaded mushrooms in batches, turning them with a perforated spatula, until golden and crispy on both sides, about 3 minutes per batch. Place the mushrooms on a paper towel–lined baking sheet, and sprinkle with salt.

To finish: Keep the fried mushrooms warm in a 200°F oven for up to 30 minutes. Serve them hot with a dollop of the corn cream on the side for dipping.

BLACK BEAN *AND* GRAPE SUCCOTASH

You might not be used to this surprising addition of grapes to a savory succotash, but rest assured you'll welcome the little bursts of fresh sweetness to lighten up the earthiness of the beans. You can make this recipe a day in advance, as it keeps very well in the refrigerator—the flavors combine thoroughly and the succotash tastes even better than when it's eaten right away. The leftovers also lend themselves to a bake, and are simply delicious mixed with some warm grains. Don't add the roasted peanuts until you're ready to eat so they keep their crunchiness.

Dosha Dos and Don'ts: *Pitta and Vata types can use half the amount of corn and add more sweet potato instead.*

SERVES 4 TO 6
1½ tablespoons extra-virgin olive oil
1½ cups chopped red onion
2 garlic cloves, finely chopped
2¼ cups corn kernels, cut from 4 ears
    of corn

2 sweet potatoes, peeled, cut into small
    cubes, and steamed for 15 minutes
1½ cup cooked black beans (page 247)
    or one 15-ounce can black beans,
    drained and rinsed
1 portion Salty Spice Mix (page 31),
    coarsely ground

To Finish:
½ cup thinly sliced basil leaves
1 cup red grapes, sliced in halves or
    thirds
½ cup roasted peanuts

Heat the oil in a large heavy skillet over medium heat. Add the onion and sauté until the onion is translucent, about 5 minutes. Add the garlic and cook for another minute. Add the corn, sweet potatoes, black beans, and spice mix.

Reduce the heat to medium low, cover, and simmer until the corn and black beans are tender and the sweet potatoes are browned, about 15 minutes, stirring occasionally. Remove the pan from the heat.

To finish: Stir in the basil. Divide among serving bowls and top with the sliced grapes and roasted peanuts.

FRENCH ONION SOUP KHICHDI

French onion soup includes the most basic ingredients cooked with patience and imagination. The caramelized and creamy flavors of the original dish are grounding, and the hot soup is the perfect comfort food for colder days. This recipe is a combination of the French classic and a nutritious and wholesome khichdi with a familiar and soothing essence of Earl Grey tea. Earl Grey tea contains bergamot, which has natural aromatherapy qualities. Bergamot has a calming effect and boosts a person's mood and thus helps to overcome stress, anxiety, and depression. Onions have a sweet taste when they're cooked and are extremely nourishing and grounding in this dish.

Dosha Dos and Don'ts: *Pitta types should limit the vinegar to avoid too much acidity. Lentils are mostly tridoshic, meaning they suit all body types.*

SERVES 4 TO 6

Khichdi:

¾ cup Puy lentils

2 teaspoons asafetida powder

½ cup red rice

1 tablespoon any vinegar or lemon juice (optional)

1 tablespoon sunflower oil

3 medium shallots, peeled and sliced

3 garlic cloves, thinly sliced

1 portion Sweet Spice Mix (page 30), coarsely ground

2 cups Ginger, Garlic, and Onion Broth (page 244)

1 teaspoon kosher or sea salt, plus more to taste

2 red onions, each cut crosswise into ¾-inch slices

2 tablespoons ghee, melted

1 tablespoon tamari sauce

2 tablespoons thyme leaves, plus 1 tablespoon for garnish

½ cup cottage cheese, strained

2 scallions, white and light green parts only, sliced

French Onion Soup:

4 large red onions, thinly sliced

2½ tablespoons sunflower oil

3 tablespoons almond flour

½ teaspoon kosher salt

¼ teaspoon freshly ground black pepper

1 cup Ginger, Garlic, and Onion Broth (page 244)

2 tablespoons sherry vinegar

1 tablespoon balsamic vinegar

1 bay leaf

2 Earl Grey tea bags

To prepare: In a medium heavy-bottomed saucepan cover the lentils with water, add 1 teaspoon of asafetida, and bring to a boil; boil for 2 minutes. Turn off the heat, cover the pot, and let the lentils soak for 60 minutes (preferably overnight). Presoaking the lentils makes them easier to digest; it also helps them cook more evenly and become tender all the way through.

It's also good to soak the rice. In a medium bowl, cover the rice with 2 cups of water and add the vinegar (if using); soak for as long as possible, preferably overnight.

After soaking the lentils and rice, drain and wash thoroughly with cold water.

If you don't have time for any soaking, you can cook the dish directly from the dry ingredients, but it will take additional time to achieve the desired tenderness.

For the onion soup: In a large skillet, sauté the onions in the oil until tender, about 7 minutes. Sprinkle with the flour, then stir in the salt and pepper. Add the broth, both vinegars, and the bay leaf, and cook, stirring,

for about 3 minutes, or until thickened. Remove from the heat, and steep the tea bags in the soup for 2 minutes. Remove the tea bags and bay leaf, and pour the mixture into a blender. Blend until smooth, then set aside to cool. If you want to make the soup ahead of time, you can keep it in the refrigerator for about 2 days.

For the khichdi: In a medium heavy-bottomed saucepan, heat the oil, add the shallots, garlic, and spice mix and cook until the shallots and garlic are translucent. Add the lentils, rice, the remaining 1 teaspoon of asafetida, and the broth, and bring to a boil.

Bring the mixture down to a simmer and cook for about 15 minutes, making sure there is always enough liquid in the pot. Add the salt after 15 minutes of simmering. Simmering the lentils gently helps them cook evenly until tender, retain their shape without losing their texture (getting mushy) too quickly, and keep their skins intact. The khichdi should have a loose risotto-like texture.

Meanwhile, preheat oven to 425°F. Place red onions

in a large mixing bowl and coat with ghee. Arrange the red onions onto a parchment paper–lined baking sheet. Roast for about 40 minutes (checking in after 20 minutes to avoid burning or blackening the onions) or until golden brown, then remove from the oven and set aside.

To finish: Pour the partly cooked khichdi into a shallow baking dish (or individual ramekins) leaving room for the onion soup. Pour 3 cups of reserved onion soup into the dish or divide between individual ramekins. Top with tamari, thyme leaves, and a layer of the roasted onions. Cover with aluminum foil and put into the oven (at the same temperature the onions were roasted). Cook for 25 minutes, tasting to make sure that the lentils and rice are tender Take out of the oven, and spread cottage cheese, the remaining thyme leaves, and scallions over the top and broil uncovered for up to 10 minutes or until golden brown. Take out of the oven and let cool for 2 minutes. Sprinkle with more salt if needed before serving.

BAKED TROUT *WITH* RADISH-CUCUMBER SALSA

A freshwater fish like trout is great for this Kapha season. For a heartier meal, you can serve it with a side of rice or some crusty bread. Just remember, the craving for carbs often has more to do with comfort than hunger, and you might be surprised how satisfying this meal can be on its own. Making an extra portion of the salsa by doubling the ingredients is a great way to quickly whip up a meal the next day—just use it as a topping on a simple salad or some toast. I don't like to use too much sugar due to its negative effects on the body—I opt for natural sweeteners instead. Honey is a great substitute, but I sometimes prefer using maple syrup because, unlike honey, it's okay to heat maple syrup, and it contains fewer calories.

Dosha Dos and Don'ts: *Pitta types can skip the lemon to avoid too much acidity.*

SERVES 4 TO 6

Salsa:
2 tablespoons rice vinegar
2 teaspoons maple syrup
1 teaspoon fresh lemon juice
1 teaspoon fresh lime juice
1 teaspoon olive or sunflower oil
2 small cucumbers, peeled, seeded, quartered lengthwise, and diced
12 radishes, finely diced
½ medium red onion, finely diced
2 tablespoons capers

Trout:
2 medium-size rainbow trout fillets
1 tablespoon ghee
¾ teaspoon kosher salt
1 teaspoon freshly ground black pepper
2 garlic cloves, smashed
One 1-inch piece fresh ginger, grated
1 jalapeño pepper, cut into ¼-inch slices
1 lemon, cut into ¼-inch slices

To Finish:
1 portion Sour Spice Mix (page 32), finely ground
2 teaspoons sunflower seeds, toasted in a dry pan
1 tablespoon chopped parsley
1 tablespoon chopped dill
2 tablespoons sliced chives

For the salsa: In a small bowl, whisk together the vinegar, maple syrup, lemon and lime juices, and oil. Add the cucumbers, radishes, onion, and capers, and toss the mixture until the vegetables are coated with the dressing. Refrigerate the salsa until ready to serve.

For the trout: Preheat the oven to 400°F.

Rinse the fillets and pat them dry with a paper towel. Rub them with ghee and season with the salt and pepper. Place each fillet on a piece of aluminum foil large enough to wrap around the fillet.

Top each fillet with the garlic, ginger, and jalapeño slices, then squeeze the juice from a lemon slice over each of them, and arrange a few lemon slices on top. Fold the foil around the fish to create sealed packets.

Place the packets on a baking sheet and bake for about 15 to 20 minutes. The fish is done when it flakes easily with a fork.

To finish: Take the salsa out of the refrigerator and let it rest until it reaches room temperature; when you're ready to serve the dish, season the salsa with the spice mix.

Place the warm trout on plates and top with salsa. Sprinkle with sunflower seeds, parsley, dill, and chives.

SPICED POACHED PEARS *WITH* ROSE-HONEY CREAM

Pears are a soothing, cooling, and Kapha-friendly fruit during this season. I recommend making the poached pears a day ahead and keeping them in the poaching liquid in the refrigerator so the flavors can really permeate the fruit. Try to buy firm pears to avoid having them become soggy or lose their shape after being cooked and soaked. The pears can be served cold or warm. If you have any extra poached pears left over, try drizzling them with a bit of their poaching liquid and eat as a healthy snack to satisfy cravings between meals.

Dosha Dos and Don'ts: *The cream cheese should be enjoyed in moderation, especially by Kapha types.*

SERVES 2 TO 4
Poached Pears:
1 lemon, zested and juiced
1 orange, zested and juiced
1 stick of cinnamon
3 cloves
4 allspice berries
1 star anise pod

½ cup maple syrup
2 cups water
2 pears, peeled and immersed in ice
    water to avoid browning

Rose and Honey Cream:
3½ ounces cream cheese, at room
    temperature

¼ cup buttermilk
2 tablespoons rose water
¼ teaspoon vanilla extract
2 tablespoons plus 1½ teaspoons honey
¼ portion Astringent Spice Mix (page
    35), finely ground

For the poached pears: In a large heavy-bottomed pot, combine the zest and juice from the lemon and orange, the cinnamon, cloves, allspice, star anise, and maple syrup, and cook over medium heat. Add the water and bring to a boil, then lower the heat and simmer for about 4 minutes.

Add the pears to the syrup and simmer gently for 12 minutes, or until the pears are soft and tender when tested with a fork. Transfer the pears to a plate and set aside to cool. Cut the pears up into rough slices. Bring the poaching liquid back to a simmer and cook until it's reduced down to a thick, syrupy consistency.

For the cream: In a bowl with a mixer, beat the cream cheese, buttermilk, rose water, vanilla, honey, and spice mix until it's a thick pouring consistency.

To finish: Assemble each serving by placing a few pear slices in a bowl and topping with cream sauce and a tablespoon of reduced poaching liquid.

UMEBOSHI ELIXIR

Umeboshi, one of my favorite Japanese delicacies, is pickled ume fruit, a hybrid of a plum and an apricot. The second it touches your tongue, it brings your taste buds to life with a unique tanginess. I was more than pleased to learn that this dramatically flavored pickle also has remarkable health benefits, and is known as one of the best cures for a hangover. Alcohol is not encouraged in Ayurveda (it has all the opposite qualities and effects to ojas, which is the vital energy of the body). That said, if you do consume alcohol, this delicious sour elixir packed with energy-boosting ingredients is a perfect way to replenish your body the next day.

Dosha Dos and Don'ts: *This drink has sweet, salty, and sour flavors, which are great for Vata types, but too much aloe can aggravate Vata, so if you're sensitive, use half the amount. If Pitta and Kapha types are planning on having more than 1 drink, they should use only half the amount of umeboshi.*

SERVES 4 TO 6

1 cup aloe vera juice

2 sweet plums, pitted and sliced

2 dried apricots

3 umeboshi plums

One 1-inch piece fresh ginger, grated

2 tablespoons honey, preferably raw

2 cups sparkling water

Pour the aloe juice into a pitcher or large jar, then add the sweet plums, apricots, umeboshi plums, ginger, and honey and stir. Let the mixture sit for an hour, or as long as you can (preferably overnight), to infuse the flavors into the juice.

When you're ready to serve the elixir, transfer the mixture to a blender, add a cup of ice, and blend until you get a smooth puree.

Fill glasses halfway and top with sparkling water.

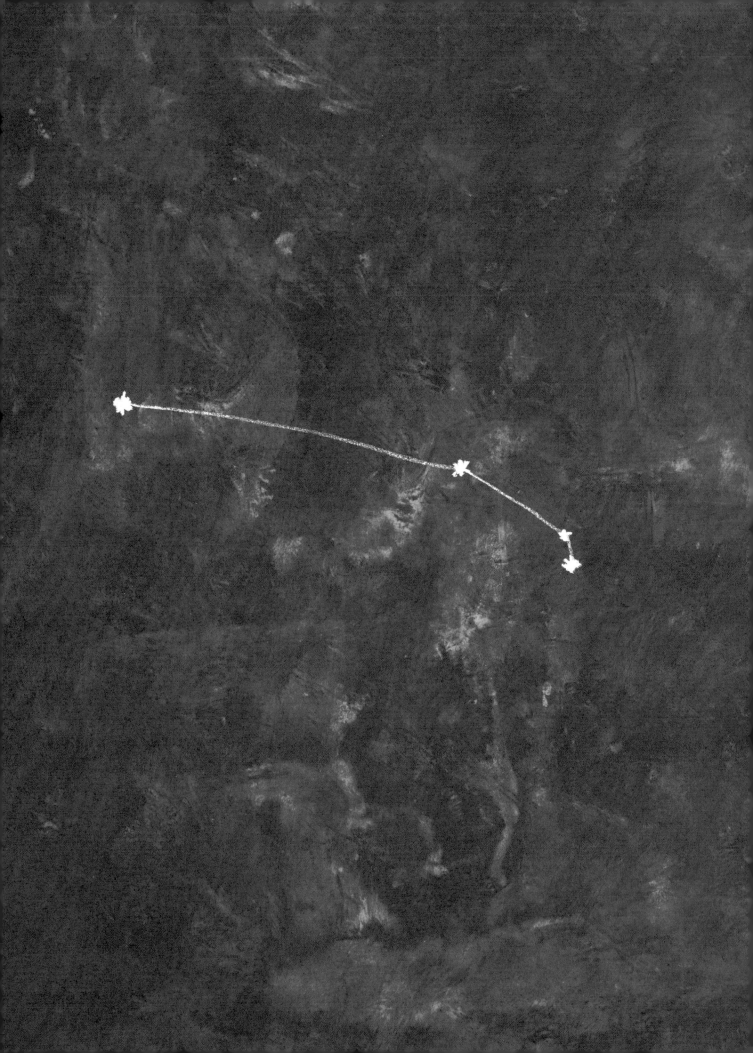

CHAPTER 4

ARIES

Essential Ayurvedic Spice

CORIANDER

» *Coriander is native to regions spanning from southern Europe and northern Africa to southwestern Asia. Egypt, Romania, and Morocco produce most of the world's coriander, while China and India also produce a limited amount.*

» *In North America, there is a distinction made between cilantro, which is known as the leaf of the cilantro plant, and coriander, which is the dried seed of the same plant. In many other countries, both the leaf and the seed are referred to as coriander. To avoid confusion, it is best to refer to them as coriander leaf (or cilantro) and coriander seed. The plant is part of the parsley family.*

» *Coriander is tridoshic—it is good for balancing all three types of doshas.*

» *Coriander is most beneficial in the hotter seasons due to its natural cooling effects on the body. It can also be used during the colder seasons in warm dishes or drinks to aid with digestion in combination with other warm spices.*

» *Among its long list of health benefits, coriander is most used to defend against allergens, enhance digestion, stimulate the appetite, and help purify the blood.*

» *A cooling spice, coriander has a sharp scent and sweet, astringent, and pungent flavors.*

» *Generally, coriander's flavor deepens the longer it's cooked. It can easily be used as a way to flavor almost any type of dish, as it complements nearly any ingredient without taking on different flavors. One of my favorite ways of using coriander seeds is whole and lightly toasted, then mixed with a bit of extra-virgin olive oil, Himalayan pink salt, and honey. I spread this mixture on top of some Homemade Cheese Curds (page 240) and warm sourdough bread.*

» *To keep coriander seeds fresh, store them in an airtight container. Whole coriander will keep for as long as a year, while ground coriander should be used within a few months.*

ARIES

Aries is Latin for "the ram" an uncastrated male sheep, and is commonly represented by a simplified image of a ram's horns. It is the first sign of the zodiac. Falling in the general Kapha season, Aries marks the new year according to the zodiac calendar. Aries begins the spring equinox with an equal balance of daylight and darkness, birthing new beginnings, new energy, and new life. The world takes on a fresh lightness after its winter rest. Springtime flourishes with wild abundance as dormant plant life begins to awaken. Roots are beginning to grow deep and strong beneath the surface.

Indulge in the bounty of spring and feel its healing effects on your body, which is now adapting to consistently warmer days—it's ready to lighten up and shed. Continue eating bitter, astringent, and pungent foods, like fennel, citrus fruits, greens, herbs, and lentils, to dislodge and detox fats and prevent any excess moisture in the body. Astringent foods keep the pores of your body toned as they start to expose themselves to the outside world with the increasing warmth, which will boost your immunity. Enjoy lightly sweet, salty, and sour foods in careful moderation for energy and warmth during this time of change and release.

In terms of life energy, spring equinox symbolizes new beginnings. This time of your life challenges you to move forward with courage and set the tone for the year by balancing your body and kick-starting metabolism. By making the recipes in this chapter, you'll delight in the abundance of spring and enjoy optimal health during this time of year.

TUNA-FENNEL SALAD *WITH* CITRUS VINAIGRETTE

Fennel is packed with fiber. It has a mild licorice flavor, which balances the bitter, sour, and minty taste of the vinaigrette, and helps manage the excess moisture that tends to accumulate in the body during this season. You can adjust this recipe and use the Sweet Spice Mix (page 30) in the vinaigrette if you make the salad in the summer. Consider this fennel slaw–like salad an alternative to the basic cabbage coleslaw. Like a lot of salads, it often tastes better after it's had time to absorb the flavors.

Dosha Dos and Don'ts: *Fennel is good for all three doshas (known as tridoshic). Kapha and Pitta types looking to balance their dosha can use lime juice instead of orange and lemon juice in the vinaigrette to moderate the acidity.*

SERVES 4 TO 6

Vinaigrette:
¼ cup fresh lemon juice
¼ cup fresh orange juice with pulp
½ teaspoon mustard
1½ teaspoons honey, preferably raw
1 tablespoon chopped mint
½ teaspoon fine Himalayan salt
1 portion Bitter Spice Mix (page 34), finely ground

½ cup flaxseed oil or extra-virgin olive oil

Salad:
1 large fennel bulb, fronds reserved
2 celery stalks, tough fibers peeled off
½ medium red onion
1 red or orange bell pepper
Two 6-ounce cans wild-caught tuna in water, drained and flaked

¼ cup chopped mint
¼ cup chopped dill
½ cup capers

To Finish:
3 tablespoons flaxseeds, lightly roasted in a dry pan
2 tablespoons chopped mint leaves
½ cup orange segments

For the citrus vinaigrette: Put the lemon juice, orange juice, mustard, honey, mint, salt, and spice mix in a blender and pulse briefly to combine. With the blender running, drizzle in the oil until well combined. Refrigerate until ready to use.

For the salad: Using a mandoline or a sharp knife, slice the fennel, celery, onion, and pepper into ⅛-inch slices. Place all the vegetables and the tuna into a large mixing bowl, and toss together. Chop all the fennel fronds and toss half of them in with the salad, adding the mint, dill, and capers at the same time.

Toss the slaw with the vinaigrette and allow it to marinate in the refrigerator, covered, for at least 1 hour.

To finish: Remove the slaw from the refrigerator, and, using a pair of tongs, divide it among serving bowls. Sprinkle each serving with about 1½ teaspoons of flaxseeds, some fennel fronds, mint, and orange segments.

GRILLED EGGPLANT ROLLS *WITH* HOMEMADE CHEESE CURDS

This small dish is a perfect way to strike a healthy balance between indulgence and healthful eating. Eggplant regulates the Kapha's sensitivity to sugar during this period, and provides an earthy, grounding taste. The miso glaze should be used in moderation during this Kapha season to avoid too much acidity. If you don't have time to make the cheese curds, you can substitute fresh cheese from the farmers' market or a good grocery store.

Dosha Dos and Don'ts: *Vata and Pitta types should limit the amount of eggplant, and Vata can add more of the cheese and miso if desired.*

SERVES 4 TO 6

2 Japanese eggplants or 4 small Italian eggplants, ends trimmed, cut lengthwise into ½-inch slices

1 teaspoon fine kosher salt, plus more for the eggplant

2 tablespoons ghee, melted

1 tablespoon balsamic vinegar

1 tablespoon dry white wine

2 tablespoons white or yellow miso

1 tablespoon jaggery, crumbled

1 portion Sweet Spice Mix (page 30), coarsely ground

1 teaspoon olive or sunflower oil

1½ cups Homemade Cheese Curds (page 240)

Place the eggplant slices on a plate, salt lightly, and let them sit for 10 minutes to release moisture.

Meanwhile, preheat the oven to 400°F. Line a baking sheet with parchment paper.

Blot the eggplant with paper towels and transfer to a mixing bowl. Add the ghee, properly coating each slice of eggplant, and place on the baking sheet. Roast for 15 to 20 minutes, until the flesh is soft. Remove from the oven and gently flip the eggplant slices over. Preheat the broiler.

In a small saucepan, combine the vinegar and wine and bring to a boil over high heat. Boil for about 20 seconds, making sure not to boil off too much of the liquid, then reduce the heat to low and stir in the miso, jaggery, and spice mix. Whisk over medium-low heat without letting the mixture boil until the jaggery has dissolved. Remove the pan from the heat and whisk in the oil.

Generously brush the eggplant slices with the glaze. Broil for about 2 minutes, until the glaze begins to bubble and looks shiny. Remove from the oven.

Top each slice with a small amount of the cheese curds and roll up into a pinwheel. Sprinkle with the salt and serve.

SPRING KHICHDI

As the heaviness of winter gives way to springtime, you'll crave fresh, seasonal greens and simple wholesome foods. This recipe is a great way to use all the beautiful young vegetables arriving at the farmers' markets and will restore vitality after a long winter of heartier root vegetables. Parsley is used in this recipe to make a chlorophyll-rich green paste, which has strong antioxidant properties. As your body detoxifies and eliminates some of the fats stored during the winter, the greens in this khichdi will help boost that process and provide you with energy.

Dosha Dos and Don'ts: *Vata types can replace the kale with spinach if they find kale difficult to digest, and they can use black chickpeas, as the white ones can cause bloating to a sensitive Vata. Pitta types can replace the sesame oil and seeds, which are warming, with sunflower oil and seeds, as they're more cooling and help balance the Pitta tendency toward excess heat in the body.*

SERVES 4 TO 6

¾ cup dry chickpeas (you can also use black chickpeas)
2 teaspoons asafetida powder
¾ cup brown rice
1 tablespoon any vinegar or lemon juice (optional)
1 cup tightly packed parsley leaves
2 cups water
1½ tablespoons sesame oil
2 medium shallots, thinly sliced

5 garlic cloves, thinly sliced
1 leek, white and light green parts only, halved, rinsed, and thinly sliced
1 portion Bitter Spice Mix (page 34), finely ground
4 cups Vegetable Broth (page 242) or water
1 teaspoon fine Himalayan salt, plus more to taste
⅓ cup chopped dill, plus some intact fronds for topping

¼ pound asparagus, tough ends trimmed, sliced on an angle
1 cup fresh or frozen peas

Toppings:
¼ cup finely sliced chives
3 scallions, trimmed and sliced
2 tablespoons toasted sesame seeds
1 lime, cut into six wedges

To prepare: In a medium heavy-bottomed saucepan, cover the chickpeas with water, add 1 teaspoon of asafetida, and bring to a boil; boil for 2 minutes. Turn off the heat, cover the pot, and let the chickpeas soak for 60 minutes (preferably overnight). Presoaking the chickpeas makes them easier to digest; it also helps them cook more evenly and become tender all the way through.

It's also good to soak the rice. In a medium bowl, cover the rice with 2 cups of water and add the vinegar (if using); soak for as long as possible, preferably overnight.

After soaking the chickpeas and rice, drain and wash thoroughly with cold water.

If you don't have time for any soaking, you can cook the dish directly from the dry ingredients, but it will take additional time to achieve the desired tenderness.

Meanwhile, place the parsley in a blender with the water. Blend until the mixture turns an even bright green, then pour it through a fine-mesh sieve into a small pot. Cook over low heat, stirring constantly, until you see green particles rising to the surface. Let the mixture cool, then pour it through a cheesecloth-lined sieve. Be careful not to push the mixture through; just let it strain on its own.

Set the strained liquid aside to add to the khichdi when serving, or drink it as a healthy chlorophyll-rich shot.

Scrape as much of the green paste off the cheesecloth as possible and put it in a bowl in the refrigerator, covered, until it's time to use it in the khichdi (you should have about 2 tablespoons of paste).

For the khichdi: In a heavy-bottomed saucepan, heat the oil, then add the shallots, garlic, leek, and spice mix. Cook until the vegetables are translucent. Add the chickpeas, rice, the remaining 1 teaspoon of asafetida, and the broth, and bring to a boil. Reduce the mixture to a simmer and cook for about 1 hour, making sure there is always enough liquid in the pot. Simmering the chickpeas gently helps them cook evenly until tender, retain their shape without losing their texture (getting mushy) too quickly, and keep their skins intact. The best time to add the salt is about 45 minutes into cooking, when they are tender enough, but still partly firm.

After an hour, taste the khichdi, and, if the chickpeas and rice are not very tender continue cooking for up to 30 minutes longer. Depending on your preference, you can adjust the texture of the khichdi for a drier risotto-like

consistency or a wetter soup-like one by either allowing the excess liquid to evaporate or adding more liquid.

Once the khichdi is cooked, remove it from the heat and stir in the chlorophyll paste and chopped dill, mix well, and cover for a few minutes.

Meanwhile, place the asparagus and peas in a steaming basket, and steam them for 5 to 10 minutes (check texture and continue steaming for up to 5 minutes more if you wish).

To finish: Serve 2 large spoons of khichdi into each serving dish. Top with the hot steamed vegetables, then with dill fronds, chives, scallions, and sesame seeds. Drizzle each portion with a squeeze of lime juice.

CHICKEN LIVER CONFIT *AND* URAD DAL CURRY

This recipe makes a wholesome curry that you can prepare ahead of time and then top with fresh ingredients when you're ready to eat. It combines iron-rich liver confit, Jerusalem artichokes, and urad dal (a bean from the Indian subcontinent). Black garlic, a Korean condiment, is the result of a month-long fermentation process; it has a strong flavor, so you don't need a lot of it (which is good news because it can be expensive). When buying liver, it's imperative to get it absolutely fresh, or it will harm your body more than help it. Be mindful not to overcook it, which ruins the delicate texture. If you know a reputable butcher who sells ready-made high-quality chicken liver confit, that might be a time-saving choice for this dish. If you're not a liver fan, you can make the recipe without it.

Dosha Dos and Don'ts: *Pitta types can moderate the amount of black garlic to avoid overheating their digestive system.*

SERVES 4 TO 6

Liver Confit:
½ pound organic chicken liver, trimmed of loose veins, fat, and membranes
1 cup whole milk
1 teaspoon sea salt
2 cups ghee
2 thyme sprigs
2 rosemary sprigs

2 pounds Jerusalem artichokes

Urad Dal:
⅔ cup urad dal
1 tablespoon ghee
2 leeks, white and light green parts only, halved, rinsed, and thinly sliced
12 garlic cloves, chopped
2 tablespoons black garlic
1 green chile, seeded and sliced

One 1-inch piece fresh ginger, peeled and grated
1 teaspoon sea salt
1 tablespoon Dijon mustard
10 basil leaves, thinly sliced
1 portion Pungent Spice Mix (page 33), coarsely ground
½ cup plain organic yogurt

For the liver confit: Place the liver in a bowl and add the milk (the milk should cover the liver). Cover the bowl with plastic wrap and refrigerate overnight. The next day, drain the liver and pat dry with paper towels. Season with the salt.

Add the liver to a saucepan that can hold them in a single layer, then add the ghee (once the ghee has melted, the livers should be immersed). Place the pan over medium heat and cook until the ghee starts to bubble vigorously, about 1 minute. Transfer the ghee and livers to a container, then add the thyme and rosemary sprigs. Cover the container and set it aside until the ghee has cooled down to room temperature. Refrigerate for at least 24 hours.

For the Jerusalem artichokes: Wash and gently scrub the artichokes under cold running water.

Cut them into ½-inch slices and immediately immerse them in a large mixing bowl with ice cold water to keep them from turning brown. Set aside.

Bring a large pot of salted boiling water to a boil. Drain the artichokes from the ice water, and transfer them to the pot. Let the water return to a boil, then reduce to a simmer and cook the artichokes, uncovered, for about 10 minutes. Set the artichokes aside.

For the urad dal: Place the urad dal in a large container and cover with several inches of cool water. Let the mixture soak for a few hours, then drain and rinse.

In a heavy-bottomed pot over medium heat, heat the ghee. Cook the leeks, garlic cloves, black garlic, chile, and ginger in the hot ghee until the leeks and garlic are golden brown, about 5 minutes. Add the urad dal and 1 cup of water to the pot and stir. Add the salt and bring to a boil. Reduce the heat to low and simmer until the lentils are tender, about 30 minutes. Then add the mustard, basil, and spice mix and stir. Cook until the lentils are cooked through, about 10 more minutes.

To finish: Place 6 to 8 slices of warm Jerusalem artichokes into serving bowls and top with 2 tablespoons of drained and chopped liver confit. Pour the hot urad dal over the artichokes and confit. Top with a dollop of yogurt.

COD *AND* VEGETABLES *IN* MUSHROOM-VANILLA BROTH

Cod has a mild flavor that just about everyone will like, plus it's an easy fish to cook, it's relatively inexpensive, and it's available throughout the year. For those looking for an alternative to red meat, cod is a great substitute and packed with healthy protein. The vanilla aroma in the mushroom broth and the bitter taste of the spinach make a perfect trio with the light sweetness of the cod. This dish is light but keeps you satisfied until your next meal, but feel free to add as much spinach as you like.

SERVES 4

Mushroom-Vanilla Broth:
1 tablespoon sunflower oil
5 garlic cloves, finely chopped
1 portion Sour Spice Mix (page 32), coarsely ground
3 cups water
3 cups Mushroom Broth (page 243)
10 thyme sprigs
5 black peppercorns
1 bay leaf
1 vanilla bean, split
2 cups spinach, washed well, stems removed
3 tablespoons sherry vinegar
¾ teaspoon kosher salt

Vegetables:
2 cups snow peas, cut on an angle into ¼-inch pieces
1 cup organic peas, fresh or frozen
1 cup carrots, lightly peeled or just scrubbed, cut on an angle into ¼-inch slices
¾ pound asparagus, trimmed, stalks cut on an angle into ¼-inch slices
3 tablespoons sunflower oil
10 garlic cloves, smashed
4 bulbs baby fennel, trimmed and halved, or 2 medium bulbs of fennel, quartered
4 scallions, greens thinly sliced, white parts halved

Cod:
1 teaspoon kosher salt
1 teaspoon coriander seeds
4 skinless cod fillets
2 tablespoons ghee

Toppings:
Cilantro sprigs, for garnish
Pinch of kosher salt

For the broth: In a large pot, heat the oil over low heat. Add the garlic and spice mix and cook, stirring, for 1 minute. Add the water, broth, thyme, peppercorns, bay leaf, and vanilla bean, then bring to a boil. Reduce the heat, cover, and simmer for 10 minutes.

Add the spinach to the broth and cook until just wilted, about 1 minute. Stir in the vinegar and salt. Remove the pot from the heat and keep covered until ready to serve.

For the vegetables: Bring a large pot of water to a boil. Working in batches, cook the snow peas, peas, carrots, and asparagus until tender but still crisp, about 1 minute for the peas and 2 to 3 minutes for the carrots and asparagus. Drain and transfer the vegetables to a plate.

In a medium saucepan, heat the oil, add the garlic, and cook until it's golden; using a slotted spoon, transfer the garlic to the plate with vegetables. Add the fennel and scallions and cook until they're golden brown, about 6 minutes, then transfer them to the plate.

For the cod: Sprinkle the salt and coriander seeds on both sides of the cod and set aside. In a frying pan, bring the ghee to medium heat, then add the cod and the seeds. Cook on one side for 2 to 3 minutes. Using a spatula, carefully flip the cod over (it's a delicate and flaky fish, so go slowly) and cook for 2 to 3 minutes longer. You can tell it's cooked when its flesh turns opaque.

To finish: Place 2 large spoons of the vegetables into shallow serving bowls and top with the cod. Pour the hot broth (reheated if necessary) over the vegetables and cod, garnish with cilantro and sprinkle with salt.

SHORTBREAD COOKIES *WITH* JAGGERY-MAPLE MERINGUE

In the decade I spent in India, I had a mixed relationship with mangoes. They were easy to come by, but they played an overheating number on my body in the already scorching summer months. I was forced to learn moderation in my consumption, and it was then that I truly got to appreciate their flavor and intensity. The cooling meringue in this recipe helps balance the heat of the mango. You can prepare this gluten-free shortbread ahead of time or serve it fresh out of the oven.

Dosha Dos and Don'ts: *Pitta types should moderate the amount of mango they consume and ensure that it is ripe.*

SERVES 4 TO 6

Jaggery-Maple Meringue:
3 egg whites
¼ teaspoon cream of tartar
⅔ cup jaggery, finely crumbled
¼ cup room-temperature water
¾ cup maple syrup
1 teaspoon lavender extract (optional)

Shortbread Cookies:
1⅓ cups white rice flour, plus more for dusting
½ cup sweet rice flour
½ cup cornstarch
1 teaspoon cardamom powder
1 teaspoon cinnamon powder
¼ teaspoon baking powder
¼ teaspoon xanthan gum
¾ cup ghee

¾ cup jaggery, crumbled
½ portion Salty Spice Mix (page 31), coarsely ground
1 teaspoon vanilla extract

To Finish:
1 cup diced mangoes or mango pulp

For the meringue: In the bowl of a stand mixer, beat the egg whites and cream of tartar until soft peaks form. In a saucepan, bring the jaggery, water, and maple syrup to a boil. Attach a candy thermometer to the pan, and cook the mixture until the thermometer reads 245°F, about 5 minutes. Remove the pan from the heat.

Turn your mixer on low speed, and slowly drizzle the maple syrup mixture into the egg white mixture while beating. Once the mixtures are fully incorporated, add the lavender extract (if using), turn the speed to high, and beat the mixture until it's light and fluffy, about 10 minutes.

For the cookies: Preheat the oven to 300°F and line a baking sheet with parchment paper.

In a small bowl, whisk together the white rice flour, sweet rice flour, cornstarch, cardamom, cinnamon, baking powder, and xanthan gum.

In a food processor bowl fitted with a paddle attachment, process the ghee, jaggery, spice mix, and vanilla on medium-low speed until well combined, about 30 seconds. Turn the processor off and add all the dry ingredients. Turn the processor on and mix until a dough forms, about 3 minutes.

Dust some rice flour on a flat surface. Turn half of the dough out onto the work surface and shape it into a disk.

Using a rolling pin, roll the dough out until it's about ¼ inch thick. Cut the rolled dough into 1- by 4-inch rectangles (this will yield about 15 to 20 pieces), then carefully place them on the parchment paper–lined baking sheet; repeat using the remaining dough. Using a fork, gently poke holes into each piece. Bake the shortbread until it's golden brown, about 30 minutes. Once the cookies are done, allow them to cool on the baking sheet for 5 minutes, then transfer them to a wire rack to continue cooling.

To finish: Place 2 spoons of fresh mangoes or mango pulp into each dessert bowl, top with a large spoon of meringue and a few shortbread cookies.

RAISIN *AND* ROSE TEA LASSI

Lassi is a beautifully cooling Indian drink, traditionally made with yogurt or buttermilk, water, and spices. Lassi usually comes in plain, sweet, or salty flavor profiles. The salty version is often flavored with coriander and black salt. The plain version usually has a small amount of salt and/or sweetener added. For the sweet lassi, any type of sweetener is common, as are mangoes. Soaked raisins are a perfect substitute for sugar, healthy for all three types of doshas, and known to promote healthy weight loss when eaten in moderation.

Dosha Dos and Don'ts: *For Pitta and Kapha types, use 1 cup of buttermilk and add 6 ice cubes to the recipe (buttermilk needs to be diluted to avoid extensive acidity). The trick to a good lassi is achieving some froth, so don't add ice or water all at once. Instead, adjust the consistency as you go, and blend at high speed.*

SERVES 4

½ cup chilled rose tea (1 cup of water steeped with a rose tea bag for 15 minutes, then refrigerated)

1 cup plain organic yogurt

½ cup buttermilk

One 1-inch piece fresh ginger, grated

4 tablespoons golden raisins, soaked in hot water for 15 minutes

4 dates, pitted

½ cup ice cubes

Organic raw honey to taste

Place all the ingredients except the honey in the blender, and blend until smooth and frothy. Pour the lassi into glasses and adjust the sweetness with honey if you like.

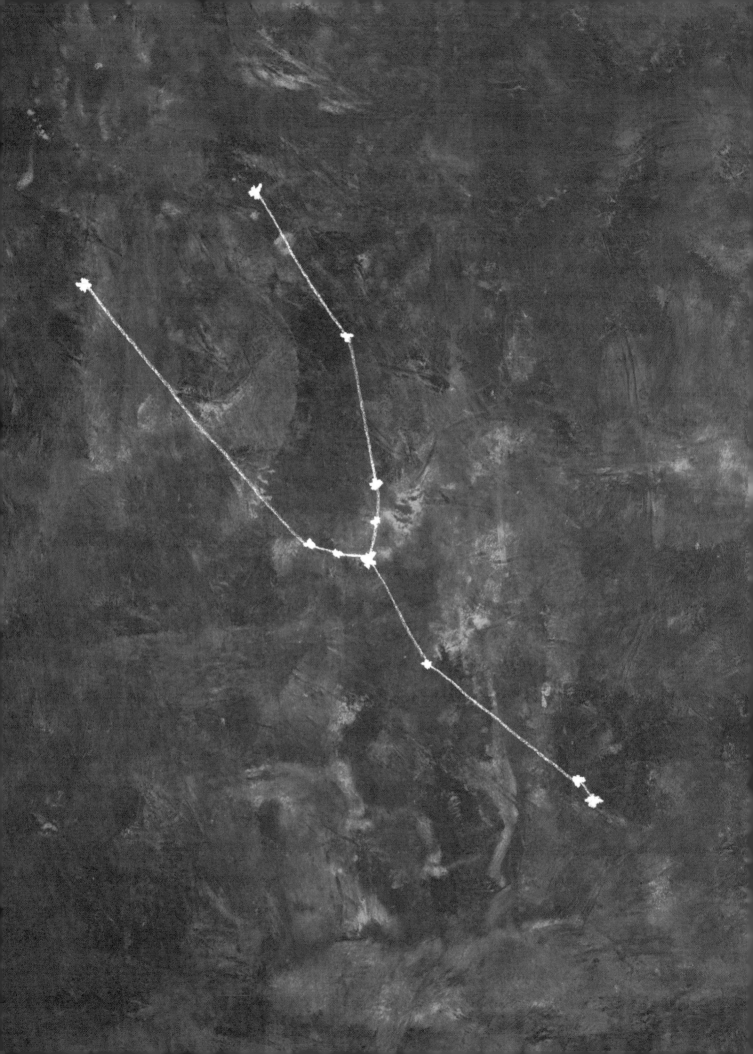

CHAPTER 5
TAURUS

GINGER

» *The origins of ginger are mysterious: No one has ever found it growing wild. It was first cultivated in China and India. Today, India is the largest producer of ginger, though it is grown in most parts of the world.*

» *The common misconception about ginger is that it is a root when in fact it's a rhizome, or a stem that grows just under the soil (generally horizontally) and sprouts shoots and roots from vertical stems.*

» *Known in Ayurveda as "a medicine for all," ginger is tridoshic, but it can be aggravating to Pitta if not taken in moderation and combined with cooling ingredients.*

» *Ginger has a pungent taste with a sweet postdigestive effect on the body. Best eaten in small amounts, ginger is usually added to other food, both in its fresh and dried forms, both raw and cooked. To replace fresh ginger with dried ginger in a recipe, use anywhere from ⅛ to ¼ teaspoon of ground ginger per tablespoon of fresh ginger.*

» *Ginger can be consumed throughout the year, and it's recommended as a daily staple. One of my mentors, Chef LaMarita, taught me how to incorporate ginger into my diet every day in a way that has significantly improved my digestive health and skin. Every morning, I roughly chop a medium-size piece of ginger root and place it in a large pot full of water. I boil it for 15 minutes and then let it steep for 15 more minutes. I make sure to sip on the drink throughout the day.*

» *Turning fresh ginger into ground ginger reduces the amount of one of its beneficial compounds, but it increases the amounts of other important compounds, which can be even more beneficial to your health in some ways. Therefore, fresh ginger isn't always preferable, and it's fine to use both types of ginger.*

April 19–May 20

TAURUS

Taurus is Latin for "the bull" and is commonly represented by the head of a horned bull. It is the second sign of the zodiac. Taurus falls into the general Kapha season for half the duration, then transitions into Pitta for the second half. Throughout this period, there is more light during the day, when the energy of spring is at its peak and seeds begin to take root. Spring is at its midpoint, and days are longer—and with the long days come shorter nights. Farmers' markets are coming back to life with an abundance of young and fresh ingredients.

Your body is struggling to manage the increase in heat and humidity. Pace yourself as the days grow increasingly longer; there is a tendency to want to tap into nature's energy and hit the ground running. By now, the heat of the season has burned off most of your winter fat. Begin increasing your intake of light and sweet foods, like new potatoes, eggs, goat cheese, honey, and yogurt, which will help boost your energy and replenish hydration. May is the best month to follow a vegetarian diet. As the weather warms up, we need less and less of heavy fats.

It's time to get your hands dirty and connect with nature. Spending time outside helps your body come into balance. Soak up the extra sunlight to replenish vitamin D levels that may be deficient after the long winter. Be sure you are getting adequate sleep as the days lengthen and it can be hard to get to bed early.

NEW POTATOES *AND* ZUCCHINI BREAD CHAAT

Chaat, one of India's most popular street foods, is also a dish made at home. It hits practically every element that makes something craveable and covers every flavor profile and texture you could want—sweet, sour, tangy, spicy, and crunchy. It usually contains some sort of boiled vegetable, sometimes fruit, some form of carbs (bread, crackers, wafers, puffed rice, etc.), sauces, chutneys, and different spices. It's light enough to be eaten for breakfast or as an afternoon snack but satisfying enough to take the place of lunch or dinner. The zucchini bread in this recipe is gluten-free and can be a wholesome alternative to toast or sandwich bread. New potatoes are harvested before they reach full maturity and they're sweeter than other potatoes. When you get the hang of this recipe, try coming up with your own version; the essence of a good chaat is innovation in pursuit of creating the perfect comfort food that's tailored to your taste.

Dosha Dos and Don'ts: *Vata types should choose new potatoes over more mature potatoes whenever possible because they are lighter than their starchy counterparts. If you can't find new potatoes, you can replace them with sweet potatoes which are more suited to the Vata dosha.*

SERVES 4 TO 6

Zucchini Bread:
⅓ cup melted coconut oil
¼ cup maple syrup
2 large organic eggs
2 teaspoons vanilla extract
½ cup unsweetened almond milk
1 teaspoon baking soda
1 teaspoon cinnamon powder
¼ teaspoon nutmeg powder
1½ cups chickpea flour
½ cup grated carrots
¾ cup grated zucchini (moisture squeezed out completely)

⅓ cup pumpkin seeds, toasted in a dry pan

Potatoes:
4 new potatoes, scrubbed and cut into 1-inch cubes
2 tablespoons unsalted butter
1 tablespoon freshly ground black pepper
8 basil leaves, thinly sliced
1 portion Salty Spice Mix (page 31), finely ground
Juice of 1 lime

Toppings:
1 tablespoon plus 1½ teaspoons olive oil
1 tablespoon coriander seeds
½ teaspoon kosher salt
4 large organic hard-boiled eggs, chopped into a crumble
1 teaspoon asafetida powder
½ tablespoon smoked paprika
2 tablespoons chopped dill
1 lime, cut in half

For the zucchini bread: Preheat oven to 350°F. In a medium bowl, add the coconut oil, maple syrup, eggs, vanilla, and almond milk and whisk together.

In another bowl, combine the baking soda, cinnamon, nutmeg, and chickpea flour. Add the dry ingredients to the wet ingredients, then mix in the carrots and zucchini. Fold in the pumpkin seeds, then pour the batter into a loaf pan, and bake for 45 to 55 minutes, or until a toothpick inserted in the middle comes out clean. Remove the bread from the oven and place on a wire rack to cool completely.

For the potatoes: Bring a large pot of water to a boil. Add the potatoes and boil for 25 minutes. Drain the potatoes and place them back into the pot. Add the butter,

black pepper, basil, spice mix, and lime juice, and stir to coat the potatoes evenly.

To finish: Cut the zucchini bread into 1-inch cubes and place in a large mixing bowl. Drizzle with the oil and mix in the coriander seeds and salt. Toast the bread on a dry skillet until crisp, about 3 minutes. Place the bread cubes in a large bowl and top with the warm potatoes and crumbled eggs.

Sprinkle with the asafetida, paprika, and dill, then squeeze the juice from both lime halves over the dish.

ROASTED EGGPLANT *AND* POTATO SALAD *WITH GOAT CHEESE*

According to Ayurveda, you should avoid vegetables that are classified as nightshades because they provide too much heat for the body and, in return, can aggravate Vata, Pitta, and Kapha. But to my great relief and after much recent confusion about eggplant, it turns out that this delicious fruit (which is often considered a vegetable), is an important exception to the rule. Native to India and later cultivated in Europe and Asia, eggplant has been widely used in Ayurveda for its rich antioxidant content and regulating effects on blood sugar. In this salad, the roasted eggplant contributes a strong earthy flavor and delicate texture.

Dosha Dos and Don'ts: Vata and Pitta types could moderate the amount of eggplant to balance its bitter taste and heating qualities, which can aggravate their dosha when eaten in excess. If you use less eggplant, add more potatoes to the salad instead.

SERVES 4 TO 6

Marinade:
2 tablespoons ghee, melted
2 tablespoons apple cider vinegar
1 tablespoon maple syrup
1 tablespoon fresh lemon juice
2 tablespoons chopped dill
1 tablespoon mustard seeds, lightly toasted in a dry pan
1 portion Bitter Spice Mix (page 34), finely ground

Salad:
2 large eggplants, cut into 1½-inch cubes
1 small red onion, thinly sliced
2 tablespoons barberries (or raisins or cranberries)
Kosher salt
1 cup cubed potatoes
4 large garlic cloves, roughly chopped
1½ cups fresh or frozen peas

To Finish:
2 tablespoons fresh lemon juice
1 tablespoon plus 1½ teaspoons tamari
2 cups arugula
½ cup smoked almonds, roughly chopped
2 ounces goat cheese, crumbled
4½ teaspoons coriander seeds, toasted in a dry pan

For the marinade: Place all the ingredients in a blender, and blend until well mixed. Set aside until ready to use.

For the salad: Preheat the oven to 400°F and place a rack in the center position. Put the eggplant, onion, and barberries in a large mixing bowl, leaving enough room to toss. Sprinkle lightly with salt and set aside for 15 minutes to allow the eggplant to release water. Dab the excess moisture with a paper towel or dish towel and add the marinade. Let the mixture marinate for 15 minutes to 1 hour.

Add the potatoes and chopped garlic to the vegetables and toss. Spread the mixture on a large parchment paper–lined baking sheet. After 30 minutes, add the peas and continue cooking for 10 minutes longer, or as long as needed for the vegetables to be soft and cooked through. Remove the baking sheet from the oven and cool slightly before transferring the mixture back into the bowl.

To finish: In a small bowl, whisk the lemon juice and tamari together, pour over the vegetable mixture, and toss. Divide the salad among serving bowls and top with arugula, almonds, goat cheese, and coriander seeds.

SCRAMBLED EGG *AND* CAULIFLOWER KHICHDI

This khichdi has the appeal of breakfast-like food that can be enjoyed any time of day. It is easy to digest, and the quinoa and dal keep your belly satisfied for a long time. Cook the eggs gently and turn off the heat before they are even done, allowing them to finish cooking with the declining heat of the pan.

Dosha Dos and Don'ts: *Vata types can moderate the amount of eggs and cauliflower and indulge in larger amounts of quinoa and lentils.*

SERVES 4 TO 6

¾ cup mung lentils
2 teaspoons asafetida powder
3 tablespoons ghee
1 large leek, white and light green parts only, halved, rinsed, and thinly sliced
1 portion Astringent Spice Mix (page 35), finely ground
¾ cup quinoa

3½ cups Ginger, Garlic, and Onion Broth (page 244) or water
1 teaspoon kosher or sea salt, plus more to taste
1½ teaspoons tahini
1½ teaspoons apple cider vinegar
1½ cups cauliflower, chopped into small florets
2 garlic cloves, thinly sliced

2 tablespoons nigella seeds
6 extra-large organic brown eggs
½ cup coconut milk
½ cup chopped dill
2 tablespoons toasted sesame seeds
1 cup bean sprouts

To prepare: In a medium heavy-bottomed saucepan, cover the lentils with water, add 1 teaspoon of asafetida, and bring to a boil; boil for 2 minutes. Turn off the heat, cover the pot, and let the lentils soak for 60 minutes (preferably overnight). Presoaking the lentils makes them easier to digest; it also helps them cook more evenly and become tender all the way through.

After soaking the lentils, drain and wash thoroughly with cold water.

If you don't have time for any soaking, you can cook the dish directly from the dry ingredients, but it will take additional time to achieve the desired tenderness.

For the khichdi: In a heavy-bottomed saucepan, heat 1 tablespoon of ghee, then add the leek and spice mix. Cook until the leek is translucent. Add the lentils, quinoa, remaining 1 teaspoon of asafetida, and the broth, and bring to a boil. Reduce the mixture to a simmer and cook for about 45 minutes, making sure there is always enough liquid in the pot. Simmering the lentils gently helps them cook evenly, retain their shape without losing their texture (getting mushy) too quickly, and keep their skins intact. Add the salt about 30 minutes into cooking, when the lentils are tender but still partly firm.

After cooking for 45 minutes, taste the khichdi, and if the lentils and quinoa are not very tender, continue cooking for up to 15 minutes longer. Depending on your preference, you can adjust the texture of the khichdi for a drier risotto-like consistency or a wetter soup-like one by either allowing the excess liquid to evaporate or adding more liquid.

Toward the end of cooking time, add the tahini and vinegar and mix in well. Cook for 2 more minutes, then add salt to taste and remove from the heat.

Boil a large pot of water, then cook the cauliflower partially, for about 5 minutes. Drain the cauliflower completely. Heat 1 tablespoon of ghee in a large pan over medium heat. Fry the garlic and nigella seeds until the garlic begins to brown. Add the cauliflower and cook for about 4 minutes. Remove from the heat.

Crack the eggs into a mixing bowl and add the coconut milk. Whisk until you get a frothy mixture. In a nonstick pan, heat the remaining 1 tablespoon of ghee to medium heat, add the eggs, and sprinkle with salt. Using a wooden spoon, scrape the bottom of the pan and mix the eggs to get a scrambled texture. Cook the eggs for about 2 minutes, then throw in the dill and cover.

To finish: Place 2 large spoons of khichdi in each serving bowl. Top with hot scrambled eggs, cauliflower, sesame seeds, and the sprouts.

MACKEREL RILLETTES
ON GRILLED LETTUCE

This recipe balances the richness of traditional French rillettes, a meat dish similar to pâté, by replacing bread with crunchy, refreshing lettuce as a bed to serve them on. The rillettes are best after being kept in the refrigerator overnight, but you can achieve a great flavor even if you reduce that time to an hour. Products made with goat milk are tridoshic, as is asparagus, so this dish is easy to cook for guests of all dosha types.

Dosha Dos and Don'ts: *Kapha types should always consume dairy products in moderation; they can enjoy a lighter version of this dish with just the mackerel, lettuce, and asparagus.*

SERVES 4

Mackerel Rillettes:
2 scallions, white and light green parts only, finely sliced
6 radishes, grated
2 thyme sprigs
1 bay leaf
1 teaspoon kosher or sea salt
½ cup Champagne vinegar
1 portion Sour Spice Mix (page 32), coarsely ground
2 large Spanish mackerel fillets, skin and bones removed
2 cups Vegetable Broth (page 242)

¼ cup pickled pearl onions, cut into thin slices
2 tablespoons Bengali kasundi or Dijon mustard
1 tablespoon apple cider vinegar
1½ tablespoons olive oil
¼ cup plain organic yogurt
¼ cup goat cheese, crumbled
2 tablespoons finely chopped parsley

Grilled Lettuce:
1 tablespoon olive oil, plus more for greasing the pan or grill

1 head romaine lettuce, cut in half lengthwise
1 teaspoon kosher salt
1 teaspoon freshly ground black pepper
Juice of 1 lemon

To Finish:
½ teaspoon smoking liquid (optional)
½ pound asparagus, tough ends trimmed, shaved thinly with a vegetable peeler
1 teaspoon sumac

For the mackerel rillettes: Place the scallions and radishes in a bowl. Add the thyme sprigs, bay leaf, salt, vinegar, and spice mix. Layer the mixture over the mackerel fillets and place in the refrigerator overnight to marinate (if pressed for time, marinate as long as you can).

In a medium saucepan, bring the broth to a boil. Meanwhile, remove the mackerel from the marinade; when the broth boils, add the mackerel and let it simmer for about 10 minutes. Remove the pot from the heat and drain the mackerel. Using a fork, separate the flesh into chunks. Put the mackerel flakes in a mixing bowl and add the onions, mustard, vinegar, and oil, then mix well.

In a separate bowl, blend the yogurt and goat cheese until smooth. Add it to the mackerel mixture and mix well to combine into a flaky and creamy mixture that shouldn't be too loose or wet. Add some salt and the parsley and toss. Refrigerate until ready to serve.

For the grilled lettuce: Lightly oil and preheat a grill or grilling pan to medium heat. Drizzle the oil over the lettuce and season with salt and pepper. Place the lettuce halves cut side down on the grill. Cook until the lettuce is slightly wilted and charred, about 5 minutes. Remove from the grill, pull apart the leaves, and drizzle with lemon juice.

To finish: Remove the mackerel rillettes from the refrigerator, and add the smoking liquid (if using). Top 2 or 3 lettuce leaves with a spoonful of the rillettes, asparagus shavings, and sumac.

CHICKPEA-FLOUR CREPES *WITH* ENOKI MUSHROOMS *AND* YOGURT CREAM

These gluten-free crepes are light and versatile; they can be made into a savory dish, as they are in this recipe, or served as dessert with fruit and honey. The chickpea flour is a great source of protein, fiber, and iron, which means the crepes will fill you up and keep you full for hours. Ayurveda advises moderate mushroom consumption, but you should nevertheless enjoy their earthy taste like the dark, rich, loamy soil itself. The earthiness that is inherent to mushrooms represents their ability to keep you grounded and calm your nervous system. I always like to make extra yogurt cream and eat it with pan-fried rice or quinoa the next day.

SERVES 4 TO 6

Crepes:
1½ cups chickpea flour
1 cup water
¼ teaspoon fine sea salt
½ teaspoon garlic powder
½ teaspoon onion powder
1 portion Sweet Spice Mix (page 30), coarsely ground
2 tablespoons ghee

Yogurt Cream:
¼ cup organic Greek yogurt
Juice and zest of ½ lime
4 dates, pitted and finely chopped
1½ teaspoons white wine vinegar
1 tablespoon chopped thyme
1 tablespoon chopped mint
1 tablespoon extra-virgin olive oil
½ teaspoon fine Himalayan salt
1 teaspoon finely ground white pepper

Enoki Mushrooms:
1 tablespoon sunflower oil
1 pound enoki mushrooms, chopped
1½ teaspoons poppy seeds
1½ teaspoons Dijon mustard

For the crepes: In a blender, combine the chickpea flour, water, salt, garlic powder, onion powder, and spice mix and blend on high speed until smooth.

Place the mixture in the refrigerator for at least 10 minutes or up to a day to allow the mixture to bind. When you take the crepe batter out of the refrigerator, you'll find some liquid accumulated on top of the batter, so gently stir the batter before making the crepes.

Lightly grease a large nonstick pan (preferably a crepe pan) with the ghee and warm over medium-high heat. (If you plan to make the crepes again soon, keep ⅛ cup of batter to use in the next batch for better flavor. You can keep it in the refrigerator for up to 4 days.) Pour a quarter of the batter into the pan and cook until the edges start to bubble, about 3 minutes. Carefully flip and fry on the other side until the crepe is firm. Set aside and continue with the remaining batter; you should have at least 4 crepes. You can prepare the crepes up to 2 days ahead of time and refrigerate them for later use.

For the yogurt cream: Place the yogurt, lime juice and zest, dates, vinegar, thyme, mint, and oil in a bowl. Stir to combine. If the mixture is too thick, you can add some more lime juice to achieve a texture similar to heavy cream. Season with the salt and pepper. Refrigerate until ready to use.

For the enoki mushrooms: Heat the oil on a flat grill to medium hot, then add the diced enoki, stirring continuously to avoid burning the mushrooms. Cook for 3 minutes, then transfer the mushrooms to a mixing bowl. Add the poppy seeds and mustard and toss to combine with the mushrooms.

To finish: Top each crepe with a large spoon of the mushrooms and fold in half or roll up. Drizzle the yogurt cream over the crepes before serving.

STRAWBERRY-TAMARIND TART

With strawberries coming into season, this tart is a perfect way to enjoy them. The light crust is gluten-free, and the turmeric adds a lovely yellow color and a smoky bitterness to both the tartness and sweetness of the strawberries. The tart is delicious right out of the oven, but it also keeps well in the refrigerator for a few days (I bring mine to room temperature or reheat it in the oven). As other delicious berries appear at the farmers' market, feel free to use them in an iteration of this.

Dosha Dos and Don'ts: *As with all desserts, Kapha types should enjoy this tart in moderation. Pitta types should cut the amount of tamarind and spice mix in half, to avoid too much sour and pungent tastes.*

SERVES 4 TO 6

Strawberry Filling:
One 16-ounce block sweet tamarind pulp
1 cup water
1 portion Pungent Spice Mix (page 33), finely ground
1 cup coconut sugar
½ teaspoon cayenne pepper (optional)
½ teaspoon kosher salt
4 cups strawberries, hulled and sliced

Crust:
1 cup brown rice flour, plus more for rolling the dough
¼ teaspoon baking powder
2 teaspoons turmeric powder
¼ teaspoon sea salt
¼ cup cold butter, cut into small pieces
1 large organic egg, beaten
3 teaspoons cold water

To Finish:
¼ cup mascarpone cheese
2 vanilla beans
1 tablespoon plus 1½ teaspoons honey, preferably raw
2 teaspoons coconut sugar

For the filling: Place the tamarind in a medium pot and cover with water. Bring to a boil, then reduce the heat and simmer, covered, for 45 minutes to 1 hour, or until the block of pulp is completely broken down. You should have a thick brown liquid puree. Remove the pot from the heat and pour the mixture through a fine-mesh sieve into a bowl, stirring to separate the pulp dissolved in the liquid. Return the pulpy seeds to the pan and add the cup of water. Once again, bring the mixture to a boil and then reduce to a simmer and cook for 15 to 20 minutes. Strain into the bowl with the first round of pulp. Stir the spice mix into the tamarind puree. Discard the seeds and rinse out the pot.

Attach a candy thermometer to the side of the pot, and spread the sugar on the bottom of pan in an even layer. Place over medium heat and cook undisturbed until the sugar begins to melt and turns golden. Add the liquid tamarind pulp to the melted sugar and whisk together. Cook for about 10 minutes, until the candy thermometer reaches 220°F. Remove the pan from the heat and stir in the cayenne pepper (if using) and salt. Let the mixture cool, and set aside.

Place the strawberries in a large mixing bowl, then pour in two thirds of the tamarind sauce. Toss to combine.

For the crust: Preheat the oven to 350°F. Put the rice flour, baking powder, turmeric, and salt in a medium mixing bowl. Add the butter, then smash the mixture together with a fork. Add the egg and water and stir until the mixture is sticky and forms a dough.

Sprinkle some rice flour on a work surface and roll the dough out into a rectangular shape, about ¼-inch thick. Trim the rough edges and transfer to a parchment paper–lined baking sheet. Spoon the strawberry filling into the crust in an even layer, leaving about a 1-inch border all around. Fold the crust edges up, then bake for about 30 minutes, or until the crust has turned golden brown. Remove the tart from the oven, place on a wire rack to cool, and set aside.

To finish: Cut the tart into squares or slices. Place the mascarpone in a bowl. Split open the vanilla beans, scrape out the seeds, and place them in the bowl with the mascarpone. Add the remaining tamarind sauce, honey, and coconut sugar; mix to combine. Serve the tart topped with a dollop of the mascarpone mixture.

CHERRY *AND* PEAR SPARKLER

Unlike many fruits that are available in the market year-round, cherries have a growing season of about four months (from late spring through early summer), so eat them while you can. They are a cooling and cleansing summer food that helps remove excess heat that builds up in the body. This drink is a perfect alternative to a cocktail.

Dosha Dos and Don'ts: *Vata types can replace the apple juice with pear juice, as the astringency of apples can aggravate you. Kapha types can leave out the jaggery and enjoy the natural sweetness of the cherries instead. Pitta types can use maple syrup instead of jaggery.*

SERVES 4 TO 6

2 cups red cherries, pitted
One 1-inch piece fresh ginger, peeled and grated
2 cups organic pear juice

Juice of 2 limes
1 tablespoon plus 2 teaspoons crumbled jaggery
¼ teaspoon celery seeds
½ teaspoon sea salt

1 teaspoon cinnamon powder
1 lime, cut into wedges
2 cups natural sparkling water

In a large bowl, combine the cherries, ginger, and pear juice, and let soak overnight, or for at least 30 minutes.

Pour the soaked mixture, lime juice, and 2 teaspoons of jaggery into a blender; blend for 2 minutes.

Grind the remaining 1 tablespoon jaggery, celery seeds, sea salt, and cinnamon coarsely, and place in a small shallow saucer. Pass a quarter wedge of lime around the rim of each glass, then dip the rim into this spice blend to coat generously.

Add 2 large ice cubes to each glass, then fill halfway with the blended cherry-and-pear juice. Top with sparkling water and serve.

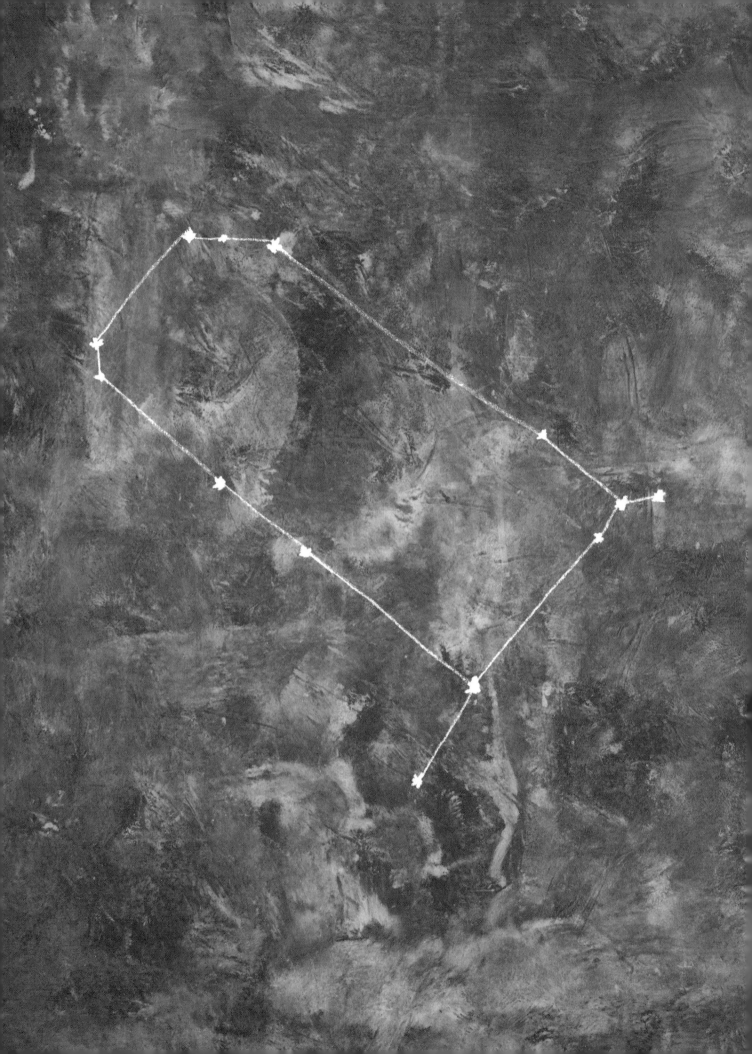

CHAPTER 6

GEMINI

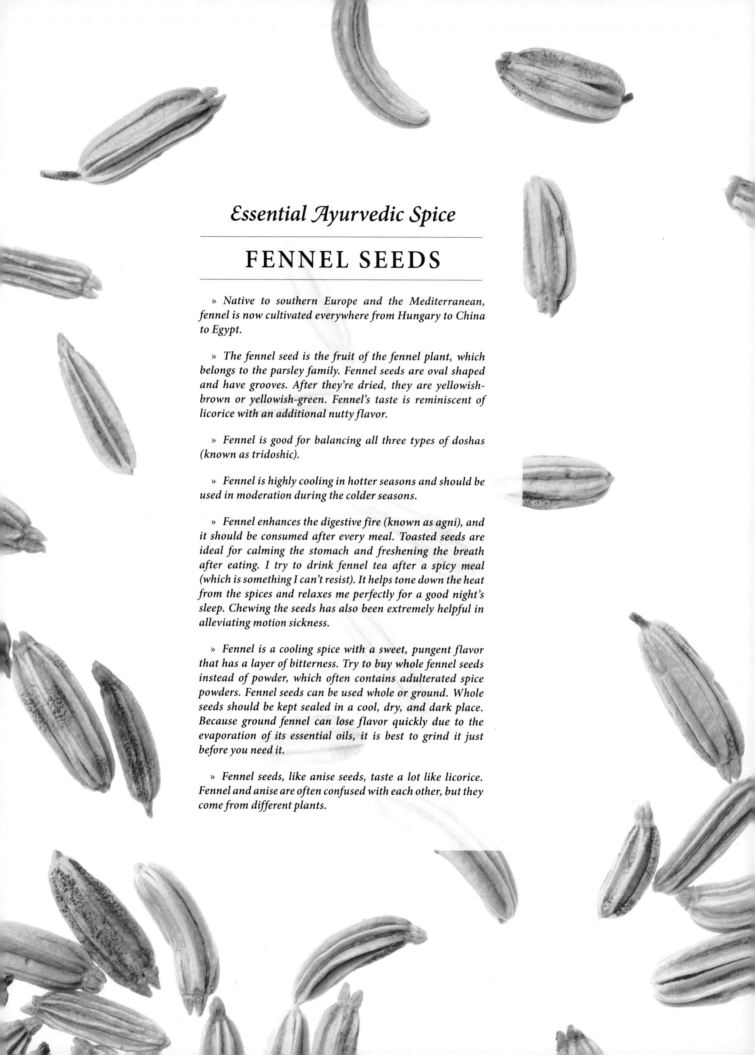

Essential Ayurvedic Spice

FENNEL SEEDS

» *Native to southern Europe and the Mediterranean, fennel is now cultivated everywhere from Hungary to China to Egypt.*

» *The fennel seed is the fruit of the fennel plant, which belongs to the parsley family. Fennel seeds are oval shaped and have grooves. After they're dried, they are yellowish-brown or yellowish-green. Fennel's taste is reminiscent of licorice with an additional nutty flavor.*

» *Fennel is good for balancing all three types of doshas (known as tridoshic).*

» *Fennel is highly cooling in hotter seasons and should be used in moderation during the colder seasons.*

» *Fennel enhances the digestive fire (known as agni), and it should be consumed after every meal. Toasted seeds are ideal for calming the stomach and freshening the breath after eating. I try to drink fennel tea after a spicy meal (which is something I can't resist). It helps tone down the heat from the spices and relaxes me perfectly for a good night's sleep. Chewing the seeds has also been extremely helpful in alleviating motion sickness.*

» *Fennel is a cooling spice with a sweet, pungent flavor that has a layer of bitterness. Try to buy whole fennel seeds instead of powder, which often contains adulterated spice powders. Fennel seeds can be used whole or ground. Whole seeds should be kept sealed in a cool, dry, and dark place. Because ground fennel can lose flavor quickly due to the evaporation of its essential oils, it is best to grind it just before you need it.*

» *Fennel seeds, like anise seeds, taste a lot like licorice. Fennel and anise are often confused with each other, but they come from different plants.*

May 21–June 21

GEMINI

Gemini is Latin for "the twins" and is commonly represented by the Roman numeral II. It is the third sign of the zodiac. A part of the Pitta season, it is the ending phase of spring in late May, when the rhythm of nature has settled and spring is about to merge with summer. Gardens flourish, humidity rises, and the summer heat accumulates.

It's important to keep your cool, but resist the temptation to crank up your air-conditioning because the constant fluctuation of extreme temperatures is taxing on your body as it struggles to adapt. You're meant to experience heat in the summer and cold in the winter, and your body is designed to gradually calibrate and adjust to each season. Seasonal harvest provides cooling and high-energy foods to help your body get through the long, hot days. Digestion is weakest in the summer, so keep your diet light and cool with ingredients like watermelon, quinoa, amaranth, red rice, turkey, and chicken, especially at lunch, to avoid lethargy during the hottest time of the day. Limit your intake of pungent foods as they further stimulate the heat produced by the body. Sour and salty tastes should be eaten in small amounts to avoid dehydration and depletion as the last bit of Kapha wetness is flushed from the body.

There is a lightness in the air and a tendency to let enthusiasm over the good weather run us into the ground. The weeks around summer solstice mark the longest days of the year, and overexertion can steer you into deep imbalance. Take the time to get inspired and use the boosting energy of summer to set your ambitions into motion.

CARROT CUSTARD TART

This tart is beautiful and can be made as one large tart or individual or bite-size tartlets. The nutrients in carrots are concentrated in the vegetable's skin, so buy organic carrots as often as possible and, for maximum benefits, don't peel them. This tart is as tasty as any sinful indulgence; it's also a great source of nourishment for your body.

SERVES 4 TO 6

Carrot Custard:
1 pound carrots, scrubbed
1 tablespoon extra-virgin olive oil
1 cup Chicken Stock (page 241)
Kosher or sea salt
1 tablespoon ghee
1 medium shallot, finely chopped

One 1-inch piece fresh ginger, peeled
    and grated
2 large organic eggs, beaten
1 portion Pungent Spice Mix (page 33),
    finely ground
4½ teaspoons goat cheese
10 chives, finely chopped

Almond Crust:
1¾ cups sliced natural almonds
½ teaspoon salt
1¼ sticks cold unsalted butter, cut into
    pieces
1¼ cups quinoa or rice flour
1 large organic egg, beaten

For the carrot custard: Cut the carrots into slices. In a skillet, add 1 tablespoon of oil and sauté the carrots for a few minutes. Add the stock and cook for 20 minutes or until the liquid completely evaporates. Add salt to taste and remove the pan from the heat. Place the carrots in a food processor and pulse until they are finely chopped. Place them in a mixing bowl and set aside.

Meanwhile, melt the ghee in a pan and fry the shallots and ginger until slightly brown, about 5 minutes, then remove from the heat.

Add the eggs, spice mix, cheese, chives, and the browned shallots and ginger to the bowl with the finely chopped carrots, then toss to mix evenly. Place in the refrigerator until you are ready to assemble the tarts.

For the almond crust: Preheat the oven to 350°F.

In a food processor, finely grind the almonds and salt. Add the butter and flour and process until you get a mixture that resembles sand. Add the egg and pulse until the mixture begins to clump together.

Transfer the mixture to a round baking pan with a removable bottom. Using floured fingers, press the dough into the bottom and sides of the pan. Bake in the middle of the oven for 5 minutes.

Take the crust out of the oven and spread the carrot custard mixture in it evenly. Place the tart back in the oven and bake for another 20 minutes, or until the custard is fully cooked (test it by inserting a toothpick in the center and seeing if it comes out clean). Remove the tart from the oven and let it cool slightly before removing the bottom of the baking pan and placing the tart on a wire rack to cool. Serve warm.

WATERMELON-RHUBARB SALAD *WITH* GARLIC DRESSING

During the hot summer months, watermelon has the perfect cooling effect on your body and thereby restores the doshic balance. To get the full health benefits of watermelon, it's important to know how to eat it properly. Heavier foods that are difficult to digest will slow down the naturally fast digestion of watermelon, which can, in turn, cause a smorgasbord of unpleasant digestive disruptions. Moral of the story: Watermelon is best consumed in light salads like this one, or on its own with some spices and herbs. Although most people are accustomed to eating only the sweet red fleshy parts, the seeds and the white part of the rind are also edible. This recipe uses these commonly ignored parts—the rind is used in the dressing, and the seeds are roasted and added to the salad for some extra crunch.

Dosha Dos and Don'ts: *Vata types can rely on the spices to help avoid bloating.*

SERVES 4 TO 6

Garlic Dressing:
4 garlic cloves
1 tablespoon thyme leaves
1 tablespoon olive oil
2 egg yolks
1 teaspoon Dijon mustard
1½ teaspoons white wine vinegar
1½ teaspoons fresh lemon juice
1 portion Pungent Spice Mix (page 33), coarsely ground
¼ cup coconut oil

2 tablespoons pink peppercorns, crushed

Salad:
1¼ cups fresh orange juice
½ cup maple syrup
⅓ cup water
2 tablespoons finely grated orange zest
One 1-inch piece fresh ginger, grated
3 cups rhubarb, leaves trimmed, cut into ⅛-inch slices

To Finish:
1 pound seedless watermelon, cut into 1-inch cubes
Coarsely ground Himalayan salt
3 cups arugula
2 radishes, thinly sliced
4 teaspoons coriander seeds, lightly toasted in a dry pan
2 tablespoons coconut chips, toasted

For the dressing: Put the garlic, thyme, olive oil, egg yolks, mustard, vinegar, lemon juice, and spice mix in a blender and blend until emulsified. With the blender running at medium speed, add the coconut oil in a slow stream. The mixture will gradually get creamy. Once you're done adding the oil, continue to blend for up to 1 minute. Add the peppercorns and pulse a couple of times. Refrigerate until ready to use.

For the salad: In a large saucepan, bring the orange juice, maple syrup, water, and orange zest to a boil. Reduce the heat to medium and add the ginger. Simmer the mixture until it thickens to a syrupy consistency, about 10 minutes.

Add the rhubarb and reduce the heat to medium low. Cover and simmer until the rhubarb is tender but intact, about 2 minutes. Using a slotted spoon, remove the rhubarb from the pan and set aside; keep the remaining syrup in the pan.

To finish: Divide the rhubarb among serving plates. If the rhubarb is no longer warm, then bring a pot of water to a boil and steam the rhubarb in a steaming basket for about 2 minutes before assembling the salad.

In a medium bowl, add the watermelon cubes, season them with the Himalayan salt, and toss with the arugula, radishes, some of the syrup from the pan, and half the dressing. Place some of the watermelon mixture on each plate and top with coriander seeds and coconut chips, plus another dollop of dressing.

RATATOUILLE KHICHDI

Ratatouille is a classic French dish, and most cultures around the world have their own version of it. It's a familiar and easy-to-love combination of seasonal summer vegetables that are easy to find no matter where you live. This khichdi version is a perfect dish to serve to a crowd at a lunch or dinner party. If you make the ratatouille a day ahead, you'll be able to split the work over two days.

Dosha Dos and Don'ts: *Sensitive Vata types can replace the kidney beans with any type of lentils in case they are already frequently experiencing bloating and latent digestion. Otherwise, the spices and herbs in this dish should make the beans easier to digest.*

SERVES 4 TO 6

Khichdi:
¾ cup dried kidney beans
2 teaspoons asafetida powder
1 tablespoon olive oil
¾ cup quinoa
1 portion Sweet Spice Mix (page 30), ground coarsely
4 cups Vegetable Broth (page 242)
1 teaspoon kosher or sea salt, plus more to taste

Ratatouille:
One 14-ounce can tomato puree
2 garlic cloves, thinly sliced
2 red onions, thinly sliced
1½ tablespoons olive oil
Kosher salt
Freshly ground black pepper
2 cups halved cherry tomatoes
1 small eggplant, trimmed and sliced into ¼-inch-thick slices
1 zucchini, trimmed and sliced into ¼-inch pieces

1 smallish yellow squash, trimmed and cut into ¼-inch slices lengthwise
1 red bell pepper, trimmed and sliced into ¼-inch pieces
1 tablespoon thyme leaves

Toppings:
1 cup grated Parmesan cheese
½ cup cashews, toasted in a dry pan and chopped

To prepare: In a medium heavy-bottomed saucepan, cover the beans with water, add 1 teaspoon of asafetida, and bring to a boil; boil for 2 minutes. Turn off the heat, cover the pot, and let the beans soak for 60 minutes (preferably overnight). Presoaking the beans makes them easier to digest; it also helps them cook more evenly and become tender all the way through.

After soaking the beans, drain and wash thoroughly with cold water.

If you don't have time for any soaking, you can cook the dish directly from the dry ingredients, but it will take additional time to achieve the desired tenderness.

For the ratatouille: Preheat oven to 375°F. Pour a thick layer of tomato puree into the bottom of a 9-by-13-inch baking dish. Layer the garlic and onion in the sauce, then drizzle on 1 tablespoon of the oil and season with some salt and pepper. Arrange slices of cherry tomatoes, eggplant, zucchini, yellow squash, and bell pepper concentrically from the outer edge toward the center of the baking dish. Overlap the sliced vegetables by less than half of their surface and try to keep a flat layer. Drizzle the remaining ½ tablespoon of oil over the vegetables and season with salt and pepper. Sprinkle the thyme

leaves over the vegetables. Cover the dish with a piece of parchment paper cut to fit the inside of the baking dish.

Bake for approximately 45 to 55 minutes, until the vegetables have released their liquid. Do a taste test after 40 minutes to see if the vegetables have reached the tenderness level you desire. Remove from the oven and set aside.

For the khichdi: In a heavy-bottomed saucepan, heat the oil, then add the beans, the remaining 1 teaspoon of asafetida, the quinoa, the spice mix, and broth, and bring to a boil.

Reduce to a simmer and cook for about 1 hour, making sure there is always enough liquid in the pot. Simmering the beans gently helps them cook evenly until tender, retain their shape without losing their texture (getting mushy) too quickly, and keep their skins intact. The best time to add the salt is about 45 minutes into cooking, when the beans are tender enough, but still partly firm.

After an hour, taste the khichdi, and if the beans are not very tender continue cooking for up to 30 minutes longer. Depending on your preference, you can adjust the texture of the khichdi for a drier risotto-like consistency or a wetter soup-like one by either allowing the excess liquid to evaporate or adding more liquid.

To finish: Add 2 large spoonfuls of khichdi to each serving bowl. Using the back of a spoon, create a small well for the toppings. Top the khichdi with a large serving spoon of ratatouille, then sprinkle with Parmesan and cashews.

HOMEMADE AMARANTH PASTA *WITH* TURKEY RAGÙ

When I was too exhausted to cook one day, my husband, Mikkel, casually mentioned a dish he'd made in the past with whatever he had in his refrigerator, which he dubbed "hippie spaghetti." Curious and bemused by the idea of him cooking anything, I ended up discovering his natural instincts for using what's available and making a dish filled with flavor and nuanced combinations. I enjoy making this gluten-free pasta and have a much easier time digesting it than wheat pasta. If you're a vegetarian, you can make the turkey ragù with mashed red kidney beans. In the spirit of of Mikkel's experimentation, I invite you to do some experimentation of your own with this recipe (always keeping your dosha in mind, of course).

SERVES 4 TO 6

Amaranth Pasta:
1½ cups brown rice flour, plus more for dusting
½ cup tapioca starch
1 teaspoon xanthan gum
¼ teaspoon fine kosher salt
4 large organic eggs, beaten

Turkey Ragù:
2 tablespoons olive oil, plus more as needed

2 garlic cloves
One 2-inch piece fresh ginger, peeled and grated
1 cup diced red onion
2 large carrots, finely chopped
½ cup raisins
1 pound organic ground turkey
One 14-ounce can diced tomatoes
3 tablespoons whole cream or coconut cream
1 tablespoon plus 1½ teaspoons maple syrup

1 teaspoon kosher salt
1 tablespoon sweet paprika
1 teaspoon freshly ground black pepper
2 portions Bitter Spice Mix (page 34), finely ground

To Finish:
½ cup sliced basil leaves
⅛ cup shredded coconut, toasted
Kosher or sea salt to taste

For the pasta: In large bowl, mix the flour, tapioca starch, salt, and xanthan gum. Add the beaten eggs. Using a silicone spatula or wooden spoon, gently fold the mixture together until it forms a dough. Be careful not to overmix, as the xanthan gum will harden the dough if it's overworked. Dust your work surface with flour and start to knead the dough gently and just enough to get it smooth. Cut the dough into four parts, rolling out one part at a time and covering the remaining parts with a clean dish cloth.

Shape the dough into a rough rectangle with your hands, dust it with flour, then cover it with a piece of thick parchment paper. Using a rolling pin, start rolling in both directions to try and maintain the rectangular shape. Lift the paper to dust the dough with flour often enough to prevent the dough from sticking to the paper. Roll the dough out into as thin a piece as possible and cut it into linguine-shaped strips. Cover, set aside, and repeat with the remaining dough.

For the turkey ragù: Add the oil to a large skillet and bring to a high heat. Add the garlic, ginger, and onions, cook until browned, then add the carrots, raisins,

and turkey. Cook for 10 minutes, adding a little more oil if needed. When the meat is browned on all sides, add the tomatoes, cream, maple syrup, salt and all the spices and bring to a boil. Reduce to a simmer and cook, covered, for 10 minutes, stirring occasionally. Remove the cover and simmer for another 15 minutes, tasting regularly to make sure the turkey isn't overcooked.

To finish: In a large pot of boiling salted water, cook the pasta for 5 minutes (test a strip to see if you're happy with the texture). Drain the pasta and divide among serving dishes. Top with ragù, a handful of basil, and shredded coconut. Sprinkle with salt and serve hot.

BREADED CHICKEN BREASTS
WITH SPICY STEWED APRICOTS

When I was a kid, I didn't like chicken at all—it always tasted like a bland, tortured piece of dry meat. When I discovered that the secret to achieving perfectly juicy chicken relies on timing, I found that it's best to finish cooking the chicken in the oven, as it tends to overcook or dry out when it's cooked in a pan. In this recipe, the chicken is prepared in the oven for that perfect crispiness. But it's the apricot stew that takes this dish to another level.

Dosha Dos and Don'ts: *Stewed apricots are suitable for all three doshas, so try adding them to your culinary repertoire. You can prepare them ahead of time and keep them sealed in an airtight container in the refrigerator for up to 10 days.*

SERVES 4 TO 8

Stewed Apricots:
2 cups dried apricots
2 cups water
1 cup jaggery, crumbled
2 star anise pods
1 whole cinnamon stick

Breaded Chicken Breasts:
⅓ cup rice flour
½ teaspoon kosher salt
1 portion Astringent Spice Mix (page 35), coarsely ground
1 teaspoon garlic powder
2 large organic eggs

1½ cups quinoa, toasted in an oven for 10 minutes
1 teaspoon sweet paprika
2 tablespoons coconut oil
4 large organic skinless chicken breasts

To Finish:
½ teaspoon Himalayan salt

For the stewed apricots: In a small saucepan, combine the apricots, water, jaggery, and spices. Bring to a boil, cover, and simmer on low heat for 30 minutes, or until the mixture takes on a loose jam-like texture (it will thicken once cooled).

For the breaded chicken: Preheat the oven to 400°F. Line a baking sheet with parchment paper.

In a shallow dish, mix the rice flour, ¼ teaspoon of salt, the spice mix, and ¾ teaspoon of garlic powder. Whisk the eggs in a second shallow dish.

In a third shallow dish, combine the toasted quinoa, paprika, the remaining ¼ teaspoon garlic powder, and the remaining ¼ teaspoon of salt. Drizzle the oil over the mixture, then mix thoroughly with a fork until all of the oil and spices coat the quinoa.

Pound the chicken breasts with a meat tenderizer, until they are about 1 inch thick. To coat the chicken, use one hand for the dry ingredients and one for the wet ingredients. Dip a chicken tender into the flour mixture, turn to coat completely, then shake off the excess flour. Dip the chicken into the eggs, coating completely, then shake off the excess egg. Finally, press the chicken into the quinoa mixture, turn to coat completely, then shake off the excess. Place the chicken tenders on a baking sheet. Continue coating the remaining chicken, one at a time.

Place the baking sheet in the oven, and bake the chicken until it's cooked through, about 20 minutes. If possible, use a digital thermometer to check the temperature at the center of the breast. The desired temperature for a perfectly cooked chicken breast is 165°F.

To finish: Place a spoon of stewed apricots on a serving plate. Slice each chicken breast in half and place on top of the stewed apricots. Top with some more apricots and sprinkle with salt.

NANAIMO CRUMBLE *WITH VANILLA CUSTARD, CHOCOLATE CREAM, AND FIGS*

This recipe was first inspired by nanaimo bars, which were one of my favorite indulgences during college. However, once I learned how to make them, I decided to develop a lighter version, which can continue being a part of my Ayurvedic lifestyle. I've now grown to love this wholesome version even more than the original one.

Dosha Dos and Don'ts: *As with all desserts, Kapha types should enjoy this dessert in moderation.*

SERVES 4 TO 6

Vanilla Custard:
2 tablespoons organic full-fat coconut milk
1 teaspoon vanilla extract
2 tablespoons vanilla custard powder
½ cup unsalted butter, at room temperature
2 cups confectioners' sugar, sifted
½ portion Sour Spice Mix (page 32), finely ground

Crumble:
¼ cup ghee
⅛ cup jaggery, crumbled
3 tablespoons dark cocoa powder, sifted, plus more for serving
1 flax egg (1 tablespoon ground flax-seeds soaked for an hour in 3 tablespoons warm water)
½ cup amaranth seeds
½ cup pearl barley
1 cup shredded coconut
¼ cup almonds, toasted and finely chopped

Chocolate Cream:
12 ounces vegan dark chocolate
1 pound organic silken tofu
1 teaspoon vanilla extract
2 tablespoons freshly brewed coffee
1½ teaspoons pure maple syrup or coconut nectar

Figs:
1 tablespoon ghee
4 fresh figs, trimmed and sliced into ¼-inch pieces

For the custard: In a small mixing bowl, whisk together the coconut milk, vanilla, and custard powder until you get a smooth consistency. In a large bowl and using a handheld mixer, beat the butter until smooth and creamy, about 3 to 5 minutes, then fold in the custard mixture. Continue beating the custard for a few minutes, then slowly add the sugar and spice mix and beat for about 3 to 5 more minutes until light and fluffy. Place the custard in the refrigerator until ready to serve.

For the crumble: In a saucepan, whisk together the ghee, jaggery, and cocoa powder, then heat on medium to low heat and stir frequently until smooth. Add the flax egg and stir well for a minute or so. Remove the pan from the heat and stir in the amaranth seeds, barley, coconut, and almonds. Stir until well combined.

For the chocolate cream: In a small heatproof bowl, melt the chocolate over a pot of boiling water, stirring frequently, until smooth and completely melted. In a food processor or blender, combine the tofu, melted chocolate, vanilla, coffee, and maple syrup, and blend until smooth.

For the figs: In a small pan, heat the ghee, then add the figs and fry for about 4 minutes on each side. Transfer the figs to a chopping board and roughly chop them.

To finish: Lightly press the chopped figs down into serving glasses. Top with the crumble and a spoon of custard, a spoon of chocolate cream, then another layer of crumble, custard, and chocolate cream. Cover and refrigerate for 45 minutes (or overnight). To serve, top the custard with a thick sprinkle of cocoa powder dusted over the dessert through a small fine-mesh sieve.

PINEAPPLE, BLUEBERRY, *AND* COCONUT CREAMSICLES

These nondairy creamsicles are a delicious dessert or a cooling meal replacement when temperatures are rising and your appetite is on the lighter side. The pineapple adds sweetness, while the blueberries contribute a beautiful color and are a great source of antioxidants. I don't believe in keeping food in the refrigerator—or the freezer—for too long, but you can definitely make extra portions of the creamsicles, freeze them, and enjoy them all week.

Dosha Dos and Don'ts: *For Kapha constitutions, use coconut water instead of coconut milk to make the recipe lighter. Vata types should limit the amount of creamsicles they enjoy to avoid aggravating their dosha with the cold.*

SERVES 4 TO 6

One 4-inch piece fresh ginger, peeled and grated

1 cup plain organic yogurt

1 cup organic coconut milk

2 cups fresh pineapple chunks

2 tablespoons shredded coconut

8 dates, pitted

2 cups fresh or frozen organic blueberries

Place all the ingredients in a blender and blend until smooth. Pour the mixture into molds or an ice tray, and freeze for a minimum of 2 hours.

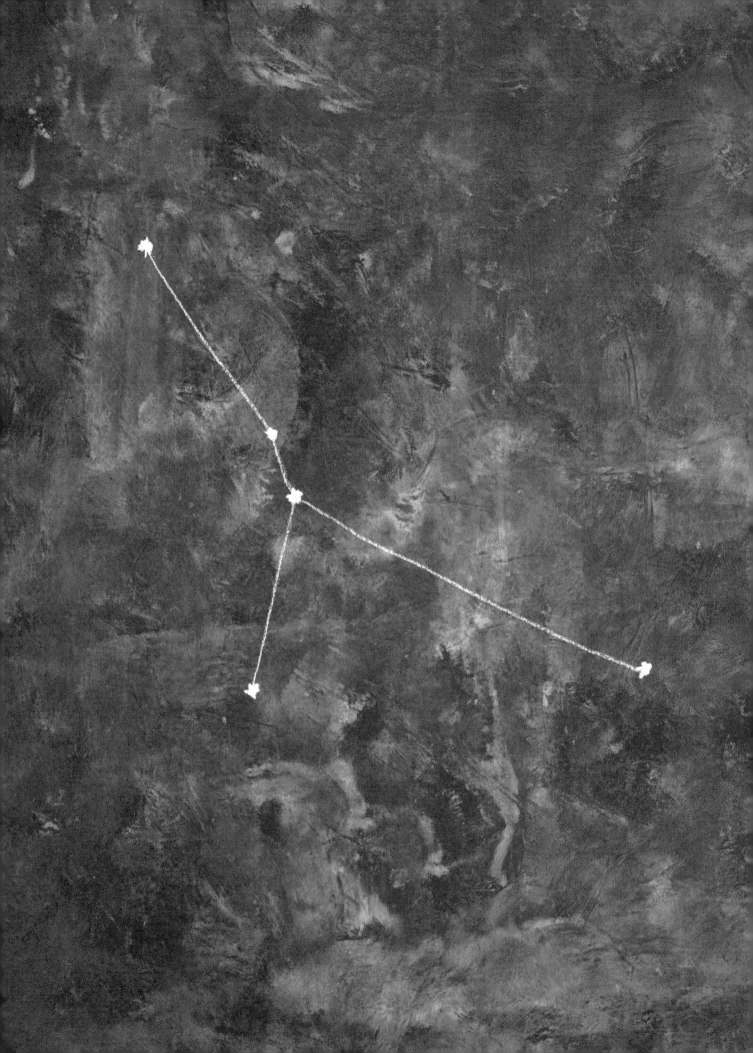

CHAPTER 7

CANCER

Essential Ayurvedic Spice

CUMIN

» *Cumin is native to Iran and the Mediterranean region. It now grows in most hot countries and countries with hot regions, especially China, Uzbekistan, Turkey, Iran, Tajikistan, Syria, Morocco, Egypt, Chile, Mexico, India, and North and South America.*

» *Cumin is the pale green seed of a small herb that is part of the parsley family.*

» *Cumin is good for balancing all three types of doshas (known as tridoshic).*

» *Cumin is beneficial year-round and needs to be consumed in moderation during the hotter seasons, which allows it to be cooling for the body. I like to balance the potent aroma of cumin by using it with sweet ingredients like sweet potato or leeks.*

» *In Ayurveda, cumin is considered invaluable for digestion, as it helps burn digestive toxins (known as ama), enhances the appetite, and soothes the stomach. A natural antioxidant, cumin relieves fatigue and anxiety by providing a boost to the immune system.*

» *Cumin is a heating spice, and it contributes the pungent and bitter tastes. It is available as a dried whole seed or a brownish-green powder and can be used raw or dry-roasted.*

» *Ground cumin has a more intense and pungent flavor than cumin seeds because the grinding process releases the compounds responsible for its distinctive pungency.*

» *To retain its pungency, cumin should be kept in an airtight container. It runs the risk of overpowering other flavors, so use it sparingly.*

June 22–July 22

CANCER

Cancer is Latin for "the crab" and it's commonly represented by a simplified drawing of the crab's rounded shape and two big claws. It is the fourth sign of the zodiac. A part of the general Pitta season, the Cancer period has some of the longest days of the year and takes place at the point when the sun is at its hottest. When summer arrives, nature is busy nurturing all that she has created. Life is lush and abundant, plants are in bloom, and the harvest is ready for the taking. Nature continues to change as the humidity of early summer gives way to the dryness of late summer. Your body also transitions from dampness to dryness, and you may start to feel parched.

At the height of Pitta season, when the sun is blazing, eat cooling foods that reduce inflammation. Make sure you don't get too dried out, and drink plenty of water. If your mind is racing and you have trouble sleeping in the summer, it could be because the heat has disturbed your electrolyte balance. Eating on time and favoring easy-to-digest foods, like seeds, coconut milk, mung beans, dates, and pineapple, will help you stay balanced, grounded, and positive. Your appetite will be naturally reduced so try to have lighter meals in the day to help avoid fatigue and lethargy. Enjoy a more substantial dinner to ensure your body gets the nutrition it needs to keep your energy high.

This is the perfect time of the year to take a break and reap the benefits of the hard work you put in during the first half of year. A pause from the everyday grind of your regular routine can give you a chance to enjoy nature in its full bloom. This time will set the tone for the second half of the year, so invest in your enjoyment and get in sync with nature's resources that are waiting to support you.

SAUTÉED MUSHROOMS *WITH* SEED CRACKERS *AND* SWEET PLUM RELISH

Due to their differing colors, textures, and flavors, mushrooms make a perfect alternative to the strong flavors we crave from meat and dairy products. When cooking different types of mushrooms for one dish, it's generally better to start with the meatier mushrooms, which usually take longer to cook and may release more water, then add the lighter and more delicate ones, which need to cook less. When adding mushrooms to the pan, don't move them until they've caramelized on the bottom. If you toss them too soon, they'll release their liquid and begin to steam. When the bottoms are caramelized, toss them and continue to cook. You can store the crackers in an airtight container for up to a week, and top them with anything sweet or savory.

Dosha Dos and Don'ts: *Vata types can cut the amount of mushrooms in this dish in half, as they can cause bloating if not eaten in moderation. However, the spices used in this recipe should relieve digestive issues caused by mushrooms for Vatas.*

SERVES 4 TO 6

Sweet Plum Relish:
Juice and zest of 2 limes
4 sweet plums, seeded, then finely
  chopped
¼ teaspoon coarse sea salt
½ cup chopped dill

Crackers:
1 cup stock, broth, or water
½ cup flaxseeds
½ cup chia seeds

½ cup raw sunflower seeds
½ cup raw pumpkin seeds
½ teaspoon Maldon sea salt
1 teaspoon cumin powder
Olive oil, for greasing the parchment
  paper

Mushrooms:
2 tablespoons olive oil
1 pound shiitake mushrooms, cut into
  ¼-inch slices

1 pound small button mushrooms,
  wiped clean
1 pound enoki mushrooms, trimmed
1½ teaspoons chopped thyme leaves
1 tablespoon finely chopped garlic
1 portion Astringent Spice Mix (page
  35), coarsely ground
1½ tablespoons ghee
½ teaspoon kosher salt
2 tablespoons fresh lemon juice
1 tablespoon chopped parsley

For the sweet plum relish: In a small bowl, toss the lime juice and zest, sweet plums, salt, and dill. Cover and refrigerate for an hour.

For the crackers: Preheat the oven to 350°F. In a large bowl, mix all the ingredients together and stir until combined. Let the mixture sit for 10 minutes to allow the flax and chia seeds to become more gelatinous. Line a baking sheet with parchment paper and brush it with the oil.

Spread the cracker mixture on the baking sheet, pressing the dough toward the edges of the sheet so that it's about ¼ inch thick or less.

Bake the crackers for 30 minutes, then remove them from the oven, place on a heatproof surface, and let the crackers cool. When they're cool, cut the crackers into squares or rectangles with a pizza cutter or a knife. Gently flip all the crackers over and put them back on the baking sheet and bake for 20 to 30 minutes longer. Remove the crackers from the oven and let them cool.

For the mushrooms: In a large skillet, heat the oil over high heat. Add the shiitake mushrooms first, and cook for 5 minutes, then add the button mushrooms and cook for another 5 minutes. Finally, add the enoki mushrooms, thyme, garlic, and spice mix and cook all the mushrooms together for 3 minutes. Add the ghee, toss the mushrooms, and cook for a few more minutes. Season with salt and drizzle with lemon juice. Cook until all the liquid has evaporated. Remove the skillet from the heat and add the parsley.

To finish: Top the crackers with mushrooms and add a dollop of plum relish.

COCONUT GREEN SOUP

Ayurveda recommends eating some leafy greens every day to help meet the nutritional requirements for optimal health. The coconut milk in this recipe creates a smooth, creamy texture that balances the bitterness of the greens. This soup is also a good base for a more substantial meal in the colder seasons. In the winter, I like to add potatoes and dill and serve it with crusty bread.

Dosha Dos and Don'ts: *Kapha body types trying to eat a lighter diet can reduce the amount of coconut milk and replace the coconut oil with ghee. Vata types can replace the kale with more spinach if they have a hard time digesting kale. Pitta and Kapha types can also limit the amount of pistachios or replace them with soaked almonds.*

SERVES 4 TO 6

1½ tablespoons coconut oil

1 pound asparagus, tough ends trimmed, cut into 2-inch pieces

2 stalks celery, tough fibers peeled off, chopped

1 large leek, white and light green parts only, halved, rinsed, and thinly sliced

2 garlic cloves, finely chopped

4 cups of Vegetable Broth (page 242) or water

1 teaspoon sea salt

1½ cups spinach, roughly chopped

1½ cups kale, roughly chopped

One portion Astringent Spice Mix (page 35), finely ground

One 13.5-ounce can coconut milk

Toppings:

½ cup pistachios, soaked overnight

2 dates, pitted and chopped

In a large stockpot, heat the coconut oil over medium heat. Add the asparagus, celery, and leek and cook, stirring occasionally, until the vegetables are tender, about 10 minutes. Add the garlic and stir for 1 minute longer. Add the broth and salt, bring to a boil, then reduce the heat and simmer for 20 minutes. Keep simmering until the mixture has a creamy texture, keeping in mind that it will thicken slightly after it's removed from the heat.

Add the spinach and kale, then stir for 1 minute, until the leaves wilt. Working in batches, fill a blender halfway with the mixture. Cover the blender with the lid but remove the clear plastic part of the lid. Cover the hole with a dish towel and quickly pulse a few times, then turn the blender on and let it run for 1 minute to puree the soup well.

Pour the soup into a large, clean saucepan. Puree the remainder of the soup and add it to the saucepan. Add the spice mix and coconut milk and simmer over medium heat for another 2 to 3 minutes. Remove from the heat.

To finish: Divide the soup among bowls and top with pistachios and dates.

HOMEMADE GNOCCHI *WITH* BALSAMIC BRUSSELS SPROUTS

Gnocchi, a fairly light potato-based dumpling, are made even lighter by using amaranth flour in this gluten-free version. Don't give up if the gnocchi don't come out perfectly the first time; once you get the hang of it, you'll realize it's one of the easiest pastas to make at home. Make the Brussels sprouts ahead of time and warm them in a pan when the gnocchi is almost ready to serve.

Dosha Dos and Don'ts: *Vata types feeling out of balance and experiencing bloating should eat this dish in moderation because the Brussels sprouts and potatoes can further aggravate these symptoms. That said, the spices should moderate the potential aggravation.*

SERVES 4 TO 6

Gnocchi:
3 Yukon Gold or Russet potatoes
4 tablespoons ghee
1 large organic egg, beaten
1 teaspoon kosher salt
1 teaspoon freshly ground black pepper
1 portion Bitter Spice Mix (page 34), finely ground
2 cups amaranth flour, plus more for rolling out the dough

Brussels Sprouts:
½ teaspoon kosher salt, plus more for boiling the sprouts
1½ cups Brussels sprouts, trimmed and shredded
1 tablespoon ghee
3 garlic cloves, thinly sliced
½ cup balsamic vinegar
¼ cup dates, pitted and finely diced
¼ teaspoon freshly ground black pepper
2 tablespoons coconut oil
2 teaspoons cinnamon powder

To Finish:
1½ tablespoon coconut oil
⅛ cup amaranth seeds, toasted in a dry pan
¼ cup almonds, toasted in a dry pan
⅓ cup thinly sliced chives
Kosher salt
1 tablespoon nigella seeds

For the gnocchi: Put the potatoes in a large pot and cover with cold water. Cover the pot and bring to a boil over high heat, then reduce the heat to medium and simmer for about 30 minutes, or until the potatoes are fork-tender. Drain the potatoes in a colander, let them cool slightly, then peel and chop them roughly.

Pass the chopped potatoes through a potato ricer or press them with a masher until the texture is free of lumps. In a small bowl, mix the ghee, egg, salt, pepper, and spice mix together, then fold the mixture into the mashed potatoes. Gently mix until the potato mixture is smooth, but don't overmix. Add the amaranth flour to the mashed potatoes ½ cup at a time, and gently fold just enough to incorporate the flour. If you overwork the mixture, the gnocchi will be chewy.

Divide the potato-amaranth paste into 6 equal portions (cover the ones you are not rolling with a dishtowel to avoid drying out the dough) and roll each of them into ½-inch-thick logs. Cut each log into ½-inch pieces. Press down on the gnocchi pieces with your fingers or a fork to imprint them with indents (optional). Make sure they are sufficiently covered in flour so they don't stick together, and cover them with a dish towel until you're ready to boil them.

For the Brussels sprouts: In a large pot, bring salted water to a boil, then reduce to a simmer and add the sprouts. Simmer for 8 to 10 minutes, leaving the sprouts slightly crunchy, then drain them in a colander.

Heat the ghee in a saucepan, add the garlic, and cook for 30 seconds, or until the garlic is translucent. Add the vinegar, dates, salt, and pepper, and cook for 5 to 7 more minutes, until the liquid is reduced to a syrupy texture.

In a nonstick pan, warm the coconut oil to medium heat, then add the sprouts. Add the cinnamon, toss, and lightly brown the sprouts.

To finish: To cook the gnocchi, bring a large pot of salted water to a boil, reduce the heat slightly, and throw in all the gnocchi. As soon as the gnocchi rise to the top of the boiling water, in about 30 seconds, remove them with a slotted spoon (carefully draining out any excess water)

or they'll start to dissolve. Lay the gnocchi out on a piece of parchment paper to cool slightly.

In a large nonstick pan, heat half of the oil to medium-high heat. Add just enough gnocchi to the pan so they have enough space to get a light, brown crust all around; cook for about 30 seconds, then flip and cook for 30 seconds more. Don't leave the gnocchi in the pan for longer than 1 minute or they'll start to melt. When the first batch is done, add the rest of the oil and gnocchi and repeat the crisping process.

Place about 10 to 16 pieces of gnocchi in each serving dish, then top with some Brussels sprouts, amaranth seeds, almonds, and chives. Top generously with the balsamic glaze. Sprinkle with salt and nigella seeds and serve.

MUSHROOM KHICHDI

You'd be hard-pressed to find a mushroom that doesn't taste good in this khichdi. A combination of rehydrated dried mushrooms and fresh mushrooms is satisfying and provides great texture. This khichdi often reminds me of the creamy mushroom risottos that are the staple of Italian cuisine, but this version is lighter and far more nourishing. You can make the Mushroom Broth (page 243) ahead of time and keep it in the refrigerator for about 4 days, then use it in a smorgasbord of soups and bowls.

SERVES 4 TO 6

¾ cup mung beans
2 teaspoons asafetida powder
¾ cup pearl barley
2 tablespoons coconut oil
1 leek, white and light green parts only, halved, rinsed, and thinly sliced
One 1-inch piece fresh ginger, chopped
4 cups Mushroom Broth (page 243) or water

2 teaspoons kosher salt, plus more to taste
¼ pound cremini mushrooms, quartered
¼ pound large shiitake mushrooms, quartered
¼ pound portobello mushrooms, gills removed, quartered
¼ pound white button mushrooms, quartered

2 garlic cloves, finely chopped
½ small yellow onion, finely chopped
1 portion Sour Spice Mix (page 32), coarsely ground
2 tablespoons chopped parsley
2 tablespoons unsalted butter
1 teaspoon freshly ground black pepper, plus more as needed

To prepare: In a medium heavy-bottomed saucepan, cover the beans with water, add 1 teaspoon of asafetida, and bring to a boil; boil for 2 minutes. Turn off the heat, cover the pot, and let the beans soak for 60 minutes (preferably overnight). Presoaking the beans makes them easier to digest; it also helps them cook more evenly and become tender all the way through.

It's also good to soak the barley, which makes it easier to digest. Cover the barley with water and soak for one hour.

After soaking the beans and barley, drain and wash thoroughly with cold water.

If you don't have time for any soaking, you can cook the dish directly from the dry ingredients, but it will take additional time to achieve the desired tenderness.

For the khichdi: In a large heavy-bottomed pot, heat 1 tablespoon of the coconut oil, then add the leek and ginger. Cook for about 3 minutes, then add the barley, beans, broth, the remaining 1 teaspoon of asafetida, and bring to a boil.

Reduce the mixture to a simmer and cook for about 45 minutes, making sure there is always enough liquid in the pot. Simmering the beans gently helps them cook evenly until tender, retain their shape without losing their texture (getting mushy) too quickly, and keep their skins intact.

After about 30 minutes, add the salt and stir (the best time to add the salt is about three-quarters of the way into

the cooking process, when the beans are tender but still partly firm).

After 1 hour, taste the khichdi, and, if the beans are not very tender, continue cooking for up to 15 additional minutes. Depending on your preference, you can adjust the texture of the khichdi for a drier risotto-like consistency or a wetter soup-like one by either allowing the excess liquid to evaporate or adding more liquid.

In a large pan over medium-high heat, heat the remaining 1 tablespoon of the coconut oil. Add all the mushrooms, toss, and cook until they're browned, about 15 minutes. Add the garlic, onion, and spice mix, and cook for about 4 more minutes. Stir in the parsley, butter, more salt if needed, and pepper; remove from the heat and set aside.

To finish: Place 2 large spoonfuls of khichdi into each serving bowl. Using the back of a spoon, create a small well on top of each serving, then add a large spoon of sautéed mushrooms. Sprinkle with salt.

STRAWBERRY-MARINATED SHRIMP *WITH* BRAISED RED CABBAGE

Banana leaves are widely used for cooking and serving food in Asia, Africa, and South America. Steaming food wrapped in banana leaves holds the heat inside and cooks the food in its juices. However, banana leaves can be pretty hard to come by (they are available in Asian specialty stores), so replacing them with parchment paper and some kitchen twine is a good alternative. Strawberries add a hint of tanginess to the shrimp, and the horseradish further brightens this dish with a bit of a kick. If you're not accustomed to using horseradish, start with smaller quantities and work your way up to avoid overpowering all the other flavors.

Dosha Dos and Don'ts: *Vata types should moderate the amount of cabbage they use in this dish to avoid bloating (to avoid cabbage entirely, replace it with thinly sliced leeks).*

SERVES 4 TO 6

Marinated Shrimp:

½ pound fresh or frozen organic strawberries, finely chopped or blended
  into a smooth puree
¼ cup sunflower oil
2 garlic cloves
1½ teaspoons chile powder
¼ teaspoon kosher salt, plus more to
  taste
1½ pound large shrimp, peeled and
  deveined

Braised Red Cabbage:

2 tablespoons ghee

1½ pounds red onions, cut into ¼-inch
  slices
1 head of red cabbage, cut into
  8 wedges, each wedge thinly sliced
2 cups chamomile tea
2 cups water
¼ cup red wine vinegar
¼ cup balsamic vinegar
1 sweet apple, peeled and coarsely
  grated
1 tablespoon plus 1½ teaspoons jaggery
1 portion Salty Spice Mix (page 31),
  finely ground
10 whole black peppercorns
2 whole cloves

1 bay leaf
Fresh ground black pepper

To Finish:

2 tablespoons horseradish paste
8 to 12 banana leaves (or 4 to 6 large
  pieces of parchment paper)
3 limes, cut into ⅛-inch slices
3 jalapeño peppers, trimmed and sliced
1 cup feta cheese, crumbled
½ cup chopped chives

For marinating the shrimp: In the bowl of a food processor, combine the strawberries, oil, garlic, chile powder, and salt, and pulse until the mixture reaches a puree-like consistency. In a bowl, pour the marinade over the shrimp, cover, and let marinate in the refrigerator for at least 15 minutes.

For the braised red cabbage: In a heavy-bottomed pot over medium heat, heat the ghee until it starts to sizzle. Add the onions and cabbage, and cook, stirring frequently, until they wilt and brown, about 20 minutes. Add the chamomile tea, water, vinegars, grated apple, jaggery, and spice mix, then bring to a boil.

Wrap the peppercorns, cloves, and bay leaf in a piece of cheesecloth and tie with kitchen twine to create a pouch. Add the pouch to the cabbage mixture, then cover the pot with a lid. Reduce the heat and simmer until the cabbage is very tender, about 1 hour. Remove the pouch and discard. Season the cabbage with pepper.

To finish: Preheat the oven to 350°F, or a grill.

In a large bowl, mix the shrimp, cabbage, and horseradish paste together.

Cut the fibrous string off the edge of each banana leaf and reserve. On a work surface, arrange 2 banana leaves in a cross. Spoon ¾ cup of the shrimp-cabbage mixture in the center and top with 3 to 4 slices of lime and 3 to 4 slices of jalapeño (reserve some for serving). Fold the top leaf like an envelope to enclose the filling, then wrap that packet in the bottom leaf. Tie the packet with the reserved banana string. Repeat with the remaining leaves and filling to make 4 to 6 servings. If you can't find banana

leaves, you can use parchment paper; if that's the case, simply bake the packets on a baking sheet and skip the grilling process.

Put the packets in the oven or on the grilling grate away from the heat source and cook or grill (covered) for about 20 minutes.

Take the packets out of the oven, place on a wire rack, and let them cool for 2 minutes. You can cut the packets open and fold back the leaves to serve each portion directly on a plate, or you can slide the contents onto a plate. Top with the remaining jalapeño, the feta, and chives.

DATE AND RICE PUDDING *WITH* CARAMELIZED PINEAPPLE

Rice pudding is sweet and delicious, and it's traditionally viewed as a cooling, easily digestible dish. It nourishes all tissues, cooling the body and calming the mind. Spices make it even easier and lighter to digest. Almonds and coconut add crunch, fiber, and protein. Dates are a substitute for sugar, and they're a great source of energy, which makes this dessert a perfect breakfast treat for special occasions.

Dosha Dos and Don'ts: *As with all desserts, Kapha types should enjoy this dessert in moderation. Vata types should soak the dates in water overnight, to avoid dryness they are prone to.*

SERVES 4 TO 6
Pudding:
½ cup short-grain brown rice (soaked overnight; optional)
1 tablespoon whole wheat flour
1¾ teaspoons cinnamon powder
⅛ teaspoon salt
3 cups whole milk or organic coconut milk

¼ cup finely chopped dates
2 teaspoons lime zest
1 teaspoon almond extract

Caramelized Pineapple:
1 portion Sweet Spice Mix (page 30), finely ground
¼ cup maple syrup
1 whole fresh pineapple

2 tablespoons coconut oil

Toppings:
½ cup almond slices, toasted
2 tablespoons shredded coconut
½ tablespoon cinnamon powder (optional)

For the pudding: In a deep heavy-bottomed saucepan, combine the rice, flour, ¼ teaspoon of cinnamon, and the salt. Stir in the milk and bring to a simmer over medium heat for about 30 minutes, or until the rice is almost tender. Stir often to avoid burning the milk at the bottom of the pan. Stir in the dates, cover, and continue to simmer, stirring often, for another 15 minutes, or until the rice is tender.

Remove the pan from the heat and stir in the lime zest, almond extract, and remaining 1½ teaspoons of cinnamon. Cover and let the pudding cool slightly and thicken (it will thicken considerably upon cooling).

For the caramelized pineapple: In a small bowl, stir the spice mix into the maple syrup and set aside. Peel and core the pineapple, then slice it into eight rings and cut each ring into 6 pieces. In a large skillet, warm the oil to medium high heat. Add the pineapple chunks and maple syrup, then cook, stirring, until the pineapple begins to brown, about 4 minutes. Remove the skillet from the heat, and transfer the pineapple to a shallow bowl, making sure to scrape the bottom of the pan. Let the mixture cool slightly, until it's warm to the touch, for about 3 minutes.

To finish: Place a few spoonfuls of pudding (warm or cool) into serving bowls. Top with the caramelized pineapple, almonds, coconut, and another sprinkle of cinnamon (if using).

GREEN TEA LEMONADE

The combination of ingredients in this lemonade has an alkalizing effect on the body. Maintaining a healthy pH (acidity level) is important and plays a role in reducing excess weight and inflammation in the body. In addition, there are theories that alkaline pH has potentially positive effects on such chronic diseases as diabetes and arthritis. Apple cider vinegar helps to flush out water retention in the body; it also adds a different flavor to a traditional lemonade. For a delicious way to stay hydrated, substitute some of your daily mandated 6 to 8 glasses of water with this concoction.

Dosha Dos and Don'ts: *Kapha and Pitta types should skip the lemon and only use lime to avoid aggravating their dosha with extra acidity. In addition, Pitta types should cut the vinegar in half.*

SERVES 4 TO 6

1 cup apple juice
1 cup water
2 green tea bags
2½ cups sparkling water
One 1-inch piece fresh ginger, peeled and grated
Juice and zest of 1 lemon, plus more zest for serving
Juice and zest of 2 limes, plus more zest for serving
2 tablespoons apple cider vinegar
10 mint leaves

Pour the apple juice into 8 sections of an ice cube tray and freeze overnight.

Bring the water to a boil and steep the green tea bags for 30 seconds. Remove the tea bags from the hot water, immerse them in 1 cup of the sparkling water, and cover for 5 minutes.

In a pitcher, mix the tea-steeped sparkling water, the remaining 1½ cups of sparkling water, the apple juice cubes, and the rest of the ingredients. Pour the lemonade into glasses, and garnish each with some lemon and lime zest or a mint leaf.

CHAPTER 8

LEO

Essential Ayurvedic Spice

TURMERIC

» Turmeric is native to southwest India. India is the top producer, but it is also grown in China, Taiwan, Sri Lanka, Indonesia, Peru, Australia, and the West Indies.

» Part of the ginger family, turmeric is also a rhizome, which is a stem that grows just under the soil (generally horizontally), then sprouts out shoots and roots up from vertical stems. The plant reproduces by spreading out underground rather than by producing seeds.

» Turmeric is good for balancing all three types of doshas (known as tridoshic).

» Turmeric can be used all year long, with some moderation in the hotter seasons to avoid overheating the digestive system.

» Among its long list of Ayurvedic health benefits, turmeric is one of the most potent natural anti-inflammatories, helps detoxify the liver, balances cholesterol levels, promotes a healthy response to allergens, stimulates digestion, boosts immunity, and enhances the complexion.

» Turmeric is a heating spice, contributing the pungent, astringent, and bitter tastes. Be careful not to overuse it in cooking, as it can create a bitter flavor and a dark golden color.

» A common hesitation when it comes to eating turmeric has to do with its strong pigment. It is consumed by millions of people every day, so rest assured, it does not stain your teeth. However, it is almost impossible to remove turmeric stains from clothing.

July 23–August 22

LEO

Leo is Latin for "the lion" and is commonly represented by a simplified drawing of a lion's head and mane. It is the fifth sign of the zodiac. It falls into the Pitta season, when summer is at its hottest and the days are long. August air is crisp, clear, and dry. The humidity seems to evaporate with the drop in temperature, leaving the lightness and clarity of fall in its wake. With the first crisp, cool morning of August, you sense that change is afoot as the days become shorter and shorter.

You can start indulging your budding cravings for slightly heavier foods. Your body recognizes that fall is coming and is starting to crave fats to build insulation for cooler times ahead. Pitta that may have accumulated in June will come to the surface in August and September once all the moisture of early summer dries up. Continue to eat astringent and bitter foods in moderation to reduce the excess heat, absorb moisture, and relieve inflammation caused by the resurfacing Pitta. During this time, it's common to completely lack energy and be unable to digest heavier meals. You can alleviate these challenges by favoring light and sweet foods, like chicken, polenta, shrimp, salmon, quinoa, and sweet potato, and adding a small amount of pungent spices to aid digestion.

With the change in temperature, August is a crucial month, so make sure to preserve your energy and keep hydrated to set yourself up for a bountiful fall. As summer begins to evaporate, be sure to enjoy the remaining good weather and spend as much time outdoors as possible.

BRUSSELS SPROUTS, NEW POTATO, *AND* CHICKEN SALAD

Brussels sprouts have always been one of my favorite green vegetables. My mother would thinly slice them, steam them, and fry them in a pan, crisping them just enough to add a delicious crunchy smokiness. Many vegetables contain small amounts of protein, but Brussels sprouts pack enough to make them a good meat substitute. Err on the side of a shorter cooking time; the sprouts lose their nutritional value and flavor—and also start to have a slightly unpleasant odor—when they're overcooked.

Dosha Dos and Don'ts: *If they're already experiencing slower digestion and bloating, Vata types should enjoy this salad in moderation; they can also swap the new potatoes for sweet potatoes and reduce the amount of Brussels sprouts they consume. The spices used in the recipe should alleviate any potential aggravation caused to a balanced Vata type.*

SERVES 4 TO 6

2 tablespoons coconut oil, plus more as needed

4 celery stalks, tough fibers peeled off, sliced into ⅛-inch pieces

2 shallots, thinly sliced

3 garlic cloves, thinly sliced

1 pound Brussels sprouts, trimmed and sliced

1 portion Salty Spice Mix (page 31), coarsely ground

4 chicken breasts, roughly chopped

2 tablespoons nigella seeds, lightly toasted in a dry pan

Juice and zest of 1 lime

24 new potatoes, washed and cut into 3 slices each

1½ tablespoons ghee

1 tablespoon freshly ground black pepper

½ cup white cheddar cheese, shredded

1 cup popcorn, popped and buttered, without salt

In a large heavy-bottomed pot, heat the coconut oil to medium heat. Add the celery, shallots, and garlic and cook for 6 minutes, or until the vegetables are soft and translucent. Add the Brussels sprouts, stir to combine, and cook for 8 minutes. Add the spice mix and more oil, if needed, and continue to cook for 10 minutes. Add the chicken and nigella seeds, and cook for 10 more minutes on medium heat, or until the chicken is tender. Remove mixture from heat and set aside.

Meanwhile, bring a medium pot of water to a boil. Once the water is boiling, add the potatoes and boil for 20 minutes. Drain the potatoes, discard the cooking water, and put the potatoes back in the pot. Add the ghee and pepper, and fry until tender when pressed with a fork. Using a pair of tongs, divide the salad among serving bowls, then do the same with the potatoes. Top with shredded cheddar and a handful of popcorn.

SHRIMP-POLENTA BITES

With a limited list of fresh ingredients to use during the long summers of extreme weather in India, I learned to innovate and appreciate ingredients sometimes taken for granted. My love for leeks developed from these windows of limitation, and I often used them as a reliable source of flavor, texture, and structure. These little bites are a perfect finger food for a picnic, or a great addition to any salad or soup to complete the meal.

Dosha Dos and Dont's: *Shrimp suits all three doshas.*

SERVES 4 TO 6

Shrimp Marinade:
½ cup olive oil
1 tablespoon Bengali kasundi or Dijon mustard
3 garlic cloves, finely chopped
Juice of 1 lemon
Juice of 1 orange
1 teaspoon dried basil

12 raw wild shrimp, peeled, deveined, and tails removed

Polenta Squares:
4 cups Vegetable Broth (page 242)
1 cup coarse polenta
2 tablespoons ghee, plus more for greasing the pan

1 portion Astringent Spice Mix (page 35), finely ground
¼ cup grated Parmesan cheese
1½ teaspoons dried thyme
Kosher salt

Leeks:
2 leeks, tops and bottoms trimmed, halved, and rinsed

For the shrimp marinade: In a glass dish, mix together the oil, mustard, garlic, lemon juice, orange juice, and basil. Add the shrimp, and stir to coat. Cover the dish and let the shrimp marinate for 1 hour in the refrigerator.

For the polenta squares: In a large saucepan over high heat, bring the broth to a simmer. Add the polenta to the pan, whisking constantly. Continue to whisk until the polenta begins to thicken, about 2 minutes. Turn the heat to medium-low, cover, and allow to the polenta to simmer until it's very thick, about 30 minutes. Add the ghee, spice mix, Parmesan, and thyme, and stir until the ghee and cheese melt. Add salt to taste.

Line a rectangular or square pan with parchment paper, then pour the polenta into the pan, smooth the top with a spatula, and let cool to room temperature. Cover the polenta and chill it in the refrigerator (still covered) for at least 15 minutes.

Preheat the oven to 350°F. Remove the polenta from the refrigerator, uncover it, and lift up the polenta slab using the parchment paper as handles. Using a large knife, cut polenta into 24 squares. Place them on a ghee-greased baking sheet and bake for 10 to 12 minutes, just until warmed through.

For the leeks: Bring a large pot of water to a boil, add the leeks, reduce to a simmer, and cook the leeks for 10 minutes. Turn off the heat and drain the leeks. Separate the leaves from each leek and spread them on a wire rack to dry.

To finish: Heat a grill to high heat. Drain the shrimp from the marinade. Cut the shrimp into 2-inch pieces, pile them on top of individual polenta squares, and add another polenta square on top, sandwiching the shrimp between 2 polenta squares. Wrap each sandwich with a blanched leek leaf and thread onto skewers. Grill each sandwich for 3 to 5 minutes.

MIXED BEAN *AND* KALE STEW

I'm sure you've noticed your natural appetite decreasing slightly during the hot summer months. This stew, filled with nourishing protein and greens, is the perfect light dinner for such summer days. You can use this recipe as a template for all kinds of seasonal adjustments and cravings. One important thing to remember, however, is that eating leftover dishes with cooked beans is a surefire way to get bloated and aggravate your digestive system. Don't remove the stems from the kale; like all leafy greens, the stems are a great source of essential fiber.

Dosha Dos and Don'ts: *Vata types experiencing digestive sensitivity can replace the beans with their favorite lentils and replace the kale with spinach.*

SERVES 4 TO 6

1½ tablespoons olive oil

3 white onions, chopped

2 carrots, peeled and chopped

2 celery stalks, tough fibers peeled off, cut into 1-inch slices

½ teaspoon kosher salt

1 portion Pungent Spice Mix (page 33), coarsely ground

2 garlic cloves, thinly sliced

4 cups Vegetable Broth (page 242) or water

7 cups chopped kale, ends trimmed and stems left intact

1½ cups cooked cannellini beans (page 247) or one 15-ounce can cannellini beans, washed and drained

1½ cups cooked black beans (page 247) or one 15-ounce cans black beans, drained and rinsed

½ teaspoon freshly ground black pepper

1 tablespoon red wine vinegar

1 teaspoon chopped fresh rosemary

Heat the oil in a large heavy-bottomed pot over medium heat. Add the onions, carrots, and celery, and sauté for 6 minutes, or until tender. Stir in ¼ teaspoon of salt, the spice mix, and garlic, and cook for 1 minute. Add 3 cups of the broth and the kale. Bring to a boil, cover, and simmer for 3 minutes.

Place half of the cannellini beans and the remaining 1 cup of broth in a blender or food processor, and blend until smooth. Add the blended mixture, the remaining cannellini beans, the black beans, and pepper to the pot. Bring to a boil, then simmer for 5 minutes. Stir in the remaining ¼ teaspoon of salt, the vinegar, and rosemary.

SALMON KHICHDI

I recommend buying only wild-caught salmon for this dish; if that's not available, buy another kind of wild-caught fish. White beans, also known as navy beans, provide extraordinary health benefits; they're packed with protein and antioxidants and naturally contain substances that help detoxify the body. I like to incorporate white or brown miso wherever I can, to take advantage of the incredible taste and probiotic properties it provides as a result of being fermented.

Dosha Dos and Don'ts: *Vata types experiencing bloating can reduce the amount of white beans in this already rich khichdi; however, the spices in the recipe should make it easier for them to digest the beans, which can otherwise aggravate their body type.*

SERVES 4 TO 6

Khichdi:
¾ cup white beans
2 teaspoons asafetida powder
1 tablespoon ghee
6 garlic cloves, sliced
One 1-inch piece fresh ginger, grated
4 celery stalks, tough fibers peeled off, cut into ⅛-inch slices
1 portion Bitter Spice Mix (page 34), finely ground
¾ cup quinoa

5 cups Vegetable Broth (page 242)
1 teaspoon kosher salt, plus more as needed
1 cup coconut milk
2 teaspoons maple syrup
1 tablespoon apple cider vinegar
4½ teaspoons tahini
1 tablespoon miso, brown or white

Salmon:
Four 2- to 3-ounce salmon steaks, skin on
Kosher or sea salt

1 tablespoon ghee
⅛ cup chopped dill
⅛ teaspoon dill seeds, toasted in a dry pan

To Finish:
2 tablespoons chopped chives
2 tablespoons sesame seeds, preferably toasted
Kosher or sea salt

To prepare: In a medium heavy-bottomed saucepan, cover the beans with water, add 1 teaspoon of asafetida and bring to a boil; boil for 2 minutes. Turn off the heat, cover the pot, and let the beans soak for 60 minutes (preferably overnight). Presoaking the beans makes them easier to digest; it also helps them cook more evenly and become tender all the way through.

After soaking the beans, drain and wash thoroughly with cold water.

If you don't have time for any soaking, you can cook the dish directly from the dry ingredients, but it will take additional time to achieve the desired tenderness.

For the khichdi: In a heavy-bottomed saucepan, heat the ghee, then add the garlic, ginger, celery, and spice mix. Cook until the celery and garlic are translucent. Add the beans, remaining 1 teaspoon of asafetida, quinoa, and broth, and bring to a boil.

Reduce the mixture to a simmer and cook for about 1 hour, making sure there is always enough liquid in the pot. Simmering the beans gently helps them cook evenly until tender, retain their shape without losing their texture getting mushy) too quickly, and keep their skins intact. After about 45 minutes, add the salt and stir (the

best time to add the salt is about three-quarters of the way into the cooking process, when the beans are tender but still partly firm).

After an hour, taste the khichdi, and, if the beans and quinoa are not very tender continue cooking for up to 30 minutes longer. Depending on your preference, you can adjust the texture of the khichdi for a drier risotto-like consistency or a wetter soup-like one by either allowing the excess liquid to evaporate or adding more liquid.

At the very end of the cooking time, add the coconut milk, maple syrup, vinegar, tahini, and miso and mix well. Cook for about 2 more minutes, then salt to taste.

For the salmon: Season the salmon with salt on both sides. Heat a pan to medium and add the ghee. Place the salmon skin-side down in the pan. Fry for 5 minutes (depending on thickness) on one side, then turn the salmon over and fry for an additional 2 minutes on the other side. Transfer the salmon to a plate, and top with some chopped dill and toasted dill seeds.

To finish: Serve 2 large spoons of khichdi into each serving bowl, and place a piece of salmon on top of the khichdi. Sprinkle with chives, sesame seeds, and salt.

ZUCCHINI *AND* SWEET POTATO FRITTERS *WITH* SWEET GARLIC DRESSING

This dish is easy on the digestion and quick to prepare, so it's a good one to incorporate into your diet for a warming energy recharge during this time of year. I've incorporated a sweet flavor profile into the dressing, for a fresh take on a creamy dip.

Dosha Dos and Don'ts: Kapha types should enjoy this dish in moderation.

SERVES 4

Sweet Garlic Dressing:
1 cup buttermilk
4 roasted garlic cloves (see technique on page 48), mashed into a paste
¼ cup sour cream
1 portion Sweet Spice Mix (page 30), finely ground

Fritters:
1 cup shredded zucchini
1 cup shredded sweet potato
2 large organic eggs, beaten
½ cup brown rice or spelt flour
1 tablespoon coconut flour
½ teaspoon garlic powder
¼ teaspoon cumin powder
½ teaspoon dried parsley
Kosher or sea salt
Black pepper
1 tablespoon ghee, plus more if needed
1 tablespoon olive oil, plus more if needed

For the garlic dressing: In a small mixing bowl, whisk together all the ingredients; refrigerate until ready to serve.

For the fritters: Combine the zucchini, sweet potato, and eggs in a medium bowl. In a small bowl, combine the brown rice flour, coconut flour, garlic powder, cumin, parsley, salt, and pepper. Add the dry ingredients to the zucchini-potato mixture and stir until fully combined.

In a medium nonstick pan, add the ghee and oil and heat them up. Scoop out about ¼ cup of the mixture at a time, put it in the pan, and fry pressing down with a fork until the fritter is ½ inch thick. Fry the fritters over medium heat, for about 2 to 3 minutes on each side, or until golden brown and crisp. Transfer the fritters to a paper towel–lined plate and repeat with the remaining mixture, adding more ghee and oil as needed.

To finish: Serve the hot, crispy fritters topped with the garlic dressing.

LEMON CAKE *WITH* PRUNE-CARAMEL SAUCE

Using chickpeas for a cake seems unusual, but you'll be pleasantly surprised by the distinct nutty flavor and lightness that chickpeas provide. The moist texture and tanginess of this cake combined with the richness of the prune caramel sauce will satisfy everyone's sweet cravings. Using prunes in the caramel sauce gives it a bright and smoky flavor and demonstrates another seamless way to add this beneficial dried fruit into your diet. This cake is a testament to using healthy ingredients to make a delicious dessert that satisfies your cravings in a nourishing way.

Dosha Dos and Don'ts: *Vata types can replace the chickpeas with white lentils if they're experiencing digestive issues or bloating.*

SERVES 4 TO 6

Lemon Cake:

¼ cup coconut oil, plus more for greasing the pan

⅔ cup all-purpose flour, plus more for dusting the pan

2 cups cooked chickpeas (page 247) or one 15-ounce can chickpeas, drained and rinsed

4 tablespoons fresh lemon juice

3 teaspoons grated lemon zest

1 cup crumbled jaggery (or coconut sugar)

2 large organic eggs, yolks and whites separated

½ cup unsweetened shredded coconut

1 portion Sour Spice Mix (page 32), finely ground

2¼ teaspoons baking powder

½ teaspoon fine sea salt

⅛ teaspoon cream of tartar

1 tablespoon fresh lime juice

Prune-Caramel Sauce:

1 cup prunes, soaked in hot water for 15 minutes

2 tablespoons fresh lime juice

2 cups maple syrup

¼ cup unsalted butter

½ cup heavy cream

½ teaspoon kosher salt

For the lemon cake: Preheat oven to 350°F. Grease an 8-inch square (or a 9-inch round) baking pan with coconut oil and lightly dust with flour.

In a blender or food processor, puree the coconut oil, chickpeas, lemon juice, lemon zest, and half the jaggery. Add the egg yolks and blend well, then pour the mixture into a large bowl.

In a medium bowl, combine the flour, shredded coconut, spice mix, baking powder, and salt. Mix well. Add the pureed chickpea mixture to the dry ingredients and mix well.

In another medium bowl, whisk the egg whites and cream of tartar until foamy. Keep whisking, slowly add the remaining jaggery, and continue to whisk until stiff white peaks form.

Fold the beaten egg whites into the chickpea mixture. Pour the batter into the prepared baking pan.

Bake the cake for 30 to 35 minutes, or until a toothpick inserted in the middle of the cake comes out clean. Remove the pan from the oven and let it cool for 10 minutes, then turn the cake out onto a wire rack. Drizzle the lime juice over the cake.

For the prune-caramel sauce: Puree the prunes and lime juice in a food processor, transfer to a bowl, and set aside.

Pour the maple syrup into a heavy-bottomed pot and bring to a boil; boil over medium heat for 15 minutes. Using a spatula, stir every few minutes to reduce the bubbles. The syrup will start to coat the outside of the spatula and cool quickly into a caramel-like consistency. Add the butter and stir until it's completely melted, then add the cream, and continue stirring constantly. Add the salt and stir to mix it into the caramel.

Pour the hot caramel into the prune puree and mix thoroughly. Using the spatula, push the mixture through a fine-mesh sieve to get rid of prune skins (this extra step is optional, but straining out the prune skins produces a nicer consistency).

To finish: When the cake is completely cool, slice it and serve each slice with a dollop of warm caramel.

STRAWBERRY, WATERMELON, *AND* AVOCADO SMOOTHIE

One of the golden rules for combining foods within Ayurvedic nutrition is to avoid eating fruit and dairy together. Because of the inherently different qualities of these two food types, they can cause aggravation in your digestive system and lead to a buildup of toxins in the body. If you want to keep drinking delicious dairy-free smoothies, you'll have to find an alternative to yogurt to provide the creaminess in the drink. This recipe uses avocado as a nourishing alternative to dairy, and it makes the drink smooth and velvety.

Dosha Dos and Don'ts: *Kapha types can halve the amount of avocado if they're feeling lethargic or heavy. Vata types can increase the amount of strawberries and halve the amount of watermelon, which can cause bloating for them (though the ginger should help make it easier to digest).*

SERVES 4

One 1-inch piece fresh ginger, peeled
2 cups fresh or frozen strawberries
1 avocado
2 cups diced watermelon
Juice and zest of 2 limes
2 tablespoons honey
12 basil leaves
2 cups coconut water

Put all the ingredients in a blender and blend until smooth. Pour into glasses and serve.

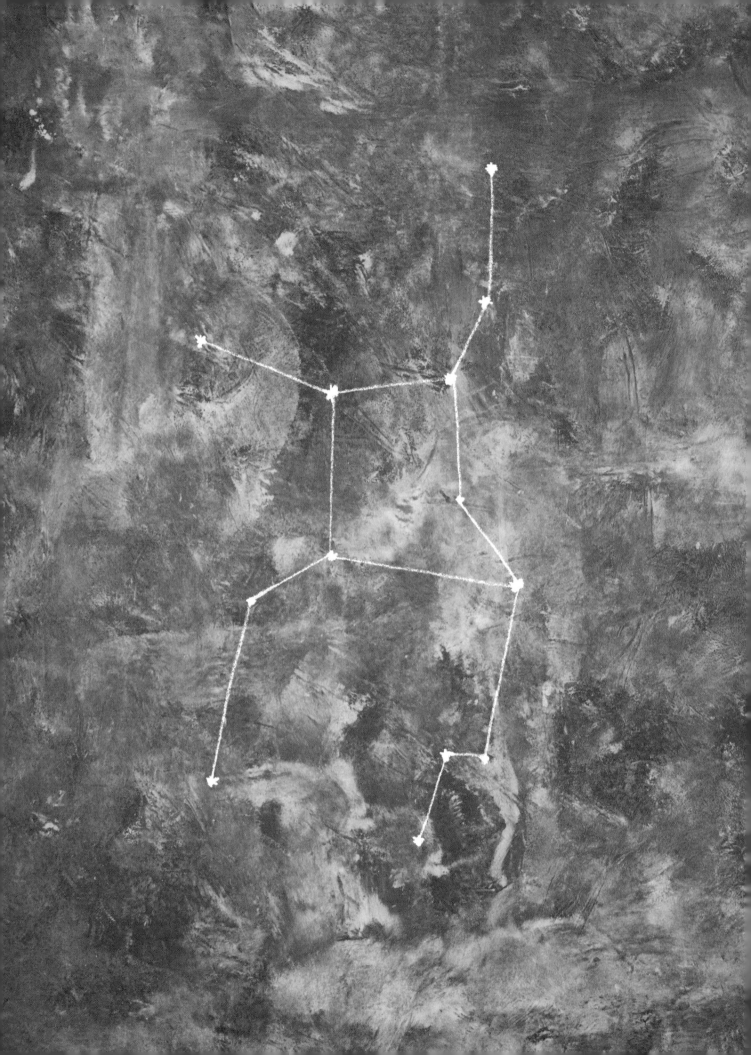

CHAPTER 9

VIRGO

Essential Ayurvedic Spice

CAYENNE

» *Cayenne is native to its namesake Cayenne region of French Guiana. Today, it grows in India, East Africa, Mexico, the United States, and in most tropical and subtropical regions.*

» *Cayenne is made by grinding up dried pods of pungent chile peppers. It is essentially the same as chile powder, but it's usually sold without other spices mixed in and in a finer form.*

» *Cayenne is good for balancing the Vata and Kapha doshas, but it can be aggravating to the Pitta dosha if not taken in strict moderation. Cayenne is a heating spice, so it should be used in moderation during the hotter seasons to avoid overheating the body.*

» *Among its long list of Ayurvedic health benefits, cayenne boosts the immune system, improves circulation, speeds metabolism, aids digestion, reduces blood sugar levels, and removes toxins.*

» *Cayenne is a heating spice that contributes a pungent flavor. Adding it to your cooking brings out the subtler flavor notes of other ingredients.*

» *Cayenne quickly loses its flavor, so it's best to buy it only as needed or in small amounts. It should be stored in a dark, cool place.*

» *While cayenne resembles paprika, it has a much stronger flavor and should be used more conservatively. I like to mix cayenne with cinnamon, as cinnamon's sweetness balances cayenne's spiciness. This mix, paired with some salt, is especially good over french fries or heated in the pan with some ghee and drizzled over popcorn.*

August 23–September 22

VIRGO

Virgo is Latin for "the virgin" and is commonly represented by the letter M. It is the sixth sign of the zodiac. Virgo is a part of the Pitta season in the first half of its period, then transitions into the Vata season for the second half. In the Virgo time of the year, the heat begins to dissipate and the last of the crops is harvested. Evenings are significantly cooler as fall draws near.

Keep hydrated to support a strong digestion and appetite. The fall weather can shock your system with changing temperatures and winds. Your body will be using all available energy to build an insulating layer of fat before the temperatures plummet in mid-October. Depleting energy during this time of year can make you feel easily scattered and distracted. Avoid any overexertion; your body needs all available energy to prepare for colder months ahead. Start eating heavy, sweet foods, like dates, cashews, pecans, cheese, and dried fruits, to insulate your body as you move into this period. Salty foods will ground you and retain moisture in your body to counteract the dryness of the season.

September sets the tone for your body's endurance through winter, so be sure to keep balanced and healthy by following Ayurveda's time-tested wisdom. There is a greater need for organization, planning, and preparation for the long, dark winter ahead. This is a time of seriousness and great forethought.

DATES STUFFED *WITH* SCALLOPS *AND* FETA

When I'm entertaining and serve these stuffed dates, they're always a huge success. I generally hesitate to tamper with ingredients as perfect as scallops—they're usually best when cooked simply and whole. But I made an exception when, after a dinner party, I found myself with leftover scallops and a craving a new, interesting way to prepare them. Like most of my favorite creations, this one has withstood the test of time. You can also simplify this dish by skipping the scallops and stuffing the dates with just feta or any other cheese and your favorite chopped herbs, nuts, and seeds.

Dosha Dos and Don'ts: *Kapha types should indulge in this delicacy in moderation to avoid feeling heavy.*

SERVES 4 TO 6
1½ tablespoons ghee, plus more for greasing the pan
1 portion Salty Spice Mix (page 31), finely ground
6 large scallops, finely diced
⅔ cup feta cheese, crumbled
12 mint leaves, finely chopped
½ cup skinless almonds, toasted in a dry pan and roughly chopped
16 large dates (preferably Medjool)

Preheat the oven to 400°F. In a medium pan, warm the ghee over medium heat, then add the spice mix and fry for 1 minute; remove the pan from heat.

Place the scallops, feta, mint, and chopped almonds in a mixing bowl and toss. Pour the warm spiced ghee into the bowl, and toss to coat the mixture evenly.

Using a small knife, make a small lengthwise incision in each date. Remove the pit and stuff 1 teaspoon of the feta mixture into the pit cavity. Lightly oil a baking sheet with some ghee, and arrange the dates, stuffed side up, in a single layer. Pour 1½ teaspoons of melted ghee over the dates. Bake until the stuffed dates are warmed through and the feta starts to brown, about 15 minutes. Transfer to a serving platter and serve warm.

HOT *AND* SOUR BUTTERNUT SQUASH SOUP

You can start introducing sour flavors into your diet as you make the transition to the fall season. Your body is naturally craving grounding and comforting foods like butternut squash, which has absorbed the sun's nutrients during the summer. Certain flavor combinations are more widely appealing to the palate, and the hot and sour combo is definitely a favorite in all types of cuisines. Some recipes try to achieve flavor by piling on processed ingredients and ready-made sauces, but it is far better to use natural flavors and play them up through simple preparation, like in this soup recipe.

Dosha Dos and Don'ts: *Pitta types should moderate the sourness in this soup by using less umeboshi and tamarind. Kapha types should enjoy this soup in moderate amounts to avoid feeling too heavy from the squash and pecans.*

SERVES 4 TO 6

2 tablespoons olive oil
1 large onion, diced
2 garlic cloves, thinly sliced
1 Indian green chile, trimmed and chopped
1 medium butternut squash, peeled, seeds discarded, and flesh cut into 1-inch chunks
One 1-inch piece fresh ginger, peeled and finely chopped
1 portion Sweet Spice Mix (page 30), coarsely ground
6 cups Chicken Stock (page 241)
2 tablespoons tamarind pulp
6 basil leaves, plus more for serving
⅓ cup fresh lime juice
2 umeboshi plums, pitted
1 tablespoon jaggery, chopped to a crumble
½ cup plain organic yogurt
Kosher or sea salt
Freshly ground black pepper

To Finish:
½ cup cottage cheese
½ cup coarsely chopped pecans, lightly roasted in a dry pan

In a large pot heat 1 tablespoon of oil over medium heat, then add the onion, garlic, and chile, and sauté until the vegetables are soft, about 2 minutes. Add the squash, ginger, and spice mix to the pot, stir to coat well, and cook for 2 minutes. Add the stock and tamarind pulp, then bring to a boil. Lower the heat and let the soup simmer for 15 to 20 minutes, or until the squash is very tender.

Pour the soup into a blender and puree in batches, then return the soup to the pot. Stir in the basil, lime juice, umeboshi plums, jaggery, and yogurt. Simmer, uncovered, for another 20 minutes.

Pour the soup through a fine-mesh sieve into another pot; discard the solids. Season well with salt and pepper.

To finish: In a 10-inch heavy skillet over moderately high heat, heat the remaining 1 tablespoon of oil until it's hot but not smoking, then fry some basil leaves until they're crisped, about 30 seconds.

Divide the soup among serving bowls and top each with a spoonful of cottage cheese, some chopped pecans, and crispy basil.

BUTTERNUT SQUASH KHICHDI

This recipe is an unusual take on khichdi, but the result is a versatile dish that can be made throughout the fall season as different squash varieties become available. Beans, lentils, and grains in the khichdi are cooked more and meant to be much more tender than they would be cooked individually for any other dish. This khichdi relies on the easy digestibility of these ingredients to give your digestion a break and serve as a vehicle for an array of nutritional components, including fibers, proteins, antioxidants, and more.

Dosha Dos and Don'ts: *All dosha types can enjoy this dish guilt-free during this time of year, as you need richer food to prepare for the approaching cold.*

SERVES 4 TO 6

Khichdi:
¾ cup mung beans
2 teaspoons asafetida powder
¾ cup red rice
1 tablespoon any vinegar or lemon juice (optional)
1 tablespoon sesame oil
1 large red onion, peeled and diced
1 portion Pungent Spice Mix (page 33), coarsely ground

3½ cups Chicken Stock (page 241) or water
1 teaspoon kosher salt, plus more to taste

Roasted Butternut Squash:
1 large butternut squash, peeled, seeded, and flesh cut into ¼-inch slices lengthwise
1 tablespoon sesame oil, plus more as needed
3 tablespoons dried oregano leaves

8 garlic cloves, thinly sliced
6 bay leaves
8 allspice berries
Seeds of 1 vanilla pod

To Finish:
1 tablespoon sesame oil, plus more for greasing the baking dish
1 fennel bulb, trimmed and thinly sliced
1 cup pearl onions, halved
1 tablespoon white miso
2 tablespoons nigella seeds

To prepare: In a medium heavy-bottomed saucepan, cover the beans with water, add 1 teaspoon of asafetida, and bring to a boil; boil for 2 minutes. Turn off the heat, cover the pot, and let the beans soak for 60 minutes (preferably overnight). Presoaking the beans makes them easier to digest; it also helps them cook more evenly and become tender all the way through.

It's also good to soak the rice. In a medium bowl, cover the rice with 2 cups of water and add the vinegar (if using); soak for as long as possible, preferably overnight.

After soaking the beans and rice, drain and wash thoroughly with cold water.

If you don't have time for any soaking, you can cook the dish directly from the dry ingredients, but it will take additional time to achieve the desired tenderness.

For the khichdi: In a heavy-bottomed saucepan, heat the oil and add the onion and spice mix. Cook until the onion is translucent. Add the beans, rice, the remaining 1 teaspoon of asafetida, and the stock, and bring to a boil.

Reduce the mixture to a simmer and cook for about 1 hour, making sure there is always enough liquid in the pot. Simmering the beans gently helps them cook evenly until tender, retain their shape without losing their texture (getting mushy) too quickly, and keep their skins intact.

After about 45 minutes, add the salt and stir (the best time to add the salt is about three-quarters of the way into the cooking process, when the beans are tender but still partly firm).

After an hour, taste the khichdi, and if the beans and rice are not very tender continue cooking for 30 minutes longer. Depending on your preference, you can adjust the texture of the khichdi for a drier risotto-like consistency or a wetter soup-like one by either allowing the excess liquid to evaporate or adding more liquid.

For the roasted squash: Preheat the oven to 400°F.

Place the squash in a bowl, then add the oil, oregano, garlic, bay leaves, allspice, and vanilla seeds, and mix until the squash is coated.

Line a baking sheet with parchment paper, transfer the squash to the baking sheet, and bake for 50 minutes. Flip the squash over every 10 to 15 minutes to avoid burning, and add more oil if it starts to dry out.

To finish: Oil a medium baking dish and spread a layer of khichdi on the bottom, then top with the squash, fennel, and onions.

In a small bowl, whisk the miso and oil together, then pour over the vegetables. Bake the khichdi for 20 minutes. Remove from the oven and top with nigella seeds.

ORZO *WITH* TURKEY MEATBALLS *AND* RAISIN CREAM

This recipe makes for a perfect, wholesome dinner bowl. Made with ground turkey, the meatballs are leaner than the beef or pork versions. You can prepare them ahead of time, which will make this meal come together in a few minutes. Be cautious when cooking turkey meat, though, as it tends to become overcooked quickly and dry out easily. Raisins have a cooling effect on the body, but they should be consumed in moderation, which is why this raisin cream recipe is the perfect way to use them.

Dosha Dos and Don'ts: *Kapha types should enjoy this meal in moderation, or simply limit the amount of cream they consume.*

SERVES 4 TO 6

Raisin Cream:
⅓ cup capers, drained
¼ cup golden raisins
¾ cup water
4 tablespoons ghee
1 teaspoon sherry vinegar
Juice and zest of 1 lime
1 Indian green chile, finely chopped
1 teaspoon kosher salt
1 teaspoon freshly ground black pepper
¾ cup heavy cream

Turkey Meatballs:
1 cup cooked green split peas

1 pound organic ground lean turkey
2 large organic eggs, lightly beaten
⅔ cup rolled oats
½ cup feta cheese, crumbled
1 red onion, finely chopped
2 tablespoons chopped black olives
6 garlic cloves, finely chopped
2 tablespoons finely chopped parsley, plus more for garnish
¼ teaspoon chopped dill
½ teaspoon kosher salt
½ teaspoon freshly ground black pepper

Orzo:
1 teaspoon kosher salt

2½ cups water
1 cup orzo
4 tablespoons ghee
1 portion Sweet Spice Mix (page 30), finely ground

Toppings:
2 tablespoons walnuts, toasted and chopped
2 tablespoons dill fronds, lightly chopped
Kosher salt

For the raisin cream: In a small saucepan, combine the capers, raisins, and water. Simmer over low heat until the raisins are plump, 10 to 15 minutes, all the while making sure the mixture doesn't start to boil. Transfer the mixture to a blender and puree. With the blender on, add the ghee, 1 tablespoon at a time, until it's incorporated. Add the vinegar, lime juice and zest, and the chile to the sauce. Season with the salt and pepper, and stir in the heavy cream. Store in the refrigerator until ready to serve.

For the turkey meatballs: In a food processor, quickly grind the split peas into a rough puree. Put them in a medium-size mixing bowl, add all the remaining meatball ingredients to the bowl, and mix well. Cover the bowl and let the mixture sit for 15 minutes in the refrigerator.

Preheat the oven to 375°F and place a rack in the center position. Line a baking sheet with parchment paper. Using your hands, form small meatballs and place them on the baking sheet, leaving an even amount of space between the meatballs. You should have about 12 to 15 meatballs. Bake the meatballs for 20 minutes, carefully turning them with a pair of tongs after 10 minutes so they brown evenly, until they're golden brown. Remove from the oven and let the meatballs cool slightly.

For the orzo: Bring a large pot of salted water to a boil, and add the orzo. Reduce the heat to a simmer, and cook for 10 minutes, or until the orzo is firm and chewy. Drain the orzo and transfer to a bowl.

Meanwhile, heat the ghee in a small pan to medium heat, add the spice mix, and fry the spices for 1 minute. Add the spiced ghee to the bowl with the orzo, and stir to combine.

To finish: Serve 2 scoops of hot orzo in individual bowls, and top with 2 to 3 meatballs per portion. Pour about ¼ cup of raisin cream on each serving. Top with walnuts and dill, and season with salt to taste.

SPICED GRILLED CHEESE *WITH* MINT CHUTNEY

Cheese toast (when I was growing up, this was the equivalent of grilled cheese) with mint chutney and a side of green chile provided many blissful food moments throughout my childhood. This version, made from scratch, is as popular with adults as it is with children. The spicy bread can also be combined with a sweet jam or some honey for a real explosion of flavors on a snack at home or for a picnic.

Dosha Dos and Don'ts: *Kapha types should reduce the amount of cheese they use in the sandwich by half. Pitta types experiencing excessive heat in the body can skip the green chiles in the chuntney. Vata types should soak the dried fruits in water overnight before using it in the bread to avoid dryness.*

SERVES 4 TO 6

Spiced Bread:

2 tablespoons ghee, melted
½ cup candied orange peel, coarsely chopped (optional)
½ cup coarsely chopped dried apricots
½ cup coarsely chopped prunes
½ cup coarsely chopped almonds, lightly toasted
2 tablespoons maple syrup
1¼ cups whole milk
1 teaspoon kosher salt
6 cinnamon sticks

3 star anise pods
3 cups brown rice flour
1 tablespoon plus 1 teaspoon baking powder
2 teaspoons baking soda
1 portion Astringent Spice Mix (page 35), finely ground
2 large eggs

Mint Chutney:

2 garlic cloves
2 Indian green chiles, finely chopped
One ½-inch piece fresh ginger, peeled

2 dates, pitted
¼ teaspoon Himalayan salt
1 cup mint leaves, finely chopped
1 cup cilantro, finely chopped
1 tablespoon fresh lemon juice
1 tablespoon water

To Finish:

1 pound Homemade Cheese Curds (page 240) or fresh mozzarella
2 tablespoons ghee

For the spiced bread: Preheat oven to 325°F. Grease a standard (9-by-5-inch) loaf pan with the ghee. Place the orange peel (if using), apricots, prunes, and almonds into a small bowl. In a saucepan over medium heat, combine the maple syrup, milk, salt, cinnamon, and star anise, and bring to a boil.

Meanwhile, whisk together the flour, baking powder, baking soda, and spice mix in a large bowl. Pour the maple-syrup mixture into the dry ingredients and whisk to combine. Add the eggs and whisk until incorporated. Using a spatula, quickly fold in the fruit-almond mixture.

Pour the batter into the loaf pan, filling it about three-quarters of the way to the top. Bake the bread until the top is golden brown and a toothpick inserted into the center of the loaf comes out clean, about 35 to 40 minutes. Remove the bread from the oven and let it cool for a few minutes in the pan, then carefully remove the loaf from the pan and transfer to a wire rack; let cool completely.

For the mint chutney: Place the garlic, chiles, ginger, dates, and salt in a food processor or blender and pulse until it forms a coarse paste. Add the mint leaves, cilantro, lemon juice, and water and blend until the mixture is smooth.

To finish: Cut 8 slices of bread and 4 thick slices of cheese. Spread chutney on one side of each slice, top half of them with cheese, and make 4 sandwiches. Heat the ghee on a griddle pan and grill the sandwiches for about 2 minutes on each side. Slice in half and serve warm.

CARROT CAKE *WITH* COCONUT ICE CREAM

The low-fat carrot cake and dairy-free ice cream in this recipe make for a lighter take on a favorite dessert. I like to cool the cake completely after baking it, then cut it into cubes and reheat it on a pan to get it crispy and serve it hot with the coconut ice cream.

Dosha Dos and Don'ts: *Kapha types can replace the coconut milk with whole milk, as it's better suited for their body type. They should generally limit the amount of sweets or desserts they eat, as they can be hard on their digestion.*

SERVES 4 TO 6

Coconut Ice Cream:

Three 13-ounce cans full-fat organic coconut milk

⅔ cup coconut sugar (or maple syrup)

2 teaspoons vanilla extract

Carrot Cake:

3 tablespoons ghee, plus more for greasing the pan

2 cups all-purpose flour

2 teaspoons baking soda

¼ teaspoon kosher salt

2 teaspoons cinnamon powder

1 teaspoon clove powder

1 teaspoon cardamom powder

¼ portion Bitter Spice Mix (page 34), finely ground

3 extra-large organic eggs

¾ cup buttermilk

¾ cup sunflower oil

1½ cups maple syrup

2 teaspoons vanilla extract

2 cups shredded carrots

1 cup coconut flakes

1 cup chopped walnuts

1 cup crushed pineapple (optional)

1 cup raisins

2 tablespoons shredded coconut (optional)

For the coconut ice cream: Chill 2 of the cans of coconut milk in the refrigerator for at least 6 hours, preferably overnight.

Pour the can of room-temperature coconut milk into a saucepan. Add the sugar and vanilla, stir, and bring to a simmer for about 30 minutes, or until the milk is reduced by half and is golden in color. Remove the pan from the heat and let cool completely.

Remove the 2 chilled cans of coconut milk from the refrigerator and scoop out the cream from the top; place the cream in a large mixing bowl, and discard the remaining liquid contents of the cans. Using an electric hand mixer, whip the coconut cream at high speed for 3 to 4 minutes, or until stiff peaks form. In a slow stream, add the previously reduced sweetened coconut milk to the whipped coconut cream while continuing to whip the mixture at high speed for another 2 to 3 minutes. Transfer the mixture to a freezer-proof container and freeze for 4 hours, or preferably overnight.

For the carrot cake: Preheat the oven to 350°F. Grease a 13-by-9-inch baking pan with ghee.

In a medium bowl, sift together the flour, baking soda, salt, cinnamon, clove, cardamom, and spice mix, then set aside. In a large bowl, combine the eggs, buttermilk, oil, maple syrup, and vanilla. Mix well. Add the flour mixture to the wet mixture and stir to combine well. In another medium bowl, combine the carrots, coconut, walnuts, pineapple (if using), and raisins. Using a large wooden spoon, add the carrot mixture to the batter, and fold it in gently until combined. Pour the batter into the baking pan, and bake for 1 hour, until a toothpick inserted in the center of the cake comes out clean. Remove the cake from the oven and allow it to cool completely. Cut the cake into small cubes.

In a large skillet, heat the ghee to medium heat, then add the carrot cake cubes and lightly fry them until they're crisped on both sides. Remove the skillet from the heat, and cool the cake for about 3 minutes before serving.

To finish: Remove the ice cream from the freezer and let it sit at room temperature for a couple of minutes to make it easier to scoop. Place 3 or 4 warm carrot cake cubes into each dessert dish, then top it with a scoop of coconut ice cream and some of shredded coconut (if using).

GOLDEN MILK

This dairy-free drink is a soothing reminder of the glass of milk we were often given to drink as children, but this is the adult vegan version with added ingredients to nourish your body. If you have it ice cold, it is a great alternative to indulging in dessert or ice cream. The smokiness of turmeric and the sweetness of cashew milk give this drink a unique flavor and a beautiful yellow color. Turmeric is nature's most effective anti-inflammatory agent and should be consumed on a daily basis. This recipe is filled with dried fruit, which provides not only delicious sweetness, but also an energy boost and healthy fiber for good digestion. Drink the milk for breakfast or as a mid-morning snack to tie you over until lunchtime.

__Dosha Dos and Don'ts:__ Kapha types should use half the amount of dates. Vata types should soak the dried fruit in warm water for 15 minutes, or preferably overnight, as they can cause bloating or be difficult for Vata types to break down due to their dry nature.

SERVES 4 TO 6

4 cups cashew milk (page 239)
2 pitted dates
2 pitted prunes
2 dried apricots

One ½-inch piece fresh ginger
One ½-inch piece fresh turmeric (or 2 teaspoons turmeric powder, heated with 1 tablespoon ghee)
⅛ teaspoon clove powder

¼ teaspoon freshly ground black pepper
1 tablespoon cinnamon powder

Place the milk, dates, prunes, apricots, ginger, turmeric, clove, and pepper in a blender. Turn the blender to medium speed and blend until you get a smooth, creamy texture. Divide the milk among mugs, sprinkle with cinnamon, and serve.

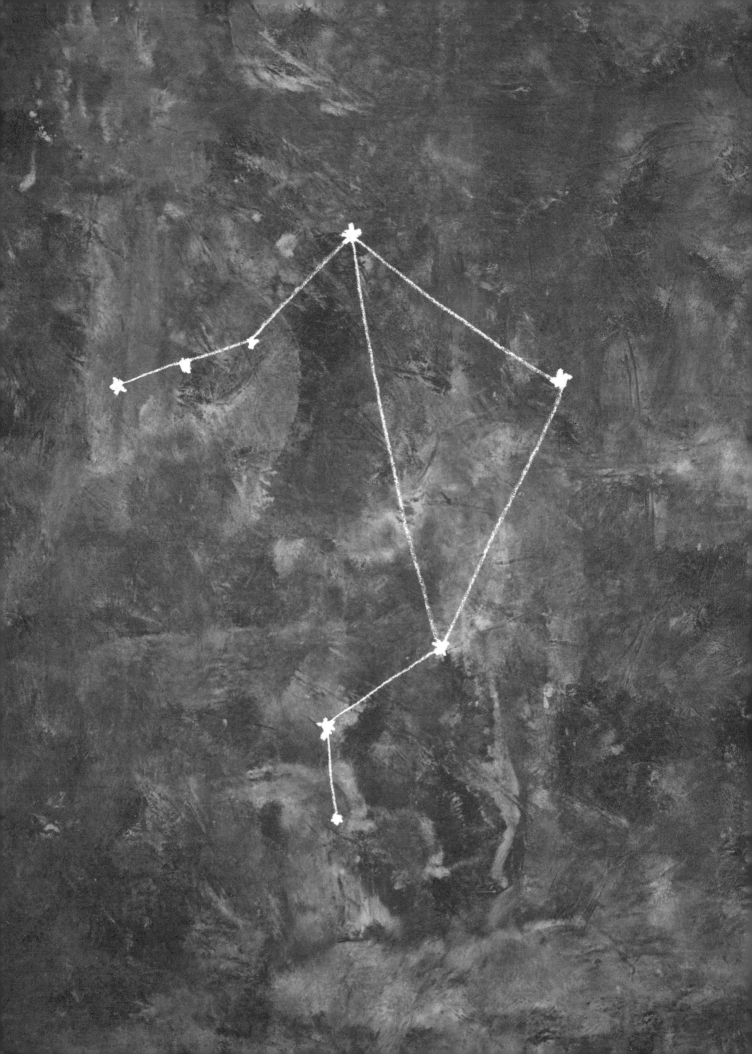

CHAPTER 10

LIBRA

Essential Ayurvedic Spice

CINNAMON

» *Cinnamon is the inner bark of various tropical evergreen trees. Today, most of the cinnamon that is available is either Ceylon or cassia cinnamon.*

» *Ceylon cinnamon is native to Sri Lanka and the southeastern coast of India. Today it is grown in Brazil, the Caribbean, and India. Cassia cinnamon is native to Indonesia, and it's also grown in Vietnam, China, and Myanmar.*

» *Cinnamon is good for balancing Vata and Kapha doshas, but it can be aggravating to the Pitta dosha if not taken in moderation.*

» *As a heating spice, cinnamon should be consumed in moderation and in combination with cooling ingredients during the hotter months. I love adding it to sautéed vegetables.*

» *Cinnamon's health benefits include strengthening and enhancing the flow of circulation, stabilizing and preventing blood sugar level spikes, and pacifying stomach disorders. It also contains antiseptic and detoxifying properties.*

» *Cinnamon contributes sweet, pungent, and astringent tastes. It is available year-round in powder form or in sticks. However, the sticks might be challenging to grind, even with an electric mixer. I recommend buying a smaller amount of the powder form and replacing it frequently so it doesn't lose its aroma.*

» *The familiar, strong scent of cinnamon announces its presence from a distance. Add cinnamon to a dish at the last minute in order to preserve its essential oils and flavor.*

» *Ceylon and cassia cinnamon are not interchangeable. Ceylon is much more expensive due to its labor-intensive production process. Compared to cassia, Ceylon has a more subdued flavor. Because cassia is much more widely used, people associate its spicier, richer flavor with the familiar taste of cinnamon.*

September 23–October 23

LIBRA

Libra is Latin for "the scales" and is commonly represented by a simplified drawing of a scale. It is the seventh sign of the zodiac. A part of the Vata season, the sun moves into Libra on the fall equinox, a time when the day and night are of equal length. October's climate is unpredictable. Nights are cool, while the days may still hold a hint of warmth amid the wind.

Like the earth, your inner landscape is also drying up. Your muscles may feel tired and your extremities cold, so you may feel like hibernating. You might experience cravings for starchy and heavy foods as your body attempts to build a layer of insulating fat to help you stay warm in the winter. Warm, oily, heavy comfort foods, like egg yolks, peanuts, duck meat, sour cream, and pistachios, build immunity and prepare the body's reserves for winter. Sweeter, heavier food is nourishing and grounding and helps you build strength. Sour foods will help increase your appetite and support digestion during this time.

The nervous system is easily scattered in fall, and October is the time for delving into a strong routine. Eat warm, cooked meals at regular times. Plan your meals the night before. Be sure to get to bed early and wake up at the same time every day.

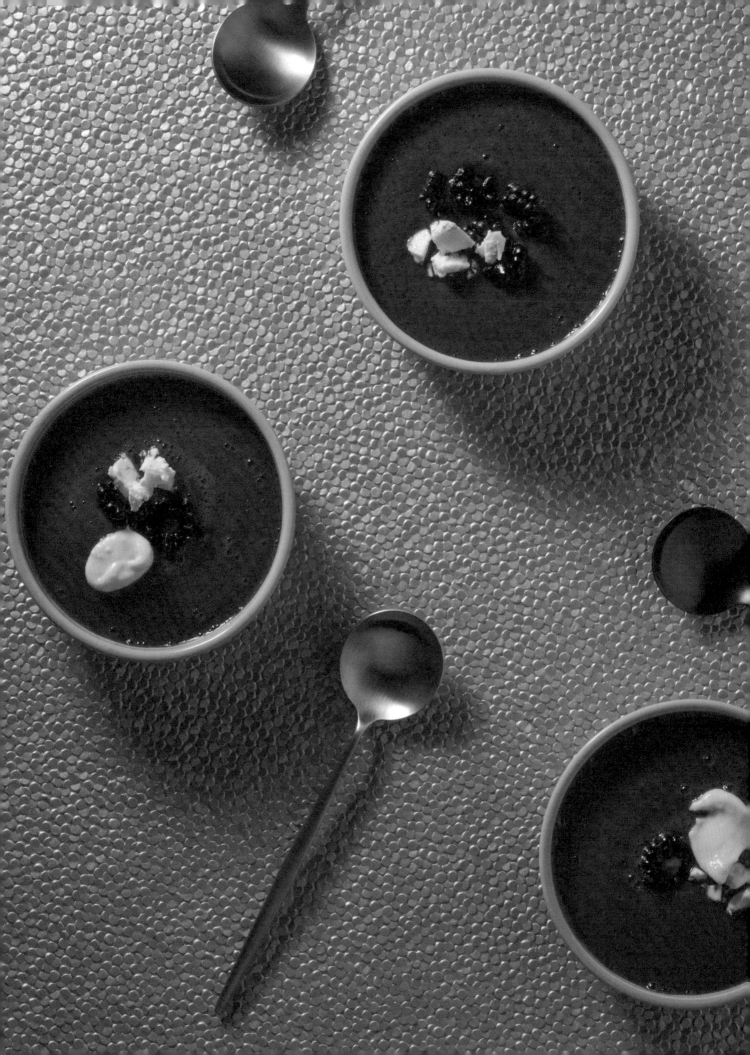

BEET *AND* BLACKBERRY SOUP *WITH* CHICKPEA BÉCHAMEL

The unlikely combination of beets and blackberries produces a wonderfully refreshing soup. The blackberries add a fruity roundness to the soup's sweet-tart flavor. Beets, like all other vividly colored vegetables, help remove toxins from the body. Paired with blackberries, a superfood known to be a potent antioxidant, this beet soup is a great way to stay energized.

Dosha Dos and Don'ts: *Beets are good for all three doshas, but Pitta types can reduce the amount of blackberries in the soup if they are too sour.*

SERVES 4 TO 6

Soup:
½ cup fresh or frozen blackberries
1 tablespoon honey (or maple syrup)
4 medium beets, washed and scrubbed
2 kohlrabies, peeled and chopped
½ cup plain organic yogurt
Juice and zest of 1 orange

¼ cup yuzu juice or lemon juice
One 1-inch piece fresh ginger, peeled
  and grated

Chickpea Béchamel:
2 tablespoons ghee
1 tablespoon chickpea flour
1 tablespoon all-purpose flour

1 portion Sweet Spice Mix (page 30),
  coarsely ground
1 cup whole milk

To Finish:
½ cup crumbled feta cheese
2 teaspoons balsamic vinegar

For the soup: Rinse and drain the blackberries and toss them with the honey in a medium bowl, then let the mixture sit so the blackberries release their juices.

Place the beets in a pot filled with water and boil them for 45 minutes, adding in the kohlrabies 20 minutes into cooking time. Once the vegetables are fork-tender drain them and let them cool. Peel the beets, and place them in a blender with the kohlrabies; add the yogurt, orange juice and zest, yuzu juice, and ginger, and blend until smooth.

Drain the berries in a fine-mesh sieve into a bowl; add the juices to the blender, and blend on high until the mixture is smooth. Set the berries aside.

For the chickpea béchamel: Heat the ghee in a small saucepan over medium heat. Add both flours and the spice mix, then whisk and cook for about 5 minutes, making sure the flour doesn't burn. Whisk in the milk, and cook until the mixture reaches a thickness similar to heavy cream. Remove the béchamel from the heat and keep at room temperature. You can make the béchamel up to a day ahead and reheat it when needed, whisking constantly to achieve a smooth texture.

To finish: Pour the soup into serving bowls, and top with a dollop of béchamel. Using the end of a spoon, swirl the béchamel into the soup. Garnish with the berries, feta, and a drizzle of vinegar.

SPLIT PEA CROQUETTES *WITH* PISTACHIO DIP

At Chez Nini, I made sure to pack all the croquettes we served with the most nutritional and seasonal ingredients, because I wanted to balance a fried indulgence with things that provided nourishment for the body. These croquettes are grounding and can be made ahead of time and frozen as a go-to snack. Split green peas are a dense food that are actually field peas that naturally split in half when they're dried. They're high in fiber, protein, and various vitamins and minerals but low in fats.

Dosha Dos and Don'ts: *Kapha types should eat this fried dish in moderation to avoid feeling heavy.*

SERVES 4 TO 6

Croquettes:
3 tablespoons ghee
2 cups cooked dry green split peas
   (page 247)
3 garlic cloves, crushed
4 shallots, chopped
3 cups Vegetable Broth (page 242)
½ cup chopped mint

½ cup chickpea flour, sifted
1 cup rolled oats
1 cup peanuts, toasted and chopped
3 extra-large organic eggs, beaten
1 portion Pungent Spice Mix (page 33),
   coarsely ground
1 teaspoon kosher or sea salt
1 tablespoon peanut oil, plus more for
   frying

Pistachio Dip:
¾ cup sour cream
1 cup pistachios, soaked in warm water
   for 15 to 30 minutes, then drained
½ teaspoon asafetida powder
½ teaspoon kosher salt
1½ teaspoons honey, preferably raw
1 tablespoon peanut oil

For the croquettes: Heat the ghee, in a saucepan over medium heat, then add the split peas, garlic, and shallots. Fry for a few minutes, then add the broth. Cook, stirring occasionally, for about 20 to 25 minutes (the split peas should start to resemble a puree). If the mixture is too dry, add some water. Remove the pan from the heat, drain the split peas, transfer them to a large mixing bowl, and allow them to cool.

Once they've cooled, add the mint, chickpea flour, oats, peanuts, eggs, spice mix, salt, and oil to the bowl, then toss to mix everything evenly. Shape the mixture into small fritter-size balls, place them on a baking sheet, and, using your fingers or the heel of your palm, press down on each to form croquettes.

Preheat the oven to 475°F. Fill a large skillet with about ½ inch of oil. Heat it over medium-high heat until sizzling. Fry the croquettes in batches for about 5 minutes on each side, or until crisp and golden brown. Transfer the finished fritters to a baking sheet lined with parchment paper and place in the oven to keep them hot while frying the remaining croquettes.

For the pistachio dip: Combine all the ingredients in a food processor or blender and blend until smooth. Add a little water if you prefer a runnier sauce. Chill in the refrigerator until ready to serve.

To finish: Remove the fritters from the oven, and transfer them to a serving platter. Place the pistachio dip in a small bowl and serve alongside the fritters.

DUCK PÂTÉ CHINOIS *WITH* ONION GRAVY

Pâté chinois is a French-Canadian comfort food that my mother appropriated by adding spices and extra vegetables when I was growing up. It resembles the English shepherd's pie in that it is a meat pie layered with vegetables then mashed potatoes but no crust. In my version, instead of beef, I use finely chopped duck for its rich, smoky flavor and butternut squash mash instead of the traditional potato one. I also use an array of spices and herbs to balance the heavy nature of this dish, making it easier to digest. You can bake this dish in one big pan or in smaller ramekins for individual servings—either way, it's sure to wow whomever you're feeding.

Dosha Dos and Don'ts: *Butternut squash can be traded for sweet potato for Vata types, and finely chopped turkey can replace the duck meat for Kapha types.*

SERVES 4 TO 6

Roasted Squash:
1 medium butternut squash, peeled, seeded, and cut into 1-inch cubes
2 tablespoons olive oil
2 garlic cloves, finely chopped
1 teaspoon Himalayan salt, plus more to taste
1 teaspoon freshly ground white pepper, plus more to taste
One 13-ounce can organic coconut milk

Onion Gravy:
1½ tablespoons olive oil
4 large onions, thinly sliced
3 tablespoons jaggery
4 cups Vegetable Broth (page 242)
¼ cup sesame oil
¼ cup all-purpose flour
½ teaspoon Himalayan salt

1 tablespoon plus 1½ teaspoons chopped rosemary
1 tablespoon plus 1½ teaspoons chopped thyme
1 tablespoon tamari
1 bay leaf
½ cup balsamic vinegar

Duck Pâté Chinois:
One 15-ounce can sweet corn or 1½ cups frozen organic corn, blanched
1½ cups fresh or frozen organic peas, blanched
½ cup pistachios, toasted in a dry pan, roughly chopped
1 portion Bitter Spice Mix (page 34), coarsely ground
2 tablespoons ghee
2 leeks, white and light green parts only, halved, rinsed, and thinly sliced

1 pound ground duck (or mince 4 breasts, including skin, with a cleaver)
8 sage leaves, sliced
¾ teaspoon Himalayan salt
1 tablespoon sesame oil
½ cup dry ricotta, crumbled

Toppings:
2 tablespoons poppy seeds, toasted in a dry pan
2 tablespoons nigella seeds, toasted in a dry pan
2 tablespoons white sesame seeds, toasted in a dry pan

For the roasted squash: Preheat the oven to 400°F.

In a large mixing bowl, toss the squash with the olive oil and garlic. Season with the salt and pepper.

Arrange the squash on a parchment paper–lined baking sheet. Place in the oven and roast until the squash is tender and lightly browned, about 30 minutes. Place the squash in a bowl and, using a potato masher, roughly mash it. Place the squash and coconut milk in a blender and puree until smooth. Season with salt and pepper, then set aside in the refrigerator.

For the onion gravy: In a medium saucepan, heat the olive oil over medium heat, then add the onions and jaggery. Cook, stirring occasionally, until the onions

are extremely soft, golden brown, and caramelized, about 40 minutes. Add 2 cups of the broth and stir, scraping up any browned bits on the bottom of the pan.

Set the pan aside and allow the mixture to cool to room temperature, then pour the gravy into the blender and puree until smooth; set aside.

Set the same pan back on the burner over medium heat and add the sesame oil. When it warms up, stir in the flour and salt. Stir constantly for 3 minutes, then add the rosemary and thyme. Drizzle in the remaining 2 cups of broth, whisking constantly. Stir in the tamari, bay leaf, and pureed onion mixture. Bring the gravy to a boil and continue stirring for about 4 minutes. Remove from the heat and discard the bay leaf. Stir in the vinegar.

For the duck pâté: Preheat the oven to 400°F and place a rack in the center position.

In a medium mixing bowl, mix the corn, peas, pistachios, and spice mix; set aside.

In a large skillet, bring the ghee to medium heat and fry the leeks until translucent. Add the duck, sage leaves, and salt. Cook for 2 minutes, or until browned. Remove from the heat.

Lightly press the meat into the bottom of an 8-to-8-inch square baking dish. Top with ½ cup of gravy. Add a layer of the corn and pea mixture, then cover with a thick layer of the squash mash.

Drizzle all over with the sesame oil. Cover the baking dish with aluminum foil and bake for 30 minutes. Remove from the oven, and turn the oven to the broiler setting. Uncover the dish and top with the ricotta. Finish cooking the dish under the broiler for up to 10 minutes, or until the cheese melts and browns. Let the pie cool for 10 minutes before serving.

To finish: Cut 4-inch-square servings and scoop them into individual dishes. Drizzle with heated gravy, top with the poppy, nigella, and sesame seeds.

TAPIOCA *AND* SWEET POTATO KHICHDI

The original version of this khichdi comes from the western parts of India, and it's known as sabudana (which means tapioca) khichdi. It's eaten during fasting times because it's easy to digest. I like to use a few different sizes of tapioca to give the khichdi some texture. Tapioca has a chewy texture, but you can add some crunchiness to it by letting it get crisp at the bottom of the pot when it's cooking or being reheated.

Dosha Dos and Don'ts: *It is essential to make sure to cook tapioca for the entire time indicated in the recipe, otherwise it continues to absorb water when it's inside the digestive system, which can cause dryness, especially for Vata types. Kapha and Pitta types can replace the peanuts with a mix of toasted seeds and top the khichdi with some popcorn.*

SERVES 4 TO 6

Khichdi:
⅓ cup red lentils
2 teaspoons asafetida powder
½ cup small tapioca pearls
½ cup medium tapioca pearls
1 tablespoon ghee
2 scallions, white and light green parts only, thinly sliced
1 portion Salty Spice Mix (page 31), coarsely ground

3½ cups Vegetable Broth (page 242) or water
1 teaspoon freshly ground black pepper

Roasted Sweet Potatoes:
3 medium sweet potatoes, washed and peeled
2 tablespoons peanut oil
5 garlic cloves, thinly sliced
2 Indian green chiles, chopped
16 curry leaves, sliced
½ teaspoon Himalayan salt

Toppings:
½ cup roasted peanuts, coarsely chopped
¼ cup toasted coconut flakes
¼ cup coriander leaves, roughly chopped
1 teaspoon fresh lime juice

To prepare: In a medium heavy-bottomed saucepan, cover the lentils with water, add 1 teaspoon of asafetida, and bring to a boil; boil for 2 minutes. Turn off the heat, cover the pot, and let the lentils soak for 60 minutes (preferably overnight). Presoaking the lentils makes them easier to digest; it also helps them cook more evenly and become tender all the way through.

It's also good to soak the tapioca, which makes it easier to digest. Cover the tapioca with 2 cups of water and soak for 1 to 3 hours, or as long as possible.

After soaking the lentils and tapioca, drain and wash thoroughly with cold water.

If you don't have time for any soaking, you can cook the dish directly from the dry ingredients, but it will take additional time to achieve the desired tenderness.

For the khichdi: In a heavy-bottomed saucepan, heat the ghee, and add the scallions and spice mix. Cook the scallions until they're translucent. Add in the lentils, tapioca, the remaining 1 teaspoon of asafetida, and the broth, and bring to a boil.

Reduce the mixture to a simmer and cook for about 45 minutes, making sure there is always enough liquid in the pot. Simmering the lentils gently helps them cook evenly until tender, retain their shape without losing their texture (getting mushy) too quickly, and keep their skins intact.

After 45 minutes, taste the khichdi and if the lentils and tapioca are not very tender continue cooking for up to 15 minutes longer. Depending on your preference, you can adjust the texture of the khichdi for a drier risotto-like consistency or a wetter soup-like one by either allowing the excess liquid to evaporate or adding more liquid. Remove the pan from the heat and add the pepper.

For the roasted sweet potatoes: Meanwhile, fill a pot with water and boil the sweet potatoes until they're tender, about 20 minutes. Make sure you don't overcook the potatoes. Drain the sweet potatoes, then chop them into cubes.

In a large pan, heat the oil to medium heat, add the garlic and chiles, and fry until the garlic starts to brown.

Add the potato cubes and cook, tossing regularly, until they're browned on all sides. Add the curry leaves and cook them until they get crispy. Remove the pan from the heat, add the salt, and stir.

To finish: Serve 2 large spoons of khichdi into each serving bowl. Using the back of a spoon, create a small well on top of each serving and top the khichdi with a large serving spoon of sweet potatoes, some peanuts, coconut flakes, coriander leaves, and lime juice.

ONION RING POUTINE

Poutine is a French-Canadian version of soul food which originated in my home province of Quebec. When I introduced it on my first restaurant menu at Chez Nini, it was a last-minute thought that ended up being one of our best-selling dishes. It includes a lighter vegetarian onion gravy—with ghee instead of butter—rather than the traditional heavy meat-based gravy. This recipe also incorporates pan-fried onion rings with a brown rice batter instead of the deep-fried potatoes you'd find in a typical poutine. The cold season allows for some more heavy foods to build fats to keep the body warm, so it is the perfect time to indulge in a more mindfully made poutine once in a while.

Dosha Dos and Don'ts: *Kapha and Pitta types should enjoy this dish in moderation, as fried foods can counter the coolness they require. This dish is meant to be a treat for special occasions.*

SERVES 4 TO 6

Onion Rings:
1 cup brown rice flour
¼ cup cornmeal
¼ cup cornstarch
½ teaspoon kosher salt
½ teaspoon freshly ground black pepper
1 teaspoon smoked paprika
¼ teaspoon cayenne pepper
½ cup whole milk
½ cup buttermilk
2 medium white onions, thinly sliced into ½-inch rings
1 medium red onion, sliced into ½-inch rings
Peanut oil, for frying

Onion Gravy:
3 tablespoons ghee
3 medium onions, thinly sliced
1 tablespoon coconut flour
1½ cups Chicken Stock (page 241), plus more if needed
2 teaspoons Dijon mustard
1 teaspoon kosher salt
1 teaspoon freshly ground black pepper
1 portion Astringent Spice Mix (page 35), finely ground

Toppings:
2 cups Homemade Cheese Curds (page 240) or ¾ pound fresh mozzarella, cut into ½-inch cubes
¼ teaspoon kosher salt
1 teaspoon freshly ground black pepper

For the onion rings: Preheat oven to 200°F.

In a large shallow bowl, mix the flour, cornmeal, cornstarch, salt, pepper, paprika, and cayenne pepper. In a separate small mixing bowl, add milk and buttermilk and set aside.

Line two baking sheets with parchment paper. Place one in the oven for keeping the rings warm after you fry them. Set the other sheet at the end of your workstation to place the breaded onion rings on. One at a time, dip the onion rings in the dry ingredients first, then the wet ingredients, then back in the dry ingredients until well coated. Place the coated rings on the baking sheet.

Heat a ½-inch layer of oil in a large skillet over medium-high heat for about 5 minutes, testing with a bit of flour to see if the oil bubbles and browns the flour. When the oil is hot, add as many onions as you can without crowding them in the skillet. Fry them for 2 minutes on each side, or until browned, lowering the heat if the rings are browning too fast. Handle them carefully with tongs to avoid breaking the crust.

Transfer the onion rings to a paper towel–lined plate and blot off extra oil with paper towels, then place them on the parchment paper–lined baking sheet in the oven to keep warm. Continue until all the onion rings are cooked.

For the onion gravy: In a heavy-bottomed pan over medium heat, melt the ghee. Add the onions and cook until they're soft, about 10 minutes. Reduce the heat to low and cover the pan, continuing to cook the onions until they're caramelized. Stir occasionally, and cook for about 20 minutes longer. Stir the flour into the onions and cook for another minute. Add the stock and mustard, and simmer until the sauce thickens, stirring often, for about 15 minutes. Season with the salt, pepper, and spice mix. Pour the gravy into a blender and blend until smooth. Add stock as needed to achieve a good pouring consistency.

To finish: Place the onion rings in shallow bowls, top with cheese and onion gravy. Sprinkle with the salt and pepper and serve hot.

MINT-CITRUS SALAD *WITH* WHITE CHOCOLATE SABAYON

This dessert is simplicity at its best. Citrus fruits practically taste like candy on their own, so they don't need much more than a simple French custard sauce known as sabayon. The dessert is light and refreshing but it satisfies my sweet cravings every time. Making a sabayon can seem intimidating at first, but once you make it a few times and get the hang of it, you'll be able to enjoy it on all kinds of desserts. You can also add a variety of different extracts to it, like orange, almond, vanilla, etc.

Dosha Dos and Don'ts: *Kapha and Pitta types trying to more strictly balance their doshas can opt for sweet oranges of all types instead of grapefruit and use lime juice rather than lemon, as it's more suitable for their dosha.*

SERVES 4 TO 6

White Chocolate Sabayon:
6 tablespoons brown sugar
5 tablespoons dry sherry
4 egg yolks
2 tablespoons water

1 ounce unsweetened white chocolate, finely chopped

Mint-Citrus Salad:
3 oranges of any kind
1 pink grapefruit

3 tablespoons honey
½ portion Sour Spice Mix (page 32), finely ground
1 tablespoon fresh lime or lemon juice
¼ cup chopped mint

For the white chocolate sabayon: In a medium metal bowl, whisk the sugar, sherry, yolks, and water until the mixture is blended. Set the bowl over a saucepan of simmering water (do not allow the bowl to touch the water). Using a handheld electric mixer or a whisk, beat the mixture continuously until it's thick and a thermometer inserted in it registers 160°F, about 4 minutes. Remove the bowl from the water, add the chocolate, and whisk until melted. Set aside at room temperature.

For the mint-citrus salad: Peel the oranges and grapefruit, removing as much pith as possible, and slice the fruit into wheels. Remove any pits. In a small bowl, whisk the honey, spice mix, lime juice, and mint together until well combined.

To finish: Layer the fruit in individual dishes, and drizzle with the juice mixture. When you're ready to serve the salad, pour the sabayon over the layered citrus.

GINGER GREEN JUICE

Juicing culture has pegged green juice as a bitter spinach- or kale-based experience. Green is the color of life and it represents growth, freshness, and renewal. This recipe makes a green juice with a fruit base—it's minty, sweet, and tangy, and flushes out toxins with the power of cucumber and coconut water. However, the fresh ginger should balance the potential aggravating effects of the sour taste. Since the drink is already quite cooling with its chilled and frozen ingredients, try to avoid adding any ice to make sure you don't dampen your digestive fire. Lightly chilled liquids are easier to digest than cold or frozen ones.

Dosha Dos and Don'ts: *Kiwi is best eaten during the Vata season, so enjoy it while you can. Pitta and Kapha types should reduce the amount of kiwi in this recipe to half. They can make another tweak by replacing the green grapes with red ones, as the sour taste of the green grapes can cause excess acidity and heat for the Pitta, while for the Kapha, it can worsen the natural tendency to retain excess water.*

SERVES 4 TO 6

One 1-inch piece fresh ginger, peeled
Juice of 1 lime

2 kiwis, peeled and frozen whole
1 medium cucumber, roughly chopped
30 green grapes, frozen

8 mint leaves
2 cups coconut water, chilled
8 dates

Place all the ingredients, except for the dates, in a blender, and blend until smooth. Add the dates and blend for another 30 seconds, until the drink is smooth but still has some small chunks in it. Pour into glasses and serve.

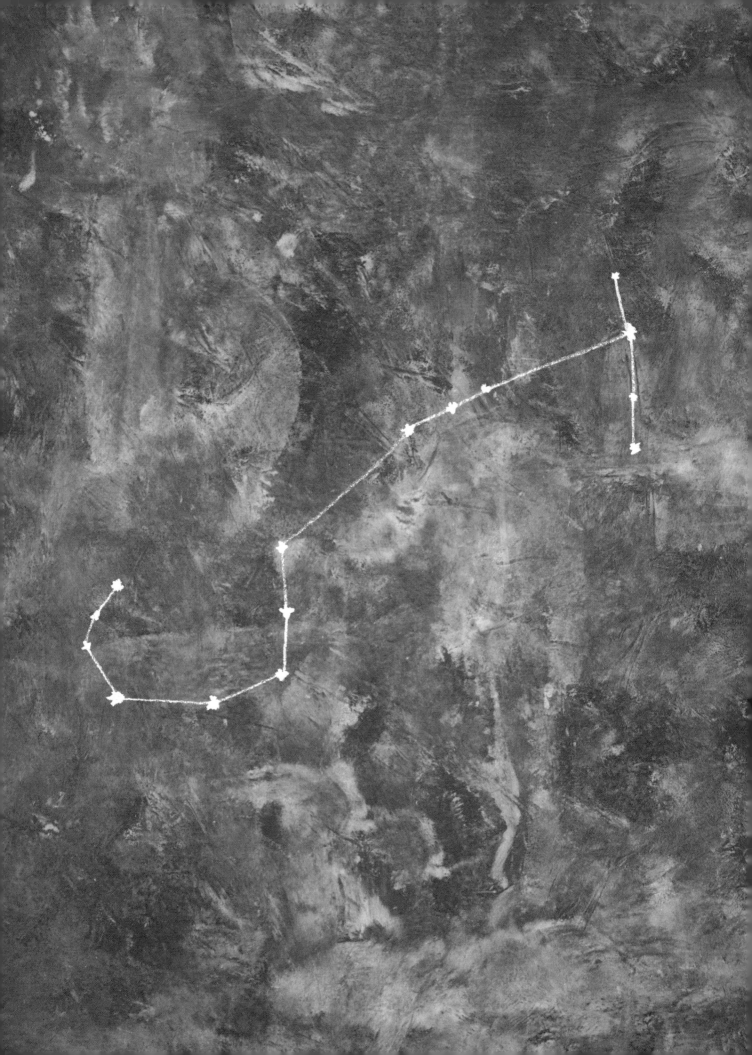

CHAPTER 11

SCORPIO

Essential Ayurvedic Spice

NUTMEG

» *Nutmeg is native to the Maluku Islands (the Spice Islands) and other tropical islands in the East Indies. Today, it is primarily grown in the West Indies.*

» *The nutmeg tree, a large evergreen, produces both nutmeg and mace.*

» *Nutmeg is good for balancing Vata and Kapha doshas, but it can be aggravating to the Pitta dosha if taken in excess.*

» *Nutmeg should be used in moderation during the warmer seasons to avoid overheating the body.*

» *Among its long list of Ayurvedic health benefits, nutmeg stimulates appetite and digestion and can be used as a sleep aid when mixed with warm milk at night before bedtime.*

» *Nutmeg is a warming spice, contributing the bitter, astringent, and pungent tastes. Fresh-grated nutmeg has a more powerful flavor and aroma than ground nutmeg. It is an intensely aromatic spice that should be used in small quantities. I like to combine it with garlic powder and just enough tamari, soy sauce, and white miso, then add the mixture to a potato mash for an irresistible, unique flavor.*

» *Although nutmeg may seem difficult to grate, avoid buying nutmeg powder. The benefits of using the freshly ground spice far outweigh the effort.*

October 24–November 21

SCORPIO

Scorpio is Latin for "the scorpion" and is commonly represented by an M with a scorpion's stinger-tipped tail. It is the eighth sign of the zodiac and is part of the general Vata season. It is the time of year when the earth is reclaiming what belongs to it. The harvest is over, and nature has nothing left to give. Regeneration takes place.

In November, your body uses the extra calories from the heavier foods you've been indulging in to store fat. This fat will be used to insulate your skin during cold winter months. Dieting during this time of year could create a serious immune system deficiency, causing you to catch a cold. Instead, enjoy the satisfaction and support of a few extra pounds. Your body's need for warmth increases your appetite for fat and lessens your desire for vigorous exercise. Due to sharp drops in temperatures, November is the time of year when one's appetite for healthy fats is greatest. Heavy, nourishing, and sweet foods, like avocado, peanuts, lamb, walnuts, and honey, help your body stay healthy during the cold. If you become dry, cold, and dehydrated in the fall, your body will compensate by craving sweets instead of healthy fats.

With shorter days, your attention naturally shifts inward as the days grow chilly and nights come early. Use these tips in November and you'll be sure to stay healthy for the upcoming season of holiday festivities. Prepare your body to weather the holidays by staying grounded, nourished, and rested.

SWEET POTATO TOAST *WITH* AVOCADO SPREAD *AND* CRISPY SARDINES

A great replacement for bread, a roasted slice of sweet potato can serve as a vessel for many light hors d'oeuvres you want to make. After sweet potatoes are roasted, they can be stored in the refrigerator for a couple of days and used as a snack with a spread or to make a form of open "sandwich" like the one in this recipe. The spread makes for an unusual but addictive combination of sweet and creamy flavors, so even if you hesitate at the idea of it, make sure to give it a try. You can use either canned or fresh sardines, but, of course, when fresh ingredients are available, it's always best to use them.

Dosha Dos and Don'ts: *Sweet potatoes are good for balancing the Vata dosha of this season. They are also unique among comfort foods for their Kapha-pacifying lightness.*

SERVES 4 TO 6

Sweet Potato Toast:
3 sweet potatoes, cut into ¼-inch slices lengthwise
3 tablespoons sesame oil
1 teaspoon kosher salt

Avocado Spread:
1 small ripe avocado, peeled and pitted

½ cup peanut butter
¼ cup warm water
Juice of 1 lemon
¼ teaspoon kosher or sea salt
1 teaspoon freshly ground black pepper (optional)

Sardines:
1 tablespoon ghee

1 can sardines in oil, drained (or 8 to 10 fresh wild-caught sardine fillets)
1 portion Astringent Spice Mix (page 35), finely ground

To Finish:
2 tablespoons finely chopped dill pickle
1 cup watercress

For the sweet potato toast: Preheat the oven to 400°F. Place the sweet potatoes in a large mixing bowl, coat with the oil, and season with the salt. Arrange the sweet potatoes on a parchment paper–lined baking sheet and roast until cooked through and browned, about 15 minutes.

For the avocado spread: In a bowl, mix the avocado, peanut butter, water, lemon juice, salt, and pepper (if using), and mash everything together until it becomes a smooth spread.

For the sardines: Heat the ghee in a pan to medium heat, and add the sardines. Reduce the heat and fry the sardines until they're warm and crispy on both sides, about 2 minutes per side. As they're frying, sprinkle them with the entire portion of the spice mix, and continue cooking for another minute, turning once.

To finish: Top each piece of toasted sweet potato with a tablespoon of the avocado spread, a crispy sardine, some dill pickle, and some watercress.

ROASTED SWEET POTATO *AND* RADISH SALAD *WITH WALNUT CREAM*

This salad is a combination of the comforting warmth of the sweet potatoes and the bitter crunchiness of the radish. Roasted, caramelized sweet potatoes are so delicious it's hard to believe they're so good for you. Unlike dairy products, regular potatoes, and other common comfort foods like pasta, the sweet potatoes in this recipe are light on the stomach.

Dosha Dos and Don'ts: *Kapha and Pitta types should reduce the amount of walnuts in the dressing or replace them with soaked almonds. Vata types can soak the radishes in a light water-vinegar mixture before roasting them.*

SERVES 4 TO 6

Walnut Cream:
2 cups walnuts, soaked in water for at least 8 hours (preferably overnight)
1 cup almond milk
Juice and zest of 2 lemons
2 umeboshi plums, pitted
2 teaspoons vanilla extract
1 teaspoon sea salt, plus more if needed
2 tablespoons extra-virgin olive oil

2 tablespoons apple cider vinegar
1 teaspoon Dijon mustard
½ portion Sweet Spice Mix (page 30), finely ground
2 teaspoons jaggery, crumbled

Salad:
2 pounds sweet potatoes, peeled and cut into bite-size pieces
1 pound radishes, trimmed and cut into

bite-size pieces
¼ cup olive oil
Sea salt
Freshly ground black pepper
½ medium red onion, diced
½ cup chopped parsley

For the walnut cream: Preheat the oven to 325°F. Drain the walnuts well and blot them dry with a paper towel. Place them on a baking sheet in a single layer, and bake for 10 minutes. Remove the walnuts from the oven and let them cool completely.

Place the milk, lemon juice and zest, umeboshi plums, vanilla, and salt in a blender. Blend for 10 seconds. Add the walnuts to the mix and blend again until smooth, up to 1 minute. You may have to stop periodically to scrape down the sides of the blender. Refrigerate the mixture for 30 to 45 minutes. In a bowl, whisk the walnut cream, oil, vinegar, mustard, spice mix, and jaggery together until the jaggery dissolves. Season with salt to taste.

For the salad: Reduce the oven to 200°F. Toss the potatoes and radishes with the oil and season with some salt and pepper. Transfer the vegetables to a parchment paper–lined baking sheet and roast for 45 to 60 minutes, or until they're cooked through and browned. Remove the vegetables from the oven, let them cool slightly, then transfer them to a bowl. Add the onion and parsley.

To finish: Pour the walnut cream over the warm salad, then toss it to make sure the entire salad is coated. Divide among bowls and serve.

KHICHDI *WITH* SAUCE GRIBICHE

Chef Daniel Morgan, my good friend and a constant source of knowledge and inspiration, introduced me to the traditional French sauce gribiche. He added it to my menu when he spent a winter in India and we had a chance to workshop and cook together. Daniel has worked in many prestigious kitchens around the world, and he sees life in flavors and ingredients. Working with him gave me the courage to try new and unique combinations and get my hands dirty without being afraid of something going wrong. Every day was an opportunity to rework previous dish ideas, and there was always so much excitement about using the abundant spices and herbs available in India as our tools of creation. This hard boiled–egg dressing enriches the flavor of virtually any savory dish.

Dosha Dos and Don'ts: *Pitta types should limit the acidity of pickled vegetables in the sauce gribiche.*

SERVES 4 TO 6
Khichdi:
½ cup urad dal
2 teaspoons asafetida powder
½ cup wild rice
1 tablespoon any vinegar or lemon juice (optional)
1 tablespoon sesame oil
1 large leek, white and light green parts only, halved, rinsed, and thinly sliced

1 portion Salty Spice Mix (page 31), coarsely ground
3½ cups Ginger, Garlic, and Onion Broth (page 244)

Sauce Gribiche:
3 celery stalks, tough fibers peeled off, thinly sliced
¼ teaspoon kosher salt, plus more to taste
¾ cup sour cream

1 tablespoon Dijon mustard
1 tablespoon white wine vinegar
1 tablespoon capers
2 dill pickles, finely chopped
1 hard-boiled large organic egg, finely chopped
Freshly ground black pepper
1 tablespoon chopped parsley

To prepare: In a medium heavy-bottomed saucepan, cover the urad dal with water, add 1 teaspoon of asafetida, and bring to a boil; boil for 2 minutes. Turn off the heat, cover the pot, and let the urad dal soak for 60 minutes (preferably overnight). Presoaking the lentils makes them easier to digest; it also helps them cook more evenly and become tender all the way through.

It's also good to soak the rice. In a medium bowl, cover the rice with 2 cups of water and add the vinegar (if using); soak for as long as possible, preferably overnight.

After soaking the urad dal and rice, drain and wash thoroughly with cold water.

If you don't have time for any soaking, you can cook the dish directly from the dry ingredients, but it will take additional time to achieve the desired tenderness.

For the khichdi: In a heavy-bottomed saucepan, heat the oil and add the leek and spice mix. Cook until the leek is translucent. Add the urad dal, rice, the remaining 1 teaspoon of asafetida, and the broth, and bring to a boil.

Reduce the heat to a simmer, and cook the khichdi for about 45 minutes, making sure there is always enough liquid in the pot. Simmering the urad dal gently helps it cook evenly until tender, retain its shape without losing its texture (getting mushy) too quickly, and keep its skins intact.

After 45 minutes, taste the khichdi, and if urad dal and rice are not very tender continue cooking for up to 15 minutes longer. Depending on your preference, you can adjust the texture of the khichdi for a drier risotto-like consistency or a wetter soup-like one by either allowing the excess liquid to evaporate or adding more liquid.

For the sauce gribiche: In a bowl, mix all the ingredients, except the parsley, until the mixture has a consistency that resembles chunky mayonnaise. When you're ready to serve, mix in the parsley.

To finish: Place 2 large spoons of khichdi in each serving bowl. Using the back of a spoon, create a small well on top of each serving, and add a large serving spoon of gribiche. Sprinkle with salt.

RICE PILAF WITH LAMB *AND* BEET RAGÙ

My husband's mother (aka Mama Hess) taught me one of the most beautiful and simple dishes, a beet and carrot soup. After learning and cooking so many dishes, it was important to come full circle and appreciate how much simplicity appeals to the palate and goes a long way for the body. Ever since I learned the recipe, I've been using this nourishing soup as a base for many different sauces and soups, including this ragù. Think of it as a replacement for tomato sauce. People often question whether someone following an Ayurvedic diet can eat meat and fish. Ayurveda first and foremost promotes moderation and high-quality ingredients. Even though vegetarian food is favored for its easier digestibility and as a source of more fiber and nutrients, meat and fish in moderation are not prohibited—or even frowned upon. In fact, meat and fish are considered to be grounding for Vata types because they're so nourishing.

Dosha Dos and Don'ts: *Kapha and Pitta types should limit their portions, but at this time of the year, everyone should be enjoying hearty food to fortify the body for the upcoming cold.*

SERVES 4 TO 6

Lamb and Beet Ragù:

4 cups Chicken Stock (page 241) or
    water
4 large beets, peeled and chopped
2 large carrots, scrubbed and chopped
One 1½-inch piece fresh ginger
1 leek, white and light green parts only,
    halved, rinsed, and sliced
1 portion Sour Spice Mix (page 32),
    finely ground

1 tablespoon balsamic vinegar
1 tablespoon ghee
1½ pounds ground lamb
½ cup heavy cream
¼ cup chopped dill

Rice Pilaf:
2 cups basmati rice
1½ tablespoons ghee
1 teaspoon Himalayan salt
¼ cup milk (preferably goat's milk)

Pinch of saffron threads
½ cup hot water
Zest of 1 orange
½ cup pistachios, toasted in a dry pan
    and chopped

Toppings:
2 tablespoons pistachios, lightly toasted
    in a dry pan and chopped
2 tablespoons chopped dill

For the ragù: Bring the stock to a boil in a medium pot. Add the beets, carrots, ginger, and leek and boil for 40 minutes. In the last 5 minutes of cooking, add the spice mix and vinegar.

Remove the pot from the heat and allow the stock and vegetables to cool for 5 minutes, then drain the mixture through a fine-mesh sieve into a bowl. Add the vegetables to a blender and reserve the cooking liquid. Blend the vegetables until they're smooth, adding cooking liquid as needed to achieve a smooth consistency.

Meanwhile, heat the ghee in a large pot, add the lamb, and start browning the meat. Cook for about 10 minutes, then pour the vegetable sauce into the pot along with the cream and dill. Continue cooking the ragù for an additional 10 minutes. Remove from heat and let it rest.

For the rice pilaf: Rinse the rice well in cold water. Bring a pot of water to a boil. Add the rice and cook for five minutes, then drain.

In a large cast-iron pan, melt the ghee over medium-low heat. Add the rice, salt, and milk and stir to combine.

Spread the mixture evenly in the pan, poking holes in the rice to let steam escape. Cover the pan and cook over medium heat for 10 minutes without stirring or uncovering.

Submerge the saffron in the hot water, then pour the liquid over the rice. Lower the heat a little and continue to cook the rice for 30 to 35 minutes, ensuring the bottom is heated evenly. Listen to the rice carefully and occasionally prop up a section of the rice with a spatula to make sure it's not burning. Once the rice starts popping and smells nutty, remove it from the heat.

Let the rice sit for 10 minutes in the pan, then invert it onto a large platter. Break up the crust with a fork and sprinkle the surface with the orange zest and pistachios.

To finish: Divide the rice among shallow bowls. Pour the ragù over the hot, crunchy pilaf. Top with chopped pistachios and dill.

ZUCCHINI PASTA *WITH* RAISIN-CASHEW CREAM

This pasta dish is as satisfying as a bowl of spaghetti, but just think of all the plant-based protein and fiber you're getting from such an indulgent-looking dish. You can make vegetable pasta with all types of potatoes, carrots, and squash, so there's a lot to experiment with. The cashews add creaminess that we normally crave when we think of a pasta dish, so you can enjoy this dish for the healthy vegan option that it is, or trick yourself into thinking you're enjoying a real plate of pasta—it's easier than you think!

Dosha Dos and Don'ts: *Kapha and Pitta types can skip the cashew topping or consume it in moderation.*

SERVES 4 TO 6

Raisin-Cashew Cream:
2 cups cashews, soaked in water at least 30 minutes
1 cup raisins, soaked in hot water at least 15 minutes
1¼ cups Vegetable Broth (page 242) or water
2 garlic cloves, crushed
2 tablespoons chopped rosemary leaves

1 portion Bitter Spice Mix (page 34), coarsely ground
1 teaspoon Himalayan salt

Zucchini Pasta:
Four 2-pound medium zucchini
½ teaspoon kosher salt
1 tablespoon sesame oil
3 large red onions, sliced into ½-inch rings

3 jalapeños, trimmed, seeded, and sliced lengthwise

To Finish:
½ cup toasted cashews, chopped
¼ cup cheddar cheese, finely grated (optional)
1 tablespoon extra-virgin olive oil
¼ teaspoon cinnamon powder

For the raisin-cashew cream: Drain and rinse the soaked cashews thoroughly. Drain the soaked raisins. Place the cashews, raisins, broth, garlic, rosemary, spice mix, and salt in a food processor or blender and puree the mixture until it's very smooth, about 2 to 3 minutes. Add a small amount of water a little at a time if needed to achieve a pouring heavy cream consistency. The raisin cashew cream can be made a day in advance and then stirred and added to the cooked vegetables prior to serving.

For the zucchini pasta: Using a vegetable turner or peeler, cut the zucchini lengthwise into long, thin strands or strips. (Stop when you reach the seeds in the middle since the seeds make the "noodles" fall apart.) Place the zucchini in a colander and toss with the salt. Let it drain for 15 to 30 minutes, then gently squeeze the strands to remove any excess water.

In a large skillet, heat the oil, then add the onions and jalapeños, and fry for about 2 minutes. Add the zucchini and gently toss until hot, about 3 minutes. Transfer the mixture to a large mixing bowl.

To finish: Mix the raisin-cashew cream into the hot pasta. Using tongs, divide the pasta among serving bowls. Top each with cashews, cheddar (if using), and a drizzle of oil. Sprinkle each serving with cinnamon.

KIWI GAZPACHO *WITH* JAGGERY SOUR CREAM

I am conflicted when it comes to combining dairy and fruits in a recipe, as it is a forbidden practice in Ayurveda. The truth of the matter is that even though we are not meant to eat sweets at the end of a meal, as they inhibit our digestion, we are going to crave them anyway. Eating can't and shouldn't be a completely restrictive and disciplined act. Your diet is never going to be black or white, but the better the choices you make, the more you are tipping the scales in your favor. Consider this as an honest disclaimer and try to enjoy this dessert in moderation.

Dosha Dos and Don'ts: *Pitta types should enjoy this dish in moderation to avoid too much of the sour taste. They can substitute coconut milk or cream for the sour cream. Kapha types can do the same to keep this dessert lighter.*

SERVES 4 TO 6

Jaggery Sour Cream:
3 medium-ripe avocados, mashed
½ cup jaggery, crumbled
6 dates, finely chopped
1 cup sour cream
½ cup heavy cream
1 teaspoon vanilla extract

1 tablespoon fresh lime juice
½ portion of Pungent Spice Mix (page 33), finely ground
Pinch of salt

Kiwi Gazpacho:
5 kiwis, peeled
1 teaspoon fresh lime juice

To Finish:
½ cup pistachios, toasted in a dry pan and roughly chopped
1½ teaspoons cinnamon powder
1 teaspoon clove powder

For the jaggery sour cream: In a large bowl, whisk all the ingredients together until the mixture is very smooth (with no lumps). Pour the mixture into a container and set aside in the refrigerator.

For the kiwi gazpacho: Combine the kiwi and lime juice in a food processor or blender. Pulse until pureed. Keep the gazpacho in the refrigerator, covered, until ready to serve.

To finish: Divide the gazpacho among dessert bowls, add 2 spoons of the chilled sour cream to each serving, then top with pistachios. Using a sifter or a strainer, sprinkle with cinnamon and clove powder.

GINGER-LEMON KOMBUCHA TEA

Kombucha is a fermented tea that has gained popularity for being a good source of probiotics. Most people usually find it to be an acquired taste, but once you get into the routine of making it, it's very easy to do. I have called for black tea here, but you can try a variety of them to construct your own versions. You can add as much or as little flavor to the kombucha when it is ready. It is naturally quite flavorful and refreshing and can be consumed hot or cold. You can also adjust the sour taste with the number of days you leave it to ferment. The scoby, a starter for kombucha that enables the fermentation process, can be found at most health food stores and is available online.

Dosha Dos and Don'ts: *Pitta types should enjoy this drink in moderation as too much of the sour taste from kombucha can increase the heat and aggravate their digestion.*

SERVES 4 TO 6
1½ teaspoons loose black tea
Two 1-inch pieces fresh ginger

2 tablespoons fresh lemon juice
¼ cup jaggery
2½ cups water, boiled for steeping tea

½ cup white wine vinegar
One 3-ounce organic kombucha scoby

Place the tea, 1 piece of ginger, the lemon juice, and jaggery in a 24-ounce glass jar. Fill the jar with the hot water, leaving about ½ inch of space at the top. Cap the jar tightly, and shake gently to dissolve the jaggery. Uncover the jar and set aside to cool, allowing the tea to steep for 15 minutes.

Strain the tea through a fine-mesh sieve, then pour it back into the jar. Add the vinegar and kombucha scoby, cover the jar with a clean dish towel or two layers of cheesecloth, and secure with a tight rubber band.

Place the jar in a cool, dark spot at room temperature for 3 to 7 days, or until the kombucha is carbonated to your liking. You can ferment it for longer, and it will continue to get more sour. Pour the kombucha into a bowl; remove the scoby (which you should reuse for making another batch). Add the remaining piece of ginger, then transfer the kombucha back into the jar, and refrigerate before consuming. You can add ingredients and spices to infuse other flavors into the drink.

When refrigerated, the kombucha will keep indefinitely, but will continue to ferment. The deciding factor on whether you keep drinking it or not will be how much sourness you can handle.

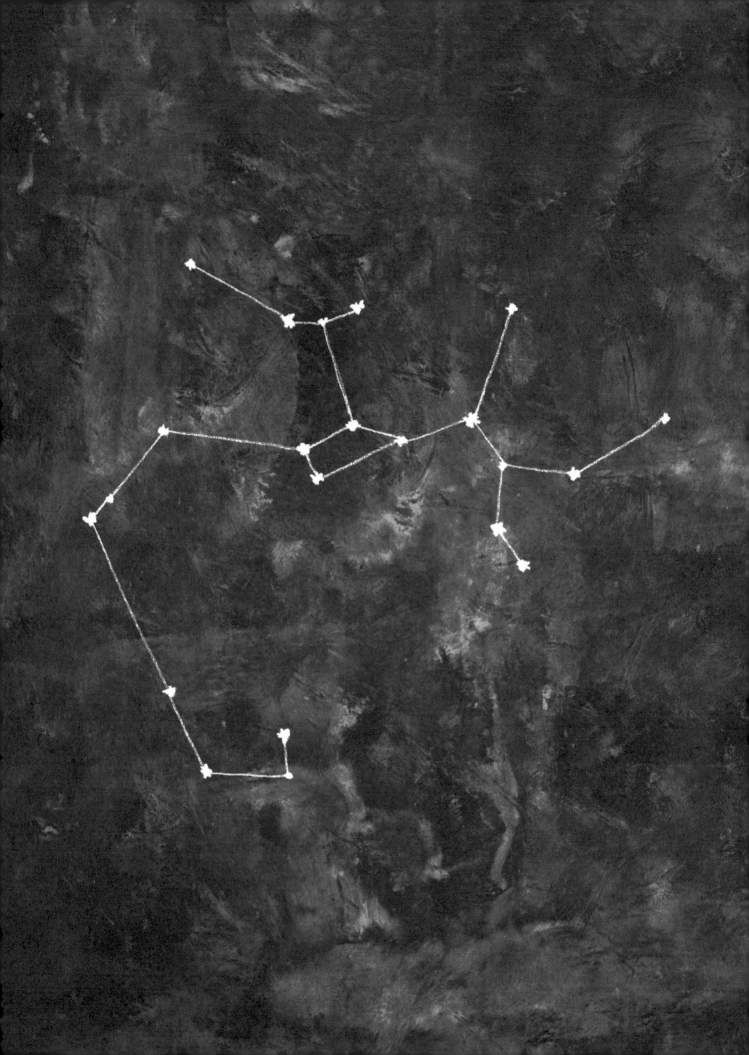

CHAPTER 12

SAGITTARIUS

Essential Ayurvedic Spice

ASAFETIDA

» *Asafetida is native to India, Pakistan, Iran, and Afghanistan, from where it is exported to the rest of the world.*

» *Asafetida comes from a perennial fennel-like plant that grows wild in large natural forests. The plant's roots are thick and pulpy, and yield a resin which is used to make the spice.*

» *Asafetida is sold in blocks as a gum, or in the form of a fine yellow powder, which can be crystalline or granulated. I recommend the use of the powder form for cooking.*

» *Described as a grounding herb in Ayurveda, Asafetida is an ancient Indian culinary ingredient, loaded with numerous health benefits, such as treating digestive and respiratory issues. I like to use it in recipes that contain beans and lentils, like khichdis, because it helps prevent bloating and indigestion.*

» *Use asafetida in very small amounts—its aroma is very potent. You can add it directly to cooking liquid, frying oil, or steeping water.*

» *It is important to keep asafetida in airtight containers. Uncooked, it has a very potent, sulfurous odor, which can affect other spices in your pantry.*

November 22–December 21

SAGITTARIUS

Sagittarius is Latin for "the archer" and is commonly represented by a simplified drawing of a bow and arrow. It is a fire sign that is ruled by Jupiter and is the ninth sign of the zodiac. Part of the Vata season, it is the last sign of the fall triad. While the sun is moving through Sagittarius, the cold weather of winter is on its way. With the arrival of Sagittarius, life energy disperses, and fall gradually changes to winter.

The holiday season is in full swing, making it challenging to adhere to routine when your social life is full of rich foods and late-night celebrations. You are naturally more sedentary during this time of year due to the cold and lack of daylight, so you won't need heavy foods. Rich, fatty foods make the blood thick and sluggish, which depresses the metabolism and causes Kapha individuals to oversleep and feel physically and mentally sluggish. Protect your immunity by keeping warm and insulated. Seek out sweet, salty, and sour foods, like nuts and seeds, tamari, lemons, yogurt, miso, cherries, and tamarind, which give you energy, keep you hydrated, and increase a wavering appetite while the air is still cold and dry.

Rather than mourning the end of light and warmth, take inspiration from others who are drawing those very things into their souls in order to sustain them during the dark months ahead. Sagittarius energy is about the celebration of life with loved ones. Sip hot water throughout the day to warm up, hydrate, and cleanse your body. Keep some form of movement in your routine to get your blood moving. Your muscles may be tense and constricted as they brace against the biting cold, so dress warmly. Go to bed early and try not to eat after 8 p.m. whenever possible.

PARFAIT *WITH* SPICY LEMON GRANOLA *AND* ARUGULA PESTO

I've never had much of a sweet tooth, so I love coming up with savory versions of desserts. For instance, when you think of a parfait, you usually imagine a sweet, creamy dessert or breakfast treat, but this version is a visually beautiful way to combine savory ingredients and flavors in a small portion. If you don't have time to make your own granola, you can buy a low-sugar or savory version. If you decide to make your own, make some extra, and sprinkle it on salads or other dishes to add a tasty crunch.

Dosha Dos and Don'ts: *For Vata types, if you're feeling bloated, you can replace the chickpeas with mung beans or any type of lentil.*

SERVES 4 TO 6

Spicy Lemon Granola:
1 cup rolled oats
¼ cup uncooked quinoa
¼ cup almonds, roughly chopped
1 tablespoon ground flaxseeds
½ teaspoon smoked paprika
½ teaspoon freshly ground black pepper
1 tablespoon olive oil
1 tablespoon low-sodium tamari
1 egg white, beaten

Arugula Pesto:
2 cups packed fresh arugula
15 large basil leaves
2 umeboshi plums, pitted
4 garlic cloves
¼ cup walnuts, soaked in warm water
    for 15 minutes
1 cup peanuts
1 portion Sour Spice Mix (page 32),
    coarsely ground
1½ teaspoons fresh lemon juice

¾ cup extra-virgin olive oil
1½ teaspoons water

To Finish:
1 cup organic Greek yogurt
½ cup cooked chickpeas (page 247)

For the granola: Preheat the oven to 300°F. In a large bowl, mix all the ingredients together. Spread the mixture out on a parchment paper–lined baking sheet in a single layer. Bake for 25 minutes, stirring the mixture a few times. Remove from the oven and let cool.

For the arugula pesto: Combine all the ingredients in a food processor and blend until you get a homogeneous mixture. Set aside.

To finish: Use small glass jars or bowls for serving. Add a layer of yogurt, then a layer of chickpeas, and a layer of pesto, then more yogurt, a layer of pesto, and a layer of granola. Or combine the layers to your liking and top the parfait with granola.

CARROTS *AND* PEAS *OVER* AMARANTH

Amaranth seeds have been cultivated as a grain for 8,000 years. They're gluten-free, have a protein content of about 16 percent (more than wheat, rice, or maize), and boast a digestibility score much higher than soy, milk, and wheat. I recommend soaking the seeds for anywhere between 1 hour and overnight to improve their digestibility and remove any harmful substances (which can be found in all raw grains and seeds). Amaranth also works well mixed with other grains, so it's worth testing different combinations to find one you enjoy. Sesame oil is considered the best of all oils in Ayurveda, and it's widely used for its nourishing effects on the digestive system.

Dosha Dos and Don'ts: *Pitta types need to use sesame oil in moderation due to its heating effects on the body; they can use olive oil instead of sesame oil in the vinaigrette if they're feeling any sort of excess heat in the body already. Kapha types need to moderate the amount of sesame oil they consume; although the oil is very beneficial to them, it can be heavy if taken in excess. Pitta and Kapha types can moderate the amount of pistachios they include, or replace them with sunflower seeds.*

SERVES 4 TO 6

Amaranth:
3 cups Chicken Stock (page 241)
1 cup amaranth seeds

Vinaigrette:
2 tablespoons sesame oil
½ portion Astringent Spice Mix (page 35), finely ground
½ teaspoon turmeric powder
⅛ teaspoon asafetida powder
1 teaspoon cinnamon powder

6 mint leaves
1 tablespoon chopped dill
1 Indian green chile, cut in half
1 teaspoon maple syrup
1½ teaspoons dry mustard
One ½-inch piece fresh turmeric, grated
1 tablespoon fresh lemon juice

Carrots and Peas:
12 young carrots with fronds, cut in half lengthwise
1½ cups fresh or frozen peas

1½ teaspoons ghee
6 garlic cloves, thinly sliced
4 large carrots, finely diced
1 teaspoon kosher salt
2 tablespoons nigella seeds
1 tablespoon maple syrup

To Finish:
½ cup pistachios, toasted in a dry pan
Juice and zest of 1 lime

For the amaranth: In a saucepan, bring the stock to a boil, then turn off the heat. Add the amaranth seeds, cover, and let the pot cool to room temperature. Put the soaking seeds in the refrigerator for at least 12 hours. When you're ready to cook, remove the seeds from the refrigerator and cook for 5 minutes before serving, just enough to warm them through.

For the vinaigrette: In a small pan, heat the oil over medium heat, then add the spice mix, turmeric, asafetida, and cinnamon, and fry the spices for 2 minutes. Turn off the heat.

Place the infused oil, mint, dill, chile, maple syrup, mustard, fresh turmeric, and lemon juice in a blender and blend until emulsified. Use immediately, or place the vinaigrette in a jar and refrigerate (shake it before using).

For the carrots and peas: Place a steaming basket in a saucepan, add enough water to reach the bottom of the basket, and bring the water to a boil. Place the young carrots in the steaming basket and steam them for 2 minutes, then move them from the basket to a plate and let them cool.

Blanch the peas in the boiling water for 2 minutes, then transfer them to a bowl of ice water to stop them from cooking more.

In a pan over a medium heat, heat the ghee and add the garlic. Once the garlic is translucent, add the large carrots and salt; cook for 3 minutes. Add the peas, vinaigrette, nigella seeds, and maple syrup, then toss in the pan for 1 minute. Remove the pan from the heat, add the young carrots and toss.

To finish: Serve 1 large spoonful of amaranth for each portion, then add the carrot and pea mixture on top. Sprinkle with the pistachios and lime zest and juice.

HOLIDAY KHICHDI *WITH* DUCK CONFIT

This is the most indulgent of all the khichdi recipes in this book, but it's still one of the lighter meals you'll eat during this holiday period. When making food for the festivities of the season, you can pack your dishes with nutritious ingredients and remain mindful of the seasonality and your dosha balance. In this recipe, the duck confit provides a smoky taste and protein (you also get protein from the lentils), and the meat fibers are broken down by the slow cooking so it's easier to digest. Eating slow-cooked meats is a great way to help your digestion during the holidays, when it's often compromised and overworked by heavy foods.

Dosha Dos and Don'ts: *Kapha types should moderate the amount of duck meat they consume, and they can cook it in sunflower oil to make it more suitable to their needs.*

SERVES 4 TO 6

Khichdi:
¾ cup red lentils
2 teaspoons asafetida powder
¾ cup brown rice
1 tablespoon any vinegar or lemon juice (optional)
1 tablespoon ghee
5 garlic cloves, thinly sliced

One 1-inch piece fresh ginger, grated
1 medium red onion
¼ cup red quinoa
3½ cups Ginger, Garlic, and Onion Broth (page 244)
1 teaspoon kosher or sea salt

Duck Confit:
4 duck legs, rinsed well and patted dry

4 thyme sprigs
4 whole garlic cloves
2 bay leaves
1 portion Bitter Spice Mix (page 34), finely ground
1 teaspoon black peppercorns
½ teaspoon kosher salt
2 cups peanut oil
2 cups coconut oil, melted

To prepare: In a medium heavy-bottomed saucepan, cover the lentils with water, add 1 teaspoon of asafetida, and bring to a boil; boil for 2 minutes. Turn off the heat, cover the pot, and let the lentils soak for 60 minutes (preferably overnight). Presoaking the lentils makes them easier to digest; it also helps them cook more evenly and become tender all the way through.

It's also good to soak the rice. In a medium bowl, cover the rice with 2 cups of water and add the vinegar (if using); soak for as long as possible, preferably overnight.

After soaking the lentils and rice, drain and wash thoroughly with cold water.

If you don't have time for any soaking, you can cook the dish directly from the dry ingredients, but it will take additional time to achieve the desired tenderness.

For the duck confit: In a large saucepan or stockpot, arrange the duck legs, thyme, garlic, bay leaves, spice mix, and peppercorns in a single layer. Add the salt and enough of the peanut and coconut oil to cover the duck legs by at least 1 inch. Set the pan over medium heat and bring the mixture just to a simmer. Reduce the heat so the mixture just barely simmers; partly cover the pot with a lid. Continue cooking the duck until the meat is very tender and falls off the bone, 2 to 3 hours.

Remove the pan from the heat and let the duck legs cool to room temperature, about 2 hours. Remove the duck meat from the bone and set aside to use as topping on the khichdi. You can transfer the duck legs to a smaller container, then add enough of its cooking oil to cover the duck, and refrigerate until you are ready to use the confit. The duck can be refrigerated in the fat for up to 1 month.

For the khichdi: In a heavy-bottomed saucepan, heat the ghee, then add the garlic, ginger, and onion. Cook until the onion and garlic are translucent. Add the lentils, rice, the remaining 1 teaspoon of asafetida, quinoa, and the broth, and bring to a boil.

Reduce the mixture to a simmer and cook for about 45 minutes, making sure there is always enough liquid in the pot. Simmering the lentils gently helps them cook evenly until tender, retain their shape without losing their texture (getting mushy) too quickly, and keep their skins intact. The best time to add the salt is about 30 minutes into cooking, when the lentils are tender enough, but still partly firm.

After about 45 minutes, taste the khichdi, and if the lentils and brown rice are not very tender continue cooking for up to 15 minutes longer. Depending on your preference, you can adjust the texture of the khichdi for a drier risotto-like consistency or a wetter soup-like one by either allowing the excess liquid to evaporate or adding more liquid.

To finish: Serve 2 large spoons of khichdi into each serving bowl. Using the back of a spoon, create a small well on top of each serving and add a large serving spoon of shredded duck confit.

SPINACH *AND* MUSHROOM GRATIN *WITH COCONUT BÉCHAMEL*

This dish is perfect for the holiday season. It can be prepared ahead of time and stored in the refrigerator until you're ready to bake (it should always be served hot!). Using coconut milk adds a unique flavor and lightness during a time when it's hard to skip rich foods and other indulgences. When using leafy greens like spinach, don't trim off the stems, which are the most important source of fiber.

Dosha Dos and Don'ts: *Kapha and Pitta types can moderate the amount of mushrooms in their dish. Also, Kapha types should generally enjoy this dish in moderation to avoid feeling lethargic and heavy.*

SERVES 4 TO 6

Coconut Béchamel:
2 tablespoons olive oil
2 tablespoons all-purpose flour
One 13-ounce can coconut milk
1 portion Salty Spice Mix (page 31),
    finely ground

Spinach and Mushroom Gratin:
4 cups spinach, washed
1 tablespoon olive oil
½ pound mushrooms, roughly chopped
Freshly ground black pepper
½ teaspoon chopped thyme
1 tablespoon unsalted butter
1 garlic clove, finely chopped

2 tablespoons ghee, melted
1 cup amaranth seeds

To Finish:
6 large organic hard-boiled eggs, peeled
    and cut in half
Kosher salt

For the coconut béchamel: In a medium saucepan, heat the oil over medium-low heat. Add the flour and stir until smooth. Cook until the mixture turns a light golden sandy color, about 6 to 7 minutes.

Meanwhile, in a separate pan, slowly heat the coconut milk until it's just about to boil. Add the hot milk to the flour mixture 1 cup at a time, whisking continuously until very smooth. Bring the sauce to a boil and cook for 5 minutes, stirring constantly, then remove from heat. Season with the spice mix. Set the sauce aside until ready to use.

For the spinach and mushroom gratin: Bring a pot of water to a boil. Add the spinach and blanch for 30 seconds, then drain the spinach and squeeze out the excess liquid. Chop the spinach up and set aside.

Heat the oil in a large sauté pan over medium heat. Add the mushrooms and season with pepper. Scatter the thyme over the mushrooms and stir to coat them with oil. The mushrooms will release quite a bit of liquid; when they do, make a well in the center of the mushrooms and add the butter. As the butter melts, add the garlic to the well and cook until fragrant. Once the garlic has cooked, stir it into the mushrooms. Cook the mushrooms until the liquid evaporates, then transfer them to a plate or work surface; let the mushrooms cool, then coarsely chop them.

Turn the broiler on and place a rack in the center position. Coat a 9-by-13-inch baking dish with the melted ghee. Add the amaranth seeds and spread them on the bottom of the dish, then place the dish under the broiler for 5 minutes, allowing the amaranth seeds to toast lightly. Remove the dish from the oven.

To finish: In a bowl, mix the mushrooms and spinach together. Layer the mixture over the amaranth seeds; using your fingers, pat the vegetables down lightly. Add the halved eggs with the yolk side facing up.

Pour the béchamel sauce over the mixture in the baking dish, then pick up the dish and gently tap it on the counter to set the sauce.

Place the baking dish in the oven and broil the gratin until the surface browns, 5 to 10 minutes. Sprinkle with a bit of salt and serve hot.

PISSALADIERE *WITH* SWEET POTATOES *AND* CHICKPEA BÉCHAMEL

Before going to culinary school, I would often shy away from making doughs or committing to anything with a crust. I was intimidated by the idea and had the wrong impression that baking is always time-consuming, but I soon realized that cooking is just a matter of habit. Once you venture into a recipe and attempt it for the first time, you should stick to it and figure out how to get it right. All of that said, I'm fond of hacks (as long as I can ensure I'm eating something nutritious). This crust is so good for you and is incredibly easy to make—thanks to a hack I've developed as an answer to my baking fears. Just like with pizza, the leftovers taste delicious the next morning.

Dosha Dos and Don'ts: *Kapha types can swap the sweet potatoes for regular white ones, or use a combination of the two.*

SERVES 4 TO 6

Chickpea Béchamel:
3½ cups cooked chickpeas or two 15-ounce cans chickpeas
1 cup whole milk
2 tablespoons ghee
1 tablespoon white miso
1 tablespoon grated Parmesan cheese
⅛ teaspoon nutmeg powder
1 portion Pungent Spice Mix (page 33), coarsely ground

¾ teaspoon kosher salt, plus more as needed

Pissaladiere:
1½ cups flaxseeds, ground to a meal in a blender or food processor
2 teaspoons baking powder
1 teaspoon kosher salt
¼ cup chopped oregano leaves
1 tablespoon coconut nectar or maple syrup

3 tablespoons sesame oil, plus more for finishing
3 extra-large organic eggs
½ cup water
2 sweet potatoes, scrubbed, thinly sliced, and stored in ice water
4 fresh figs, thinly sliced
2 scallions, white and light green parts only, thinly sliced
1 cup low-fat feta cheese, crumbled
½ cup Garlic Confit (page 64), drained of oil and chopped

For the chickpea béchamel: Place the chickpeas, milk, ghee, miso, Parmesan, nutmeg, spice mix, and salt in a medium pot. Bring the mixture to a boil, then reduce to a simmer and cook for 5 minutes. Transfer the sauce to a food processor or blender, and blend until smooth, about 3 minutes. Taste and add salt as needed, then set aside in the refrigerator until ready to use.

For the pissaladiere: Preheat the oven to 425°F. In a medium bowl, whisk together the flaxseed meal, baking powder, salt, oregano, and coconut nectar. Add the oil, eggs, and water and mix very well. Let the mixture sit for 5 minutes until it thickens. Spread the mixture into a greased pizza pan. Bake for 10 minutes and remove from the oven to finish with toppings.

To finish: Spread the sweet potato (make sure it's dry), figs, scallions, and feta onto the half-baked crust and cook for 15 more minutes, checking after 10 minutes to make sure the pissaladiere isn't burnt. Remove the pissaladiere from the oven, top with garlic confit, and drizzle with oil. Slice and serve.

BANANA SPLIT *WITH* KHOYA *AND* CHERRIES

Khoya is a delicious base in many traditional desserts of the Indian subcontinent. It is basically a milk solid made by slowly cooking and evaporating the moisture from milk. Making it at home is very easy but slightly time-consuming. You can get a similar flavor from store-bought condensed milk (though the texture will be different).

Dosha Dos and Don'ts: *Kapha and Vata types can moderate the amount of bananas.*

SERVES 4 TO 6
Khoya:
5 cups whole milk

Bananas and Cherries:
2 bananas, sliced in half lengthwise

2 cups sweet or sour cherries, pitted
2 tablespoons coconut oil
2 tablespoons coconut nectar or maple
  syrup

Toppings:
3 tablespoons shredded coconut
2 tablespoons honey, preferably raw
½ portion Sweet Spice Mix (page 30),
  coarsely ground

For the khoya: Heat the milk in a heavy-bottomed nonstick pan over medium heat and bring to a boil. Reduce to a simmer, scraping the bottom and sides of the pan continuously to prevent the milk from burning. As you continue to simmer the milk, it will reduce and take on a grainy texture. After 40 minutes, the milk will be quite grainy, and you need to scrape even more frequently, as the chances of burning are higher. The milk will start to resemble a porridge; cook for another 35 minutes. The total cooking time should be about 1 hour and 15 minutes. Pour the mixture, which should look like a wet cottage cheese, into a large mixing bowl and allow it to cool and get thicker and drier.

For the bananas and cherries: Preheat the oven to 400°F and line a baking sheet with parchment paper.

Spread the bananas and cherries on the baking sheet, drizzle with the oil, and roast for 15 to 20 minutes, until the bananas are golden brown. Remove the baking sheet from the oven and drizzle with coconut nectar, then broil for 10 minutes, checking to make sure the fruit doesn't burn. Remove from the oven.

To finish: Serve this dessert while the fruit is still hot. Place a banana half and 1 large spoon of cherries in each serving bowl, then top with khoya and shredded coconut flakes. In a small bowl, combine the honey and the spice mix. Drizzle some spiced honey over each serving.

GRAPEFRUIT, PEACH, *AND* TAMARIND ICED TEA

The heat, bitterness, and tanginess of grapefruit makes it perfect for the cold season, and all the vitamin C in this drink is a much better alternative to taking vitamin supplements when you're trying to ditch a cold.

Dosha Dos and Don'ts: *Pitta types should use orange juice instead of grapefruit juice. Kapha types should use half the amount of grapefruit juice to avoid too much acidity.*

SERVES 4 TO 6
4 tablespoons loose black tea
One 1-inch piece fresh ginger
2-inch cube dried tamarind
½ cup mint leaves

1 tablespoon whole cloves
2 cups hot water
2 cups fresh peaches, peeled and cut into wedges, or frozen peaches

2 cups freshly squeezed grapefruit juice or orange juice
1 tablespoon maple syrup

Steep the tea, ginger, tamarind, mint, and cloves in the hot water for 30 minutes. Strain the tea through a fine-mesh sieve into a bowl or pitcher; discard the solids. Allow the tea to cool to room temperature, then add the peaches and grapefruit juice. Mix everything to evenly incorporate the grapefruit juice and tea.

Place the tea in the refrigerator for 30 minutes, stirring intermittently for better results. Remove the tea from the refrigerator and add the maple syrup, then stir well. Serve over ice.

CHAPTER 13
BASICS

BASICS

This section gathers the staple recipes that are used in many of the dishes in this book. They are time-consuming, but in my experience, it's a cost worth bearing for the freshness of the basics you're using in your cooking, and for knowing exactly what's in your food. Once you get the hang of making these recipes, they'll become second nature to you, and you'll start to build an efficient routine around them. It's often more about forming the habit of making things from scratch, so I encourage you to give them an honest try. Ayurveda strongly urges eating freshly made foods. That said, most of the basics in this section can be stored for a later use. Although freezing does retain a lot of the nutritional value, try to limit the amount of time you keep things in the freezer—you'll always reap the greatest benefits from fresh ingredients.

NUT *AND* SEED MILKS

I have spent a good portion of my life following a vegan diet, so learning to make these milks came in handy. This easy template recipe has become second nature—I've made almond milk, cashew milk, peanut milk, walnut milk, pistachio milk, and pumpkin-seed milk on a weekly basis using this master recipe. You can easily adjust the amount of milk you make by proportionally increasing or decreasing the amounts of all the ingredients. Many nuts require soaking to activate their enzymes and make their nutrients easier to absorb. They include almonds, walnuts, hazelnuts, Brazil nuts, pistachios, pumpkin seeds, sunflower seeds, brown or black sesame seeds, and any other nut or seed with a skin. You do not need to soak cashews, macadamia nuts, or hemp seeds before blending them into a milk, though in my experience, soaking them gives the milk a smoother texture. Once you get the hang of making milks from the different nuts and seeds, you can mix two or more together to get an array of flavors and textures. I love mixing almonds, pistachios, and cashews or black sesame and walnuts. If you plan on using the milk for hot drinks, I recommend straining it after blending. Also, remember to shake the milk when you take it out of the refrigerator to use it.

MAKES 4 CUPS

1 cup raw unsalted nuts and/or seeds

4 cups water, plus 3 cups for soaking
    where needed

¼ teaspoon fine sea salt

Apple cider vinegar, for soaking where
    needed

To prepare nuts or seeds with skins: Place the nuts or seeds in a glass or ceramic bowl or jar and cover with 3 cups of the water. Add ½ teaspoon of salt and a splash of vinegar and stir the mixture well.

Cover the bowl with a clean dishtowel and allow the nuts to soak at room temperature for at least 1 hour and up to 12 hours if possible. Drain and rinse the nuts or seeds in tap water three times.

For all nuts or seeds: Place the nuts or seeds and the 4 cups of water in a high-speed blender. Blend until smooth.

You can use the milk unstrained or strain it through a fine-mesh sieve for a smoother texture.

The milk can be stored sealed in the refrigerator (preferably in a glass container) for up to 5 days.

HOMEMADE CHEESE CURDS

Making your own fresh cheese is deeply satisfying. It took me a few trials and some tweaking to get the perfect cheese. You can strain the cheese more if you want a firmer consistency; otherwise, it's best to gently press the cheese and let it hang so the excess moisture can drip out slowly. Then tie it into the shape of your choice. If you can get goat's milk, try it—it gives the cheese a wonderful taste. Otherwise, grass-fed organic cow's milk will work just as well.

MAKES 1 POUND OF CHEESE
1 gallon whole milk (not ultra-pasteurized)

⅔ cup fresh lemon or lime juice or white wine vinegar
Kosher or sea salt

Line a colander with 4 layers of cheesecloth or 2 layers of food-safe paper towels and set it over a large bowl.

Heat the milk in a large heavy-bottomed pot over medium heat, stirring frequently, until an inserted instant-read thermometer registers 165°F to 180°F. (Getting the most precise temperature results in the best cheese.)

Add the citrus juice or vinegar, 1 tablespoon at a time, stirring gently after each addition. Stop adding the acid when the curds separate from the whey; you will see white clumps suspended in a pale translucent liquid. Let the separated milk sit in the pot for at least 5 minutes and preferably for 20 minutes to let it separate completely. Using a slotted spoon, scoop out the curds and transfer them to the lined colander.

Cover the mixture with plastic wrap, and allow it to drain until you get the desired texture of cheese. This usually takes me about 20 minutes for softer pressed cheese, and 1 hour if I want to make drier fresh curds. Add salt to taste.

Gather the curds into a ball in the middle of the towel and press them into a flat oval shape. Tie the towel around the cheese. Place the wrapped cheese back into the colander and place any kind of heavy weight on top. After making it the first time, adjust the weight you press the cheese with, as well as the cooking and the drying times to try out different combinations and find the texture you enjoy the most. Let the wrapped fresh cheese sit for about 1½ hours.

Unwrap the cheese and dig into it or add it to your recipe right away. The cheese will keep, wrapped and in the refrigerator, for 3 to 4 days.

CHICKEN STOCK

Contrary to a lot of people's perception of Ayurveda, it doesn't prescribe a strictly vegetarian diet. Bone broth is an ancient healing remedy and has been used in Ayurvedic medicine for thousands of years. One very important thing you can do for yourself when consuming meat is to buy organic and grass-fed meat to avoid the antibiotics and hormones often found in nonorganic versions. If you're using this broth in a recipe, go light on the salt—the saltiness will get more concentrated as the broth reduces during cooking.

MAKES 8 TO 10 CUPS
Bones of two whole organic chickens
½ pound organic grass-fed chicken
    breast, roughly cubed
6 garlic cloves, crushed
3 carrots, scrubbed and roughly
    chopped
4 celery stalks, roughly chopped

2 small beets, roughly chopped
1 medium onion, roughly diced
One 2-inch piece fresh ginger, chopped
¼ teaspoon turmeric powder
¼ teaspoon fennel seeds
¼ teaspoon coriander powder
¼ teaspoon fenugreek powder
¼ teaspoon ajwain powder

¼ teaspoon brown mustard seeds
¼ teaspoon cumin seeds
1 teaspoon freshly ground black pepper
12 cups cold water (10 cups if using a
    slow cooker)
Kosher, Himalayan, or sea salt to taste
Juice of 1 to 2 lemons or limes

Place the chicken bones and breasts, garlic, carrots, celery, beets, onion, ginger, and all the spices in a large heavy-bottomed pot (a slow cooker works well, too).

Add the cold water and bring to a boil, continuously skimming the impurities that accumulate on the top for the first 30 minutes. Reduce the heat to a simmer. If using a slow cooker, set it to low temperature and cook for 12 to 20 hours.

Continue to simmer gently for 3 to 4 hours, skimming as necessary, then remove the pot from the heat, pick out all the solids, and strain the stock through a fine-mesh sieve into a large bowl. Add salt to taste.

Add the lemon or lime juice and let the stock cool for about 30 minutes.

If you're not using the stock immediately, pour it into plastic containers with a lid and store in the refrigerator for up to 1 week, or freeze for up to 1 month.

VEGETABLE BROTH

This recipe has a bit of an extensive list of ingredients, but using what you can find is okay, too. Even though making homemade broth feels like work, think of it as a labor of love for your body. This broth can be used to add flavor and nutrients to soups, sauces, to cook grains, drink on its own, and much more. Using a good homemade broth in your home cooking not only adds another wholesome level of flavor to your food, but it also does wonders for your health. I find that building habits and rituals around these more laborious tasks makes them fun and meaningful. If you get together with friends or family to cook, you can make large batches of this broth and share it—I call it the broth-making "party." People often keep broths in the freezer and use them over long periods of time, but Ayurveda encourages eating fresh foods as much as possible, so I limit myself to storing the broth to a week or two.

MAKES 8 TO 10 CUPS

2 medium carrots, scrubbed

3 celery stalks

1 small to medium leek, halved, rinsed, and sliced

3 garlic cloves, crushed

½ large sweet potato, peeled

1 large or a few smaller seasonal squashes, cubed

½ bunch seasonal leafy greens, stems removed

¼ cup dried shiitake mushrooms

1 handful fresh flat-leaf parsley

1 large kombu piece

One 2-inch piece fresh ginger, grated

One 2-inch piece fresh turmeric, grated, or ½ teaspoon turmeric powder

½ teaspoon kosher, Himalayan, or sea salt

¼ teaspoon freshly ground black pepper

12 cups cold water

Place all the ingredients in a large heavy-bottomed pot (a slow cooker works well, too). Cover them with the water and bring to a boil. Reduce the heat and barely simmer on low for about 1½ hours. If using a slow cooker, set it to high temperature and cook for 5 hours, or cook at low temperature for 10 hours.

Remove the pot from the heat, pick out all the solids, and strain the broth through a fine-mesh sieve into a large bowl.

If you're not using the broth immediately, pour it into plastic containers with a lid and store in the refrigerator for up to 1 week, or freeze for up to 1 month.

MUSHROOM BROTH

I like to use this recipe to add an earthy flavor to dishes (I also drink it warm on its own). Like all broths, it takes time and some work, but the flavors and nutrition you can achieve are well worth it. You can experiment with different mushroom varieties. Making a broth from mushrooms is a great way to mimic the strong flavors of meat stocks, and it's also a great way to use up mushrooms that might otherwise go to waste.

MAKES 8 TO 10 CUPS

1 large yellow onion, halved
½ pound button mushrooms (or your choice of mushrooms)
1 celery stalk, roughly chopped

1 medium carrot, scrubbed and roughly chopped
4 garlic cloves, crushed
1 bay leaf
3 thyme sprigs

One small bunch of parsley
½ teaspoon freshly ground black pepper
½ teaspoon kosher, Himalayan, or sea salt
12 cups cold water

Heat a grill pan or small cast-iron skillet to high heat. Place the onion halves on the pan flat side down and cook until the bottoms are charred, about 3 minutes. Transfer the onion to a heavy-bottomed pot and add the remaining ingredients. Bring to a boil, then reduce the heat and barely simmer on low for 1½ hours. If using a slow cooker, set it to low temperature and cook for 8 hours.

Remove the pan from heat, pick out the solids, and strain the broth through a fine-mesh sieve into a large bowl.

If you're not using the broth immediately, pour it into plastic containers with a lid and store in the refrigerator for up to 5 days, or freeze for up to 1 month.

GINGER, GARLIC, *AND* ONION BROTH

The three grounding ingredients in this broth help us stay healthy, detoxify our internal organs, regenerate our creative and sexual energy, stimulate our immune system, and help clean and rebuild our brain function. All three ingredients are often used as base flavors for different recipes, so this broth has a similar effect. It's strong in flavor, but it doesn't overpower a dish. I prefer making it in the oven, as it comes out more flavorful, but you can also make it on the stovetop (simmer on low-medium heat for 1 to 3 hours). When cooking in the oven, the longer you cook the broth, the better it's going to taste. After straining the broth, reserve the solids; you can blend them into a smooth paste and use as a delicious caramelized spread, which you can flavor with spices and herbs.

MAKES 8 TO 10 CUPS

3 tablespoons ghee

6 pounds medium white onions, cut into ½-inch slices

12 garlic cloves, crushed

One 3-inch piece fresh ginger, peeled

1 teaspoon kosher salt

3 thyme sprigs

1 bay leaf

3 rosemary sprigs

12 cups cold water

Preheat the oven to 175°F.

In a large heavy-bottomed stockpot, heat the ghee on medium heat. Add the onions, garlic, and ginger. Cook until the onions are golden brown, about 20 minutes, reducing the heat if they start to get caramelized and dark too quickly. After 20 minutes, add the salt, thyme, bay leaf, and rosemary, and continue to cook for 2 minutes to allow them to bloom in the heat and release their oils. Add the water, cover the pot tightly with a piece of aluminum foil, and transfer it to the oven. Cook for 2 to 12 hours.

Strain the broth through a fine-mesh sieve lined with a double layer of cheesecloth. Reserve the solids for another use. Cool the broth, then pour it into a plastic containers. If you're not using the broth immediately, store it in the refrigerator for up to 5 days, or freeze for up to 2 weeks.

GHEE

Ghee is butter that has been processed to remove the milk solids. It can be used in place of butter and is an ideal cooking oil, as it doesn't burn unless heated to a very high temperature. Known as liquid gold in Ayurveda, ghee is said to improve overall health, lubricate joints, improve memory, and aid digestion. It doesn't need to be stored in the refrigerator and it will keep, in an airtight container, for up to 1 month. Don't use a wet spoon to scoop out the ghee or allow any sort of water to get into the container because the presence of moisture allows bacteria to grow and spoil the ghee. The taste of ghee is quite nutty, and some people need a bit of time to get used to it. Once you get into the habit of using ghee, you will appreciate the sweetness and creaminess it adds to food. Since the milk solids are removed from butter to make ghee, people who have a light sensitivity to dairy can usually use it. Unsalted butter makes the best ghee, but you can use either salted or unsalted. When used in moderation, ghee is beneficial for all three doshas (known as tridoshic).

**MAKES SLIGHTLY LESS THAN
1 POUND**
1 pound organic butter

Place the butter in a heavy-bottomed saucepan over medium heat and heat until the butter melts. Line a fine-mesh strainer with a single layer of cheesecloth and set over a heatproof bowl for straining the hot butter when it is ready.

Bring the butter to a boil; this takes about 3 minutes, but keep a close eye on the pan, as butter can burn easily. Once the butter starts to boil, reduce the heat to medium for a fast simmer. The butter will form a layer of white foam, which you should gently skim with a spoon and discard. After about an additional 8 minutes of simmering, a second layer of foam will form, and the butter will turn a golden-brown color. Skim the foam and discard it so you can get a better view of the color and clarity of the butter.

Strain the hot ghee through the lined fine-mesh sieve and into a heatproof bowl, allowing it to cool completely before storing. Store the ghee in a cool and dark place, but don't refrigerate it.

COOKING LENTILS

Lentils are considered one of the healthiest foods in Ayurveda. They're a rich source of protein, fiber, minerals, and vitamins, and are low in calories (a whole cup contains only a little more than 200 calories). Lentils don't require soaking, but letting them soak—and then rinsing—reduces the cooking time by about half and makes the lentils easier to digest. After soaking but before rinsing, pick over the lentils to remove impurities (little stones, dirt, and bad lentils) and then drain. Nobody likes a mushy lentil, but you can avoid mushiness by bringing the lentils to a boil quickly, then slowly simmering for the remaining cooking time. The cooking time for different lentils varies quite a bit, so check the list below. Lentils can be used in a huge variety of ways, and there's a vast array of types, which makes them great for salads, soups, veggie burgers, mashes, dried snacks, etc. Lentils will keep in the refrigerator for 1 week if stored in an airtight container in some of their cooking liquid.

MAKES ABOUT 2½ CUPS
1 cup dry lentils
5 cups water

2 teaspoons asafetida powder
½ teaspoon kosher salt

Place the lentils, 2 cups of the water, and 1 teaspoon of asafetida in a mixing bowl. Soak the lentils for at least 30 minutes (and as long as overnight). After soaking, wash the lentils in cold water, then drain them.

Place the lentils in a large heavy-bottomed pot and the remaining 1 teaspoon of asafetida, then cover them with the remaining 3 cups of water. Cook over medium-high heat, and bring the mixture to a boil. As soon as the mixture comes to a boil, reduce the heat to a low simmer for the listed cooking time. Add salt about 10 minutes before the end of the cooking time.

When the lentils are ready, remove the pot from the heat and let them cool in their cooking liquid. When they're cool, drain the lentils and discard the cooking liquid if using immediately. To store the lentils, transfer them to airtight containers with some of their cooking liquid, and keep in the refrigerator for up to 1 week.

Cooking times (for soaked lentils):
BELUGA LENTILS: 25 minutes
GREEN AND BROWN LENTILS: 35–45 minutes
GREEN SPLIT PEAS: 45 minutes
PUY LENTILS: 25–30 minutes
RED SPLIT LENTILS: 15–20 minutes
URAD DAL: 30 minutes
YELLOW LENTILS: 15–20 minutes

COOKING BEANS *AND* CHICKPEAS

Soaking beans in water (preferably overnight) reduces cooking time, helps them cook more evenly, and makes them easier to digest. Before soaking, pick over the beans and discard any impurities (little stones, dirt, and bad beans). If you like firm beans, cook them in an uncovered pot, and if you like creamier beans, partly cover the pot with the lid. Beans can take from 1 to 3 hours to cook depending on the variety and the desired texture. Don't increase the heat, as simmering them too fast will make them mushy. Beans will keep in the refrigerator for 1 week if stored in an airtight container in some of their cooking liquid.

MAKES ABOUT 3 CUPS
1 cup dried beans

6 to 7 cups water
2 teaspoons asafetida

½ teaspoon kosher salt

Place the beans, 3 cups of water, and 1 teaspoon of asafetida in a mixing bowl. Soak the beans for at least 30 minutes (and as long as overnight). After soaking, wash the beans in cold water, then drain them.

Place the beans in a large heavy-bottomed pot, add the remaining 1 teaspoon of asafetida, and cover with 3 to 4 cups of water. Bring to a boil over medium-high heat. As soon as the mixture comes to a boil, reduce the heat to a low simmer for the listed cooking time.

Cook the beans for 1 hour, then taste to see if they are tender or firm enough for your recipe. If you need to cook them longer, keep the beans at a gentle simmer and taste frequently as they start to become tender. Add more water as needed to keep the beans submerged; stir occasionally. When beans are tender but still too firm to enjoy eating, add the salt.

When the beans are ready, remove the pot from the heat and let them cool in their cooking liquid. When they're cool, drain the beans and discard the cooking liquid if using immediately. To store the beans, transfer them to airtight containers with some of their cooking liquid, and keep in the refrigerator for up to 1 week.

Cooking times (for soaked beans):
BLACK BEANS: 1 hour and 30 minutes
BLACK-EYED PEAS: 1 hour and 30 minutes
CANNELLINI BEANS: 1 hour
CHICKPEAS: 1 hour and 30 minutes
KIDNEY BEANS: 1 hour
MUNG BEANS: 25 minutes
WHITE BEANS: 30 minutes

AYURVEDIC GLOSSARY

Agni: The Sanskrit term for "digestive fire," agni breaks down the food and everything else we ingest from our environment (experiences, emotions, and impressions), from which it produces prana, the vital life force that sustains us. Agni assimilates what is useful and eliminates the rest. It controls metabolism, digestion, and the immune system. By balancing the agni energy and digestive system through Ayurveda, the individual enjoys better health, reduced stress, and a calm mind.

Ama: A toxic, illness-causing substance that can accumulate in the body when foods, emotions, or experiences are not fully processed, digested, or assimilated.

Kapha: One of the three doshas (functional energies in nature), it is dominated by the earth and water elements and governs structure and cohesion.

Pitta: One of the three doshas (functional energies in nature), it is dominated by the fire and water elements and governs transformation.

Prakruti: A person's unique constitution; the ratio of Vata, Pitta, and Kapha established at conception. It manifests in a unique set of physical, emotional, and mental traits, strengths, and vulnerabilities.

Prana: The vital life force that enters the body primarily through the breath, but can also come from other things we experiences, like food, water, and things we assimilate through our skin. It is the flow of cellular intelligence, perception, and communication, and a subtle energy that encompasses all of reality.

Subtle body: The energetic aspects of self that permeate and inform the physical body, but that also extend beyond the physical form.

Tridoshic: A food that is pacifying or balancing for all three doshas.

Vata: One of the three doshas (functional energies in nature), it is dominated by the ether and air elements and governs movement and communication.

Vedic: Pertaining to the Vedic period in ancient India; the time during which the Vedas, the spiritual literature of the ancient Indian culture, were composed. They are the first texts to describe the origins of Ayurveda and Yoga.

Vikruti: A person's current state of health; the specific ratio of Vata, Pitta, and Kapha that currently exists within one's body, as opposed to the natural ratio of the three doshas represented by one's prakruti (constitution).

Vipaka: A postdigestive effect that food has on our doshic constitution. It is the taste essence (rasa) of a food substance after it has been completely digested with the help of digestive fire (agni).

Yoga: A sister science to Ayurveda, Yoga originates from the ancient Vedic texts. The practice of Yoga is a collection of physical, mental, and spiritual disciplines intended to transform and liberate the mind and the body. In the West, Yoga usually refers to the third limb of Yoga, the practice of physical postures.

ACKNOWLEDGMENTS

I am grateful to have had the chance to continue my journey in Ayurveda with the opportunity to write this book. I want to thank the team at Dovetail Press, especially Mura Dominko, Nick Fauchald, Scott Gordon Bleicher, Chris Santone, and Olivia Mack Anderson, for making this book come to life and showing me the ropes on how it's done. I could not have found anyone better or more open and encouraging of all my ideas.

I also want to thank:

My parents, Sushma, Josee, and Madan Kehar—yes, I have three of them!—for making me tough as nails and giving me food and flavor as my language for love.

My sisters, Seema and Mona, my first and most beautiful companions in life, for shaping my personality ("cheese whiz") and giving me the courage to be myself.

My cousins, especially Komal, for all the love, both tough and gentle, and making sure I stay true to myself.

Malika Verma, Vir Kashyap, Noelle Kadar, Akshat Ghiya, V. Sunil, Anand Ahuja, Addavail Coslett, Chris Davies, Mehtab Mann, Suchita Salwan, Uzma Ullah, Uzair Siddiqui, and Meher Varma, for being the truest and most supportive friends.

Vif, Em, and Mogens Hess, for living by their own rules and showing me how to do the same.

Chef Richard LaMarita, for serving as a true example and inspiration with his decades of dedication to Ayurveda and teaching.

Jay Ruttenberg, Susan Shapiro, and Rebecca Couche, for teaching me how to get my stories into words.

Peace Arnold, for her continuous support and advice.

Lisa Brick, for acting like an inspiration, mentor, and motherly figure.

Neelu, Analjit, Tara, Piya, and Veer Singh, for being a loving and supportive family over the years.

Dr. David Frawley for bringing Ayurveda to us, in the most comprehensive and relevant way, with his incredible books and courses, and through a life of true dedication to this science.

Gina Hamadey, for guiding me into this journey.

And last and most importantly, to my husband and truest partner in crime, Mikkel C. Hess, for being my cheerleader, pillar of strength, clown, and inspiration, through thick and thin.

INDEX

ABOUT THE AUTHOR

Nira Kehar, a native of Montreal, Canada, attended culinary school in Québec, before embarking on a decade-long culinary journey in India. She was the chef-owner of New Delhi's beloved French brasserie Chez Nini, and a collaborator on multiple food projects for different organizations, most notably India Art Fair. Her first book, a self-published art book about storytelling through food, *Eating Stories*, was created for an event she hosted at the James Beard Foundation in 2014. This is Nira's first cookbook, born out of a passion and lifelong study of Ayurveda.

"There is no greater agony than bearing an untold story inside you."
—Maya Angelou

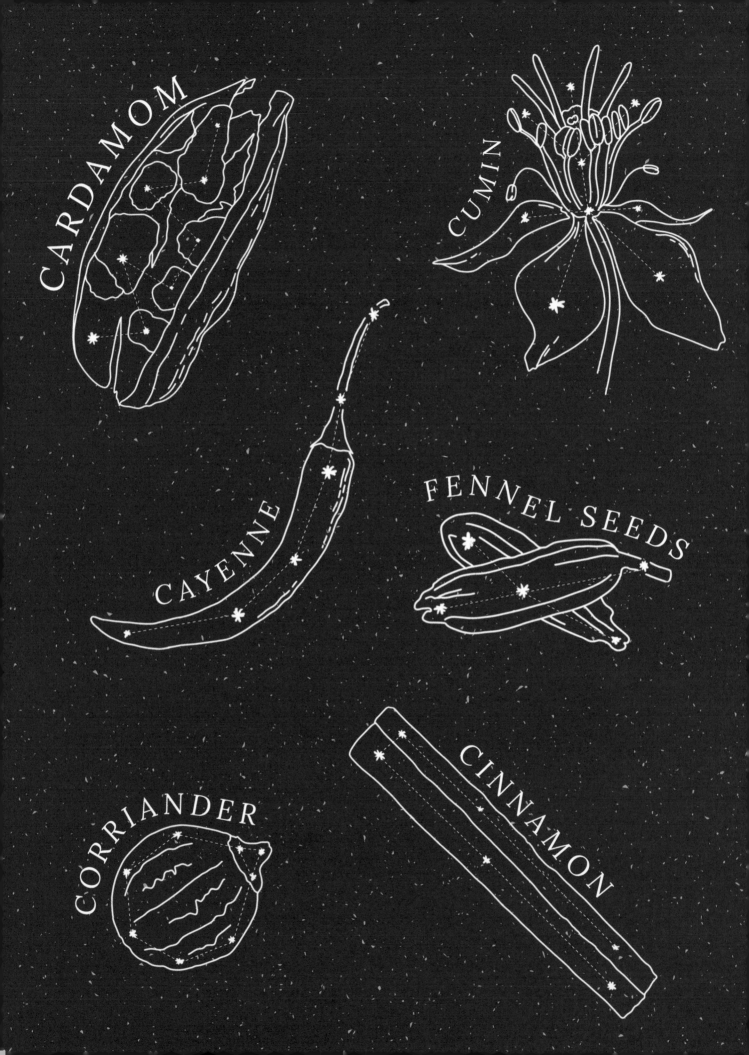